Spiritual Healing

Spiritual Healing

Selections From the Writings of
Joel Goldsmith

A Citadel Press Book
Published by Carol Publishing Group

First Carol Publishing Group edition 1994

A Citadel Press Book
Published by Carol Publishing Group
Citadel Press is a registered trademark of Carol Communications Group
Editorial Offices: 600 Madison Avenue, New York, N.Y. 10022
Sales and Distribution Offices: 120 Enterprise Avenue, Secaucus, N.J. 07094
In Canada: Canadian Manda Group, P.O. Box 920, Station U, Toronto,
    Ontario M8Z 5P9
Queries regarding rights and permissions should be addressed to:
Carol Publishing Group, 600 Madison Avenue, New York, N.Y. 10022

Carol Publishing Group books are available at special discounts
for bulk purchases, for sales promotions, fund-raising, or
educational purposes. Special editions can be created to
specifications. For details, contact Special Sales Department,
Carol Publishing Group, 120 Enterprise Avenue, Secaucus, N.J.
07094

Manufactured in the United States of America
ISBN 0-8065-1521-X

10   9   8   7   6   5   4   3   2   1

Contents

From LIVING NOW

From THE CONTEMPLATIVE LIFE

From CONSCIOUS UNION WITH GOD

From THE MASTER SPEAKS

From MAN WAS NOT BORN TO CRY

From CONSCIOUSNESS UNFOLDING

Joel S. Goldsmith

Even in his own lifetime Joel Goldsmith was recognized as an authentically *American* mystic and religious teacher. His vision was most comprehensively expressed in a series of books whose message he referred to as The Infinite Way. These titles have sold more than two million copies both in the United States and abroad and each year additional translations are commissioned. Goldsmith has truly become a global phenomenon.

Born in New York City on March 10, 1892, in his youth he became a partner in his father's import business. Though raised in the Jewish religion he became interested in Christian Science when his father was helped by a Christian Science practitioner.

Shortly thereafter, as he himself described it, he "became reborn into a new state of consciousness." He then ventured out on his own, giving expression to his newly found vision in a series of books and lectures which became known as The Infinite Way writings.

From his home in Hawaii, Goldsmith wrote and lectured ceaselessly, amassing twenty-odd published volumes whose purposes were to help the reader establish a practical way of life which could lead to the discovery of *self* and awaken the awareness that it was possible to live *in the spirit*.

Many regard him as a twentieth-century embodiment of the school and spirit of Ralph Waldo Emerson and Walt Whitman. Above all he strove to affirm the reality of mystical experience and the possibility of a life lived in constant awareness of spiritual realities.

Joel Goldsmith never allowed himself to be referred to as "doctor" or "reverend," but simply as "mister," since he refused all offers of titles and honorary degrees, fearing that they might set up a barrier between him and his followers. It was also for this reason that he never encouraged an organization to develop to spread his thought. Rather, he taught his Infinite Way doctrine personally and directly by his lecture tours, his books and a monthly letter he mailed directly to those who requested it.

Joel Goldsmsith died on June 17, 1964, at the age of 72. He was in London on a lecture tour.

Spiritual Healing

From

Realization of Oneness

Pure Being

For thousands of years, man has held God responsible for the evils of this world, believing that He rewards and punishes, that He is responsible for the accidents, diseases, and disasters of this earth, that tornadoes, cyclones, hurricanes, and tidal waves are acts of God. For thousands of years, too, man has been commanded: "And thou shalt love the Lord thy God with all thine heart, and with all thy soul, and with all thy might."[1] But is it possible for a person to love a God who at one moment may reward and bless and who at the next moment, for no reason whatsoever, may visit horrible diseases, accidents, and death upon him?

There is no way to "love the Lord thy God" except by understanding and becoming convinced that evil does not have its rise in

EDITOR'S NOTE: The material in *Realization of Oneness* first appeared in the form of letters sent to students of The Infinite Way throughout the world as an aid to the revelation and unfoldment of the transcendental Consciousness through a deeper understanding of Scripture and the principles of The Infinite Way.
[1]Deuteronomy 6:5.

God, and that neither sin, disease, accident, death, famine, storm, nor drought—none of these—comes forth from God. Only in the degree that we can disassociate God from being the cause of evil can we become free of it, because the evil in our experience stems from the belief that God, in some way, is responsible for it.

This misconception as to the nature of God was evident in the earliest days of the Hebrew people when they turned hopefully to God for their blessings, but at the same time feared His cursing. This is well illustrated in the story of Noah and the Ark. Because Noah was a good and upright man, God was going to save him, and He, therefore, instructed him to build an ark and fill it with all manner of beasts, with cattle, creeping things, and fowl with which to provide for him and his family. But the same God who was going to do that for Noah was going "to destroy all flesh, wherein is the breath of life."[2]

Is it possible that Noah was the only holy or righteous man on earth? Even were that true and all other men wicked, from whence would come their capacity to be evil? Where but from God, and if from God, why, then, would God punish them? And if God did not give man the capacity to sin, where would he receive this capacity, since God is his Father, his creative Principle, and the Source of all there is?

Perhaps in those days the people did not have the wisdom to raise such questions. They had only the darkness of superstition and ignorance and, therefore, they blessed God when He blessed them and cursed Him when disaster overtook them, believing that good and evil came forth from God.

With the advent of that spiritual light which was embodied in the consciousness of Jesus Christ in its fullness, we are presented with a different God, a God in whom there is no darkness, a God too pure to behold iniquity, a God who demands of us that we be so pure that we even forgive our enemies and pray for those who despitefully use us. The God Jesus gave to the world is a God that

[2]Genesis 6:17.

demands of us that we hold no one in condemnation, that we visit no punishment on the sinner.

IS MAN MORE LOVING AND JUST THAN GOD?

Is not God greater than we are? Is not the love of God greater than any love that we can express? Are not the wisdom and the justice of God greater than the wisdom and justice of man? To ascribe evil in any form to God is to make God lower than man, for of man it is demanded, "Be ye therefore perfect, even as your Father which is in heaven is perfect."[3] No one would ever consider any man perfect who visited sin, disease, or death on another—not for any reason! Even in this modern day when civilization is still in its infancy, man is developing enough love and understanding so that capital punishment is gradually being eliminated. If man can be that just and considerate, how much more compassionate and understanding must God be!

In some instances, this same consideration is now being extended to international relationships, so that today instead of wreaking vengeance on a country which has waged war against us we help bolster its tottering economy and strengthen its financial structure. If nations can do that, how much more can and does God do? How much more of love, intelligence, life, and purity is there in God! To ascribe less than perfection to God is sinful. It is blasphemy.

Many of the discords from which we suffer have their roots in the universal belief that God visits these evils upon us, either to punish us, to teach us a lesson, or for some other reason. There are those who even believe what is often preached at some funeral services, "God has called this dear one home." The "calling home" has often come about by way of cancer, consumption, or an automobile accident. It is blasphemous to believe that God operates in such a fashion. Nevertheless, the universal belief is that God is responsible for our troubles, and you and I are suffering from our

[3]Matthew 5:48.

ignorant and unconscious acceptance of that belief. We may not be aware of this, but it is so ingrained in consciousness that we suffer from it.

To begin to set ourselves free from the penalties of universal beliefs, we must release God from all responsibility for the sins, diseases, deaths, droughts, lacks, and limitations of this world. We must honor our Father which is in heaven. We must love the Lord our God with all our heart and with all our soul in the realization that He is too pure to behold iniquity or to cause it. He is the very light of the world, and in Him is no darkness at all.

ONENESS OF GOD AND MAN

When that conviction becomes bone of our bone and flesh of our flesh and when we have a God wholly good, we ourselves then are wholly good, for "I and my Father are one.[4] . . . Son, thou art ever with me, and all that I have is thine."[5] All the qualities we now attribute to God—all the purity, goodness, justice, love, and for-giveness—are in reality qualities of man, for God and man are one, just as the glass and the tumbler are one. What is the nature of the tumbler? Is there a tumbler or is there just glass? Is the tumbler merely a name for the form as which the glass is appearing? Glass is the essence of the tumbler; glass is its quality. How strong is the tumbler? As strong as the glass of which it is made. How beautiful is the tumbler? As beautiful as the glass of which it is made.

And what of man and his relationship to God? Is not man but the form or the temple, and God the essence of his being? Is it any more possible to separate God from man than glass from the tumbler? Is not God the substance of man's life, of his mind, of his Soul, and of his Spirit? Is not even his body the temple of God?

Once we perceive that oneness is the true relationship of God and man and, at the same time, perceive the pure nature of God in whom there is no propensity for evil, man is also recognized as pure and upright in whom there likewise is no propensity or capac-

[4]John 10:30.
[5]Luke 15:31.

ity for evil. Before we can wipe sin, disease, death, accident, poverty, or injustice off this earth, we must first remove it from God. Then we shall have a universe showing forth God's glory, and God's glory can be only perfection itself.

"He that hath seen me hath seen the Father[6] . . . [for] I and my Father are one."[7] The Father is greater than we are because the Father is the substance and essence of being, and we are but the form which appears in infinite variety. Just as the glass is greater than the form it takes and can be molded into a tumbler, a saucedish, or a pepper shaker, with the glass always retaining the quality, essence, character, and nature of whatever form it takes, so is God the nature, essence, activity, and the law unto every form, including man, animal, plant, and mineral.

The nature of man, then, is the nature of God expressed individually, and this man, therefore, must be the image and likeness of God, the showing forth of God. For man to be holy, God must be holy; for man to love his enemies, God must have no other feeling than love; for man to be forgiving, God must express no condemnation, no judgment, no punishment.

Is it not clear, then, that the beginning of freedom for you and for me is to have God wholly good, God from whom can come forth nothing but Spirit, eternality, and justice? God looked on what He had made, and behold, He found it very good. The goodness that is in God is innate in the goodness of His creation.

But if we claim that God is wholly good, that still has no effect on our life as long as we are separate and apart from God. God may be wholly good, but we do not share in that goodness until we can perceive our oneness with God as heir of God and joint-heir to all the heavenly riches, and accept the promise, "Son . . . all that I have is thine." Unless we can see that oneness, it will be like believing that Jesus was wholly good, that he was the son of God, but that we are not. What good is Jesus' perfection if it is not also our perfection? What good would come from God's being perfect,

[6]John 14:9.
[7]John 10:30.

if you and I were something separate and apart from God, subject to other influences?

But we are not something separate and apart from God. "I and my Father are one," and in that relationship of oneness the perfection of God is our perfection, and God's freedom from the capacity to sin or to suffer disease, lack, or limitation is also our freedom. Whatever goodness is being made manifest through us is God's goodness; whatever immortality is the immortality of God; whatever of love or of justice is the love or the justice of God; whatever of intelligence is God's.

"His understanding is infinite."[8] But what good is that to you or to me unless we are one with Him? In that relationship of oneness, His infinite understanding becomes the measure and the capacity of our understanding. Only in oneness can that happen, and so the moment We declare the infinite, perfect, spiritual nature of God, we are also declaring the perfection of our own being.

GOD IS FOREVER POURING ITSELF FORTH

In order to free ourselves from the limitations of human sense, we must understand the nature of God. God is not a power over evil, and we have no power over evil. To believe that God is a power over evil is to believe that evil has an existence, and then we either must believe God to be the cause and creator of it or we must accept another cause and creator, and the acceptance of any other cause or creator does away with Omnipotence, Omniscience, and Omnipresence.

We must have only one Creator, and that One without capacity for sin or any evil. Then we do not need a power over sin, disease, or death because these have no existence in God, and if they do not exist in God, they do not exist. They can exist only as beliefs in the human consciousness that believes in two powers, even believes that God has within Itself[9] two powers: the power

[8]Psalm 147:5.
[9]In the spiritual literature of the world, the varying concepts of God are indicated by the use of such words as "Father," "Mother," "Soul," "Spirit," "Principle," "Love," or "Life." Therefore, in this book, the author has used the pronouns "He" and "It," or "Himself" and "Itself," interchangeably in referring to God.

to reward and the power to punish, the power to give and the power to withhold.

How we "finitize" God! How we limit God! How we make God just a bigger edition of mortals when we make Him something that has the power to give or withhold sunshine, something that has the power to give or withhold crops! Such a belief places God in the same category as mortals. God is not like that at all. God cannot give sunshine, and God cannot withhold sunshine. God cannot give us life, and God cannot give us death. God *is* eternal life, and His life is the life of our being. He does not give it: *He is it.*

God does not give us purity. God is our Soul, and the Soul of God being pure, our Soul is pure. God does not give us wisdom. God is wisdom, but being infinite, God is our wisdom. There is no giving, and there is no withholding. There is only *"Is-ing."* If there were a God-life and our life, God-life might be immortal and ours mortal; but if God is infinite, God is infinite life, and that means your life and my life.

THERE IS NO GOD IN EVIL

To know Him aright is life eternal, and as we begin to know God as complete, pure Being, without any capacity to wipe out a nation or punish sinners, God that cannot visit disease on inno-cent persons or even on guilty persons, God that does not permit conditions of war or poverty, we have freed ourselves, because much of the cause of evil in our lives is the belief that in some way God is the cause of it, the author, the creator, and the main-tainer of it.

When we come to know God aright, we have a God that we can love with all our heart and with all our soul, because we can look upon this world with its injustices, sins, and disasters and be thank-ful that there is no God in any of the evils besetting mankind. When we have removed God from them, we have removed the substance from them, and they begin to destroy themselves. They begin to dissolve.

God is never in any form of force—"not by might, nor by power, but by my spirit."[10] There is no evil where *My*[11] Spirit is, for where *My* Spirit is, there is liberty.

The world must awaken. It must awaken to the realization of the true nature of God in order to remove the cause of evil. Some persons believe that wars are righteous, and that God is on one side or another. God on the side of people out killing! God on the side of people murdering innocent men and women and children! God could not be in a war. God is not in the whirlwind; God is not in the storm: God is in the still small voice.

OVERCOMING IDOLATRY

When we come face to face with our fears, what do we find? We are usually fearing some person, thing, or condition, or, on the other hand, very often we may be worshiping some person, thing, or condition. Habbakuk had a word for it:

> What profiteth the graven image that the maker thereof hath graven it; the molten image, and a teacher of lies, that the maker of his work trusteth therein, to make dumb idols?

> Woe unto him that saith to the wood, Awake; to the dumb stone, Arise, it shall teach! Behold, it is laid over with gold and silver, and there is no breath at all in the midst of it.

> But the Lord is in his holy temple: let all the earth keep silence before him.

>   Habbakuk 2:18-20

Many persons place their hopes and fears in persons or things. It may be in gold or silver; it may be in land or in securities, or even in social security; but when hope, ambition, and confidence are in something external, that is nothing more nor less than idol-

[10]Zechariah 4:6.
[11]The word "My," capitalized, refers to God.

atry. All this disappears when we understand that the nature of God is the nature of individual being; and, therefore, there is no need to want some particular person, thing, or circumstance, for we embody our good. "Son, thou art ever with me, and all that I have is thine." All that *I*[12] have! Let us not worry about what somebody else has! "All that *I* have is thine."

In the realization that God is our very own being, how can we fear, love, or hate gold or silver, germs or poisons, bullets or bombs? How can we fear that God or God's being can be destroyed? And is not God's being the essence and substance of our being? We are the tumbler, the form, but God is the essence and substance even of our bodies. We need not fear what mortals can do to us. We need not fear what mortal circumstances or conditions can do to us. God is the essence of our being, and in Him there is no darkness. Therefore, in that of which we are formed, there is no capacity for negative activity of any form or nature. But, if we do not know the nature of God, how can we know the nature of our perfect Self? If we do not credit God with being pure, how then can we be pure? We can be no more pure than our Source, our Essence, our Substance.

When we see evil in any form—in our own experience, in the experience of the world or of our neighbor—we can smile within ourseles as we realize:

There is no God in this. This never had its rise in God: it has no God-substance, no God-law, no God-life, no God-being. It is the "arm of flesh,"[13] nothingness.[14]

[12]The word *"I,"* italicized, refers to God.
[13]II Chronicles 32:8.
[14]The italicized portions of this book are spontaneous meditations that have come to the author during periods of uplifted consciousness and are not in any sense intended to be used as affirmations, denials, or formulas. They have been inserted in this book from time to time to serve as examples of the free flowing of the Spirit. As the reader practices the Presence, he, too, in his exalted moments, will receive ever new and fresh inspirations as the outpouring of the Spirit.

This immediately takes from evil its sting. We let it dissolve of itself and disappear from sight by removing from it that which gives it life, that is, the belief that it is of God, that it emanates from God, and that God is responsible for it. But if there is no evil in God, there is no evil at all for God is the source of all creation. We need only to look at any situation and realize: "There is no God in this, no power to sustain it, and no law of God to maintain it. There is no power but God." Then it must dissolve and disappear.

This removes idolatry. It prevents us from loving, fearing, or hating that which has form, because we know that the real essence of all form is God. Any erroneous form that may appear has no existence except in the belief in two powers, or except in the belief that God caused it. Once we remove God as the cause, foundation, and source of evil, we have begun its dissolution.

As human beings, we are living a life separate and apart from God, and as long as we do that, there is certain to be some good and some evil. This is because we have no clear-cut principle by which to live. We have not grasped the meaning of the omnipresence of God. We do not understand that where God is, *I* am, that the place whereon we stand is holy ground, that the presence of God is within us, that there is a God "closer . . . than breathing, and nearer than hands and feet,"[15] and that wherever we go God goes with us. If we mount up to heaven, we find God there; if we make our bed in hell, there, too, we find God; if we "walk through the valley of the shadow of death,"[16] God is there.

But what is the nature of this Presence that is with us? Is the presence of God going to reward us? Is It going to punish us? Is It going to heal us? Is It going to visit iniquity upon us "unto the third and fourth generation,"[17] or is this God that is with us a wholly good influence, a perfect influence, an influence for freedom, joy, and for infinite good in our life?

The first step on the spiritual path is to become aware of God's

---

[15]Alfred, Lord Tennyson. *The Higher Pantheism*, Stanza 6.
[16]Psalm 23:4.
[17]Exodus 20:5.

presence, to live always as if God were bearing witness with us, as if God were going before us. Once that is attained, our next great unfoldment must be the nature of God because this is the step that brings freedom and release from what the Master called "this world."[18] To know God as that pure Being in whom evil has no rise, no source, no foundation, no cause, and no power is to live in freedom because if He is not the cause of evil, it has no cause, for God alone is law, life, substance, activity, and being.

This makes it possible to overcome idolatry, because when we have a God of purity, there is nothing to fear, there is no person or thing which can have any qualities of evil derived from God. Anything derived from mortal consciousness is not of God, and therefore not power. So when we behold injustices, inequalities, sins, persecutions, and revilings, our answer should be, "So what! Be not afraid! None of this emanates from God, and therefore, you, Pilate, 'couldest have no power at all against me.'[19] The only power that you have is that which is derived from God. What is not derived from God is not power."

CHRISTHOOD AROUND THE GLOBE

Every kind of evil in international affairs will be dissolved, but it will be dissolved because there are now persons on earth knowing that these evils have no existence in God; and therefore, they have no existence. They do not have their rise in God; therefore, they have no power. Just ten righteous men in a city can save it—a few hundred or a few thousand who can face every situation of human experience in the realization, "You do not have your rise in God, so you are not power. You have no foundation in God; you have no power. You have no law of God to maintain or sustain you; you have no power."

Then rest! Rest in His word. Rest in this Word; abide in this Word; dwell "in the secret place of the most High,"[20] always looking out at these forms or formations without hate, love, or fear,

---

[18]John 18:36.
[19]John 19:11.
[20]Psalm 91:1.

knowing that if they do not have their rise in God, they have no substance, no law, no cause, no effect.

As we are able to prove a degree of freedom from these universal beliefs in our individual experience, we begin to free our neighbor—not because he asks us to pray for him, but because when we see his sins or his diseases, we know within ourselves: "This has no rise in God, no foundation in God; it has no law of God. Be not afraid."

Such a response to evil makes of every person an influence in the world because, even though he cannot physically be present all over the world, by his influence he will be imparting the truth of the all-power of God and the nonpower of evil, so that he will be a part of a circle of Christhood around the globe. What is a circle of Christhood except a circle of those who realize that evil does not have its rise in God and, therefore, it has no law and no substance to sustain it? By abiding in that truth, they watch it as it dissolves and disappears.

That is the circle of Christhood: those who do not accept evil as real, because they do not accept evil as having a foundation in God.

The Secret of The Infinite Way

The secret of The Infinite Way is revealed in the truth that the only God there is, is Consciousness, and since God is the one Consciousness, this is the Consciousness of individual man and, therefore, the Consciousness of individual man is his creator, maintainer, and sustainer. Out of the Consciousness of individual man must come all that is necessary for his fulfillment.

The Master, repeating the revelation of Moses, "*I AM THAT I AM*,"[21] gave *I* as the secret name of God: *I* am the bread, the meat, the wine, and the water; "I am the resurrection.[22] . . . I am the way, the truth, and the life."[23] So you must see that even if you destroy this temple, whether it is the temple of your body, of your home,

[21]Exodus 3:14.
[22]John 11:25.
[23]John 14:6.

of your family, of your fortune, or of your business—whatever temple you may destroy—I will raise it up again because *I* is Consciousness, or God.

When man turns anywhere other than to the Withinness of his own being for life, supply, harmony, health, wholeness, completeness, success, wisdom, purity, or any other imaginable thing or thought, he is turning to where it is not, and the result is that there are persons of every religion and denomination praying in churches throughout the world. How many of such prayers are answered? And why is this? Because the prayers are addressed to a Presence and Power separate and apart from the one praying; whereas if the prayer were addressed to God in the inner sanctuary of his own being, in secrecy, where the Master told us to address it; and then, were the person to pray not for *things*—not for his life, or what he should eat or drink, but pray for a realization of the nature of the kingdom of God—then all these *things* would be added unto him from within the divine Consciousness which is his own being.

Why does Isaiah say, "Is there a God beside me? yea, there is no God; I know not any"?[24] This "Me"[25] is *I*, and this *I* is the infinite, divine Consciousness of my individual being. Therefore, I am not Its master, nor do I have the wisdom to tell It what I want, or when, how much, or how little; nor do I have the wisdom to direct It to anyone else, because the *I* of me is infinite, divine Consciousness, the All-knowing.

As revealed in Scripture, God is in the "still small voice,"[26] and so the only form of true prayer is the inner listening ear. It is for this reason that the most important part of our work in The Infinite Way is meditation, because no one has access to the inner sanctuary of his being, his inner consciousness, except through the listening ear. Meditation is the practice of listening for this still small voice, creating within one's self practically a vacuum in which the presence of God can announce Itself.

[24]Isaiah 44:8.
[25]The word "Me," capitalized, refers to God.
[26]I Kings 19:12.

Students complain that this is difficult. It is difficult largely because it has not been practiced for hundreds of years, and they must now learn something that has been out of consciousness for generations. That is not easy. If students are seeking an easy path, they are not going to find it in The Infinite Way because The Infinite Way has no other access to the kingdom of God than through meditation.

Any degree of good that a student may receive from a practitioner or a teacher is only of temporary help because it is still true that while a Moses can lead his flock *to* the Promised Land, he cannot take them *into* it. That, they must do for themselves. The Master later confirmed this in his statement, "If I go not away, the Comforter will not come unto you."27 By "Comforter," he meant that which completes your demonstration, that which provides you with the ultimate comfort, the full peace, and the fulfillment of your destiny. And even as it came to the Master, as it came to Moses, Elijah, and Isaiah, so must it come to you.

Remember that not even Jesus took his disciples into the kingdom of heaven. He left them on earth and told them to remain in that consciousness until they were imbued from on High with spiritual power, a clear indication that the Master felt that his disciples had not yet attained the necessary vision to know how to meditate properly and draw forth from the Father within all that He had been teaching them, which, in the last analysis, must come from the Father within, and not from any external source.

Why do you think the Master made it so clear that the kingdom of God is neither "Lo here! or, lo there!"28 and that it is not to be found in holy mountains or in holy temples, but rather it is within you? And why do you think that the mystical poet, Robert Browning, had the vision that Truth is within you and that you must open out a way for the imprisoned splendor to escape? How are you going to do this without meditation, without creating within yourself a vacuum through the listening ear, so that from this divine Consciousness can come forth your meat, wine, bread,

27John 16:7.
28Luke 17:21.

water, resurrection, and even "restore to you the years that the locust hath eaten."[29]

If you have not learned from the message of The Infinite Way that the only good you are ever going to receive is from within your own consciousness, then you have failed to perceive the nature of its message and mission, which is that God constitutes your consciousness and that through meditation you must draw forth from within your own consciousness the allness and the fulfillment of life.

Infinity and immortality are made manifest as the consciousness of the individual, and the name of this divine Consciousness, which is our individual consciousness, is *I*. You must understand that you are not to direct this *I*, enlighten It, plead with It, or try to be a master of It, but that you are to submit and yield yourself servant to the *I* of your own being, so that your prayer is that *I* fulfill Itself as your individual experience, that *I* be the Grace which is your sufficiency, and then *let* this *I* which is your true Selfhood govern your life in Its own way.

When you then go into prayer and meditation, there must be no preconceived idea as to what you want or how you wish your prayer to be answered. There must be a complete yielding as you daily realize, "Not my will, but thine, be done."[30] Do not go to God with your thoughts and do not try to have God fulfill your way, because you will fail. You must go to God, the divine Consciousness of your own being, the very *I* which you are, with this prayer: "Reveal to me Thy way, Thy will, Thy thought, and this, then, will be my way, my will, and my thought."

Now we come to the revelation of The Infinite Way that must startle those who are not prepared for it. Nevertheless, until this revelation has been discerned, the fruitage of the Message cannot fully come into the experience of an individual. I ask you to look at a tree. It does not make any different what tree you look at, but look at some tree. You know that from this tree seeds develop and that these seeds drop into the ground at the foot of the tree, or are

[29]Joel 2:25.
[30]Luke 22:42.

carried away by birds and dropped into the ground somewhere else, and that, in time, these seeds become new trees.

As you look at the tree, if possible, visualize a seed still on the tree, and then watch the seed drop into the ground. While you are doing this, remember that the life of the tree is the life of the seed. When the seed drops into the ground, the life of the tree is still the life of the seed, and when the seed gets into the earth and breaks open and becomes a root, the life of the tree, which was the life of the seed, is now the life of the root. The root now grows up into a tree, and it is still the life of the tree, which was the life of the seed, which is now the life of the tree. While, to sight, you have tree, seed, and tree, actually you have only one life manifesting itself as a tree, a seed, and the new tree—always the same life.

In using the tree as an example of Life expressing Itself, what I want you to see is that you are not the tree, that you never were the seed, and that you are not the new tree: you are the life of that first tree, of the seed, and of the next tree. Therefore, your life has been, and is, continuous since "before Abraham was."[31] As a matter of fact, the life of God is your life; therefore, your life coexisted with God in the beginning, and down through all the ages of fathers, mothers, grandfathers, grandmothers, great-grandparents, and on into infinity, but always it is the one Life which *I AM*.

Actually, therefore, *I* am the life of all my ancestors, and *I* will be the life of all my children, grandchildren, great-grandchildren, and great-great-grandchildren, because it will be the same life appearing as me, as the seed, as my child, as his seed, and as his child. Always it will be *I* appearing *as*. This is my immortality, the immortality of my life manifested as many forms in many generations.

When you look in the mirror, please remember that you are not seeing "you": you are seeing your body, just as, when you look at the tree, you are not seeing a tree at all: you are seeing the body of a tree, for the tree itself is life. So the Self of you, which is *I AM*, is the real you, and the body is only the form, and as you drop

[31]John 8:58.

a seed, it will still be your life. Then, as your child appears, it will be the life which *you* are, appearing as another form, and therefore, you are immortalized in your children, and as your children, all the way down to the end of time. The secret is, "'I will never leave thee, nor forsake thee.'[32] *I* will be with thee unto the end of time, for *I* am thee."

Since there is but one Consciousness, and therefore, there can be but one *I*, remember that *I* am not only the life of my children and the life of my parents, *I* am the life of my neighbors, of their cats, their dogs, and their crops, and *I* am the life of my enemies. It is for this reason that the Master taught us to forgive seventy times seven, to pray for our enemies, and to do unto others as we would have others do unto us. The reason is that anything you do to another you are doing unto yourself because there is but one Self, and *I* am that Self.

Be assured that even the money that you give to benevolences is only being transferred from your right-hand pocket to your left-hand pocket, because *I* is the only Selfhood, and therefore, what you give never leaves you. This is the bread that you cast on the water of life which comes back to you. The forgiveness that you give to those who have offended you is the forgiving of yourself because there is no other Self than *I AM*, and without the forgiving of others, there can be no forgiving of yourself, for *I* am the only other.

When you pray for your enemies, you are praying for yourself. You are doing unto others as you would have others do unto you, and the reason is that the enemy is yourself. Therein is one of the great secrets of mysticism. The twelve disciples of Jesus were not men: they were facets of his own consciousness. The Master embodied within himself the qualities of Peter, John, and Judas. Like it or not, this is the mystical truth.

You may think that you have loving friends and unloving ones, but you have neither. These loving friends and unloving friends are qualities of your own consciousness, which are you being external-

[32]Hebrews 13:5.

ized. It is as if you were to draw pictures of twelve men and women, any twelve you like, and when you had drawn them, you may be assured that you would have drawn your own concepts of manhood and womanhood, and nothing else, and there would be no use in blaming anybody for how your men and women looked.

So you have drawn the pictures of your loving and of your unloving friends, and they are ideas in your mind. You have projected them, and they are your images in thought. The only way they will ever be changed is by changing your concepts of manhood and womanhood, and the higher the ideal of manhood and womanhood you attain, the higher manifestation of men and women will be drawn into your experience.

Across the Desk

This comes to you from London as the year 1963 draws to a close—the most momentous year of my work since receiving my initiation and instructions in The Infinite Way in 1946. This year, 1963, the word came to me to take our students from metaphysics to mysticism.

My personal life has had many difficult periods since my first spiritual experience in 1929 because that experience lifted me into the fourth-dimensional consciousness, and yet I had to live in two worlds in order to carry on first a healing ministry and then both healing and teaching. Except when done in absolute silence, spiritual healing and teaching are conducted out from the ordinary consciousness, and yet the inspiration is always from above. To live in two worlds has always been difficult for me, but it has been necessary as there must be the metaphysical consciousness on earth before the mystical can be attained.

In 1959, I was instructed to give a full year of classes on the basic principles of The Infinite Way and then begin raising up the son of God in man. Finally, this year the word came to lift our students out of the metaphysical into the mystical, and this mission was immediately undertaken.

First, I gave instructions to ministers and Infinite Way teachers, instructions which are contained in five teaching tapes which have now become available to all students. These give the principles which for all time will establish students on a firm foundation for healing and teaching The Infinite Way. Regardless of whether anyone ever heals or teaches others, this is his foundation for spiritual unfoldment.

Then, with students coming to Hawaii from near and far, I began the transition in consciousness for our students from the metaphysical to the mystical. This work is embodied in the three *1963 Princess Kaiulani Sunday Series* tape recordings and the nine *1963 Kailua Private Class* tapes.

What measure of Grace these bring to anyone is wholly dependent on the measure of dedication he brings to the study, and especially to the meditation and practice. You may accept this as a major spiritual principle: you receive only in proportion to what you bring or give. There is no such thing as *getting* spiritually. What you bring or give to any spiritual life is reflected back to you.

A Parenthesis in Eternity[33] is given us at this particular time to make it clear to you and to the world that the day of spiritual grace has come upon the world. Furthermore, ever since its publication, *The Contemplative Life*[34] has been my Infinite Way bible. I know that as you come to understand this book, it will be your bible, too.

Regardless of the progress, or lack of it, in our students, the Message is now in consciousness, and its purpose is being served. The unfoldment of truth in consciousness is not dependent on man, but when truth is released, it serves the purpose whereunto it is sent. God's will is being done on earth.

If they wish, our students can be instruments of God's grace, but whether they are or not, be assured that God has sent His word into consciousness, and it is now being established and will bear fruit, rich and ripe and abundant.

[33]By the author (New York: Harper and Row, 1963; London: George Allen and Unwin, 1964).
[34]By the author (New York: The Julian Press, 1963; London: L. N. Fowler and Co. Ltd., 1963).

Lifting Up the *I*

There is no one mode, means, method, or system which can correctly be called metaphysical or spiritual healing. In fact, there are as many different approaches to spiritual healing as there are in *materia medica* with its allopathy, homeopathy, osteopathy, chiropractic and naprapathy, all different forms of *materia medica*.

In the world of metaphysical and spiritual healing, there are the evangelists who, by the grace of God, have received some special state of consciousness through which they heal without knowing how, why, or wherefore. For the most part, they do not have the slightest idea of any principle involved in healing: they only know that healings do take place, sometimes through the spoken word and sometimes through the laying on of hands. Apparently, it is something that is just a part of their being, something that has come to them at a particular period in their life, and something over which they have no control.

Then there are those approaches to healing which employ mental means and, by suggestion, attempt to change a diseased or evil condition into a good one. There are also methods which attempt to combine the mental and the spiritual.

A person who has had any experience with other forms of metaphysical or spiritual healing and decides to practice healing through Infinite Way healing principles may have to unlearn most of what he has previously known in order to grasp these principles, and if he encounters difficulty on the way it is probably because he has not yet unlearned enough.

AN UNDERSTANDING OF IMMORTALITY, BASIC TO HEALING

The Infinite Way begins with an infinite, ever present, omnipotent God. Its premise is that there is no imperfection in any part of God or of God's creation, none whatsoever! God is perfect being, and so, therefore, is God's creation. No one was ever born, and no one will ever die; no one ever had a beginning, and no one will ever have an ending.

One way to understand the continuity of life is through the word "I." This *I*, which is our identity, is actually coexistent with God. It is the eternal part of our being. It has no knowledge of birth or death. It is that part of our being which has existed for billions of years, and will continue to exist without interruption for many more billions of years. As long as there is God, there will be a "you" and a "me" because we are one with God: "I and my Father are one,"[1] and not two. The *I* which I am and the *I* which is God are one and the same *I*, and therefore, *I* is immortal.

Very often, when we think of immortality, we think of life beyond the grave, but we do not stop to realize that if there is any truth to immortality it must also mean life before birth. We cannot be immortal if we have a life that ever began: immortality is from everlasting to everlasting. God can no more begin than He

[1]John 10:30.

can end, and if God and I are one, the *I* of me, in that oneness, has never begun and will never end.

Our identity remains intact, spiritual, and perfect, not only after the grave, but it was so even before we were born. Our life from the cradle to the grave is that experience which has been likened to a parenthesis, but when the parenthesis is removed we live in the full circle of immortality. It is true that while we may be aware of ourselves as living only in this particular parenthesis, slowly or rapidly moving from birth to death, actually it is possible for this parenthesis to be removed and for us to become aware of our true identity as one with the entire circle of life and its immortality and eternality.

Once we can realize ourselves as *I*, separate and apart from personality, separate and apart from a physical body, as *I*, the incorporeal, spiritual *I*, we will have the secret of the eternality and immortality of life: without beginning, without birth; without ending, without death.

Since the *I* that God is and the *I* that we are, are one, we can understand that the infinite perfection of God is the infinite perfection of our being. "Son, thou art ever with me, and all that I have is thine."[2] This does not refer to material things: dollar bills, bank accounts, property, fur coats, or automobiles. "All that *I* have" means all the immortality, spirituality, integrity, all the life, all the perfection, all the holiness of God. All that is of God is of you and of me because the *I* of you and of me and the *I* of God are one and the same *I*, and all the qualities of God are the qualities of spiritual eternal, immortal man: of you and of me.

This is the premise in Infinite Way healing work, and if we want to heal, we must first of all remind ourselves of this truth. We must be conscious of the truth that the *I* of you and of me and the *I* of God are one, and all that constitutes the *I* of God constitutes the *I* of you and of me, for we are forever one with the Father. All that is of God is ours: all the immortality, eternality, spiritual perfection, harmony, peace, justice, infinity.

[2]Luke 15:31.

DISCORD, THE FRUITAGE OF SOWING TO THE FLESH

When we have established ourselves in that spiritual truth, the next question on which we must be clear is: But what about this sin, this disease, this false appetite, this lack or limitation, this unemployment, this lost baggage?

All the writings of The Infinite Way clearly reveal where evil comes from and why it comes. They explain its relation to karmic law, as it is called in the Orient, or the as-ye-sow-so-shall-ye-reap of the Bible. "He that soweth to his flesh shall of the flesh reap corruption; but he that soweth to the Spirit shall of the Spirit reap life everlasting."[3] And the Master taught, "He that abideth in me, and I in him, the same bringeth forth much fruit."[4] If we do not abide in the Word and let the Word abide in us, we will be as a branch of a tree that is cut off, withers, and dies. Every moment of every day determines what our tomorrows will be. As we sow, in this moment, so will we reap tomorrow, next week, next year, or ten years from now.

This teaching has often been interpreted to mean that if we obey the Ten Commandments we are sowing good and will reap good; and if we disobey the Ten Commandments, we are sowing to the flesh and will reap corruption. This is utter nonsense. It has no such meaning whatsoever! The as-ye-sow-so-shall-ye-reap doctrine means that if we abide in the spiritual truth of being, we will reap harmony because then we are sowing to the Spirit and will reap spiritual fruitage. But if we accept the world's belief in two powers, its belief in Spirit and matter, in good and evil, then we are going to experience both good and evil.

While we are part of this human race into which we were born, we are sowing to the flesh, and we are going to reap corruption, even if we obey the Ten Commandments to the letter. This is what the Master meant when he said to his followers, "Except your righteousness shall exceed the righteousness of the scribes and Pharisees, ye shall in no case enter into the kingdom of heav-

[3]Galatians 6:8.
[4]John 15:5.

en."[5] These two Hebrew sects lived in complete obedience to the laws of the Temple. They dotted every "i" and crossed every "t." They spent every moment required by theological law in worship; they observed every feast day, every fast day, and every holiday; they tithed; they sacrificed; they lived up to the Ten Commandments and to all the laws of the Temple, but Jesus said, "Your righteousness [must] exceed" that of those persons who are 100 per cent perfect! It sounds impossible, but it is not.

If we sow to the Spirit, we will be obeying the Ten Commandments without even being aware of so doing and without any temptation to do otherwise. Therefore, we do not have to concern ourselves with the Ten Commandments. What we have to concern ourselves with is to abide in the spiritual word of truth. This is not easy of accomplishment because it means that what we accept into our consciousness is going to determine our experience. We have to begin with the acceptance of the universal belief in good and evil, and we have to reject that and say to ourselves, "No, I accept neither good nor evil: I accept only God, Spirit, as infinite All, and in God there is neither good nor evil: there is only spiritual, perfect, harmonious being."

When Satan stands in front of us insisting that there are two powers—spiritual powers and material or mental powers—we have to be quiet enough so that the *I* of us can reply, "No, no, I accept God, I accept spiritual being as the All. I accept the scriptural truth that nothing can enter God 'that defileth . . . or maketh a lie,'[6] nothing! Only God is God, and God is infinite perfection, so there cannot be powers of good and of evil; there cannot be spiritual powers and mental or material powers. There can be only God-power, infinite, spiritual God-power." This refusal to accept in our consciousness good and evil, spiritual and material or mental powers, and this holding steadfastly to the word *I* is sowing to the Spirit.

[5]Matthew 5:20.
[6]Revelation 21:27.

CONCESSIONS IMPOSED BECAUSE OF LIVING IN "THIS WORLD"

We are constantly faced with good persons and bad persons, but we cannot accept either good persons or bad persons, sick persons or well persons: We must accept only the children of God, spiritual identity.

It is true that in our daily affairs and in our speech we make concessions to appearances. For example, every time anyone asks a practitioner for help, and he responds with "I will give you help," that is a concession to appearances, but it is something that must be done. No one can be completely absolute in such a situation and say, "No, I will not give you any help because you are already perfect."

The patient's response would very likely be, "Well, if you won't give me any help, then I will find somebody who will."

So an Infinite Way practitioner makes concessions and says, "Of course, I will give you help at once," but within himself, he cannot believe that. The *I* of him has to be knowing inwardly, "No, the *I* which is God is my Self, and the *I* which is God is your Self. There is only one Power; there is only one Presence; there is only one Law; there is only one Being." By the time the practitioner has attained this realization, the patient will probably be beginning to feel better. Nevertheless a concession to the call for help has been made, and in a measure we do that in all our affairs.

Politically, we will speak of one candidate as a good candidate, and another as a bad one. This is only a part of the human drama. Inwardly, we realize that for voting purposes we are judging those candidates from a personal standpoint in terms of our own frame of reference. Actually, we know better: we know that *I* am he. Even though he does not know it, we know! If we are not knowing that the *I* of me is the *I* of you, and the *I* of you and of me is the *I* of God, for we are one, we are sowing to the flesh.

So it is that in normal, everyday conversation, especially with those who are not on this Path, in speaking of the weather, the climate, germs, and all other so-called material powers, we are not going to argue with anyone and try to show how bright we are, or how stupid. "Agree with thine adversary."[7] Do not start an argument with anyone who is talking about what bad weather, bad crops, or bad times we are having. It is not so important what we do in the way of lip service: what counts is what we are doing within.

SEEING THROUGH UNIVERSAL BELIEFS
IN THE AREA OF RELATIONSHIPS

In no area is this better illustrated than with parents and their children. There are many occasions when parents have to discipline their children, and times when they may appear quite angry with them; but they must be sure that they are doing this only outwardly, not inwardly. In their hearts, they cannot accept this. Their outward show of displeasure is only for the purpose of correcting the young, immature thought that could not possibly grasp this idea of perfection in one explanation and, because of the universal belief, could not live up to it.

For the most part, children are not children at all: they are just ages. There are one-year-olds, two-year-olds, six-year-olds, and twelve-year-olds. Those falling into a particular age bracket act alike, and they are very much alike in their responses. It is only through the spiritual work and training of their parents that eventually they become individuals, but left to themselves, they all pattern their conduct according to the accepted standard of their peers at the different ages through which they pass. But this can be changed as parents understand that what they are being faced with as ugly behavior on the part of their child is merely a belief, universal to that age group.

In the same way, we can bring out a different relationship with our neighbor and with the persons that we deal with in business,

[7]Matthew 5:25.

not so much by acting differently outwardly as by an inward real-ization of the truth of their identity. They are neither good nor bad; they are neither sick nor well; they are neither rich nor poor: they are spiritual. Spirit has no shifting, changing qualities, and Its only quantity is infinity. To sow to the Spirit we must be continu-ously entertaining a spiritual awareness, having uppermost in our consciousness a spiritual understanding of the nature of God, man, and the universe. We must inwardly know that the only law is spir-itual law, and in the knowing of this, mental and material laws are nullified.

Once we have raised up the *I* in ourselves, so that this *I* that does not accept appearances is governing our experience, we will less and less accept powers of good and evil, or material and mental powers, but will recognize only spiritual power. This *I* that we have raised up within us that will not permit a negative thought to get past It, this *I* now governs our life and the lives of those who turn to us.

This *I* we have had with us from the beginning. We brought It into this world with us, but because of the world's ignorance of truth, we also came into the world ignorant of truth. Because of that ignorance, what handled us, therefore, what has governed our lives, and what now governs the lives of all human beings is a form of hypnotism or malpractice—whatever it is that makes us think good and evil, hear good and evil, see good and evil, and act from the standpoint of good and evil. In short, it is whatever makes us accept appearances at face value.

"JUDGE RIGHTEOUS JUDGMENT"

Those who are not familiar with the optical illusions engendered by atmospheric conditions on the desert will probably accept the appearance of a big beautiful lake with a wonderful city built around it which looms up before them, and will start driving their car toward that beautiful lake, even looking for a hotel where they can spend the night. However, those who understand the phenom-

enon of a mirage do not for a moment accept the appearance of a
lake or a city at face value: they instantly recognize that this is
mirage.

In "this world," where an ignorance of truth predominates, we
are constantly being faced with sin, disease, death, lack, and limitation, with evil of every kind. We accept the world of appearances
and pay the penalty for that acceptance. If, on the other hand, we
have been spiritually taught, we will instantly recognize that these
suggestions that come to us are appearances like the mirage on the
desert. The Master taught, "Judge not according to the appearance,
but judge righteous judgment."[8] So I say to you, "Having eyes, do
you not see through this appearance? Having ears, do you not hear
beyond this appearance? Do not accept appearances of good and
evil at face value. Accept them only as mirage, illusion, a form of
malpractice, or hypnotism, and above all things, do not accept
them as something that has to be healed, reformed, changed, or
corrected."

Every day we meet up with material laws, mental laws, and legal
laws. Every day we meet up with appearances of sin, false appetite,
disease, evil men in government, and spiritual wickedness in high
places. There is not a day in which these suggestions do not cross
our path. We cannot avoid them, not by going away to a convent,
a monastery, or an ashrama because wherever we are we take the
world right with us. Wherever we go, the newspapers will shout,
and the radios will blare.

As a matter of fact, the higher we go in spiritual realization, the
more of evil and discordant appearances will be brought to our
doorstep, because sick persons, sinning persons, and poor persons
gravitate to those of spiritual light to pour out their burdens. And
this is right; it is right! The Christ of us says, "Drop your burdens
at My feet. My yoke is light. Just pour them all out. They are of
no weight to Me."

We really do not have to get rid of any of the sins, diseases,
lacks, or limitations of the persons who come to us. We merely

[8]John 7:24.

have to refuse to accept the appearances and realize that whatever is presented to us is a state of hypnotism producing an illusion, a mirage.

We must stand fast in spite of every appearance, in spite of every cry of pain, in spite of everything: *I* within you and *I* within me must stand fast and not accept it. Because the *I* within us has been lifted up, we see through the mirage to Reality. In God's kingdom, there is not a sin, disease, death, lack, or limitation. In the whole of God's kingdom, there is not an evil of any nature. We have to stand fast in that truth, and let the appearances hit up against us until they break.

Some of them break rapidly, some of them will not break so rapidly, and a few refuse to break at all. Why? One reason may be that as practitioners we are not rising quite as high into heavenly consciousness as we should be. I will admit that if our practitioners could be a little more separate and apart from the ways of the world they could do better works, but because we all have to live in this world and with it, it may be that we do not rise high enough in spiritual consciousness to do all the works that we should do.

The other reason is that the patients will not yield. They usually have in mind the changing of an evil condition into a good one, and this acts as a block. Spiritual healing is not changing an evil condition into a good one: healing is really the changing of consciousness, and very often there is a reluctance or unwillingness to yield up whatever it is that is acting as a block.

This is never done consciously. We never blame anyone for whatever it is that he is holding onto because he cannot help it, any more than we can help whatever it is that we hold onto. It is something deep down in our consciousness, and the answer lies in keeping on until there is a yielding.

WE CANNOT GET RID OF AN APPEARANCE

In Infinite Way healing work, we are not turning to God to heal anybody. We do not have the kind of God who would let anyone be sick if it were within His knowledge, and if we recognize God to be Omniscience and Omnipotence we surely could not find any-one outside of God's knowledge. It is entirely a matter of the indi-vidual called a practitioner being able to rise to that state of con-sciousness which refuses to accept the appearance, knowing its hypnotic and illusory source, and the nothingness of it because it is not supported by a law of God.

No sin and no disease are supported by a law of God. If they were, they would be eternal. We can never hope to change any-thing that is supported by God. If it has a law of God to maintain it, we cannot hope to break it, and the very fact that we do break through our sins, our diseases, and our lacks is sufficient proof that there never was any law of God supporting them. A law of matter, yes; a law of mind, yes; but these are not laws of God, and for this very reason, any form of evil can be dispelled.

We need never be afraid to try to heal, regardless of the name or nature of the claim, because, to begin with, we have the aware-ness that there is no law of God supporting or maintaining any erroneous condition; and we know that no law of God created it. God never made it.

Humanly it is true that we are sick and we die; but let us this moment free ourselves from the superstition that God has anything to do with any of this, and let us put the blame on our own shoul-ders. It is our ignorance, yours and mine, nobody else's; but if it is your ignorance and mine, it is only our ignorance because we are a part of the universal ignorance which has been handed down to us.

Anyone can undertake healing work at any time if he will real-ize the basic principle that he is not trying to remove a disease, a condition, a sin, or a false appetite. The moment anyone tries to do that, he is trapped, and there will be no healing.

We are not dealing with a sin, with a disease, with a false appetite, or with a lack. We are dealing with an illusory appearance that must be recognized as having no God-law, God-ordination, God-presence, or God-power. We are not dealing with a condi-tion, but with a universal belief in a selfhood apart from God. Any condition or situation is always a universal belief, always a universal claim. It is never the fault of our patient; it is never the fault of our student; it is never the fault of ourselves: it is a universal claim of two powers, a universal claim of a selfhood apart from God, a universal belief in good and evil. But the truth is *I*:

> *I and the Father are one. All that is true of the Father is true of me because of oneness. God is Spirit, and I am spiritual. God is immortal and eternal, and I am immortal and eternal.*

This is not only the truth about us: it is the truth about the patient, the student, or anyone who has called upon us for help.

We are dealing with an appearance, an appearance produced by a universal malpractice, a universal ignorance, a universal hypnotism, *but only an appearance*. We are not to attempt to get rid of the appearance. *We can no more get rid of an appearance that we can get rid of the mirage on the desert*. We can only see through it and understand it to be a mirage, and then go on about our business. Usually in the moment of our recognizing it as mirage, the picture dissolves. So it is, too, in healing. In our realization of the illusory nature of the appearance, the appearance dissolves, and then the patient says, "I am better," or "I am healed."

DO'S AND DONT'S IN HEALING WORK

In The Infinite Way, we never give a treatment to a person. We give the treatment to ourselves. We are the one under treatment because we are the one to whom the appearance has been brought, and it must be met in our own consciousness. We never touch the mind of our patient or student: we never enter his mental home. We have no business there! Every person is a sacred being, sacred unto God, and we do not intrude into his mind or thought. If we do, we are practicing hypnotism or suggestion, and we are meddling in somebody else's mind. That is no part of The Infinite Way. In fact, we never mention a patient's name in our treatment; we never mention the name of his disease, sin, or fear, nor do we ever reach out to send a thought to him. Never! To do so is a serious offense in a spiritual teaching!

What we do when the appearance is brought to us is to go immediately to the *I* of our being, and abide there until we come to the conclusion that "I and my Father are one," and that this is a universal truth. We wrestle with this truth within ourselves until we come to the point of conviction that there is only Spirit. This teaching does not permit anyone ever, under any circumstance, to enter the mind or thought of a patient or to address him by name and say, "You are well," or "You are spiritual." None of that is acceptable practice in The Infinite Way!

When in The Infinite Way a person says, "I have a headache," I immediately forget him and deal with myself. The appearance of a headache has been presented to me; the appearance of a sick person has been presented to me. What am I going to do with it? And so I realize, "Ah, Joel, you are not going to accept that for one single moment. You know better! You know that 'I and my Father are one,' and that you have nothing to do with healing any person out there! You know, Joel, that all that God is, you are. You know that there is only spiritual law, spiritual being. You know that there are not good people and bad people; you know that there are not sick people and well people. You are dealing with God and His perfect spiritual creation, and all other appearances are but the product of a universal hypnotism, a universal malpractice, a universal belief in two powers."

If I keep that up within myself, eventually it comes, "Ah, yes, that is truth." Then I am quiet, and in a few moments a deep sense of peace comes, a "click," a deep breath, something or other, and I know that God is on the scene, and that is all there is to it. As you can see, I have had nothing to do with the patient.

The person may call, write, or cable me an hour later or the next day, and I may have to go through this same process again. If he does not respond quickly, I may have to stay with him for months and months, but the procedure is always the same. Never do I work through suggestion; never do I work through hypnotism; never will I enter the consciousness of any person.

My object is not merely to change a person's sickness into health. My object is to lift him in consciousness, not by doing something to him, but by raising up the *I* in me, and then, if *I* be lifted up, he is drawn to that level of consciousness, but without my having to do anything humanly about it, or about him as a person.

That is why it is necessary, first, to establish ourselves in the absolute conviction that there is a "My kingdom,"[9] a spiritual kingdom, and that nothing "that defileth . . . or maketh a lie"[10] can ever enter that spiritual kingdom of God and His spiritual universe and spiritual man.

PRACTICE IS ESSENTIAL

Through conscious realization we must establish the truth of our oneness with God, our oneness with spiritual perfection. Then, from there on, we are not dealing with persons or conditions: we are dealing only with the world of appearances, or illusion. The illusion in one place may be a lake, and the illusion in another may be a city, but it is all illusion, and the substance of an illusion is nothingness, whether it appears as a lake or a city. The substance of illusion is the same, whether it appears as a cold, a headache, a cancer, tuberculosis, a broken bone, poverty, or unemployment. It is always nothingness, the "arm of flesh,"[11] appearance. Behind it is the activity of a universal malpractice or hypnotism, which is produced by the universal belief in two powers.

The healing principle of The Infinite Way is simple, but no one can bring about healings quickly just through knowing the letter of truth: it is working with it that develops this consciousness. It becomes second nature not to take in the appearance as if it were a condition, not to condemn a person, not to react to any appearance presented by a person, and that is when the healing consciousness is in full bloom, and then is when our healing ministry begins. Up to that time, we are practicing, practicing, and practic-

[9]John 18:36.
[10]Revelation 21:27.
[11]II Chronicles 32:8.

ing to develop that consciousness. The consciousness that does not respond to appearances, the consciousness that is aware of the spiritual nature of creation and of the illusory nature of appearances, is a healing consciousness.

Every serious student must work with these principles and practice them with the most insignificant claims that arise. Many times letters come hesitatingly asking for help for a cat or a dog. My answer always is the same: "I am not interested in whether it is your cat or your dog: I am interested in the appearance that is being presented to me, and that is what must be met." By meeting it when it appears in their cats or their dogs, later on they are enabled to see how to meet it in a human being. Never, never for a moment think that there is anything so small, so tiny, or so insignificant that these principles should not be applied to it, because I can assure you that in applying them to the small things of life, you help to develop the consciousness for undertaking the greater ones.

Keep yourself in the consciousness into which this lesson lifts you because it is all too easy to come down to the human level and be frightened by an appearance of disease, sin, or lack, whether that appearance is presented as a child or a grown-up. It is only by abiding in these principles that fear is dissipated, and automatically every error is wiped out through the recognition: illusion, hypnotism, malpractice, an appearance! The more you can deal with all error in that way, the better healing work you will accomplish.

The deeper you go into the healing consciousness, the more you find yourself living so in meditation that you do not have to go into a deep meditation with every claim that comes because you are in it nine tenths of the time. You will find, however, that it is necessary to go into meditation ten, twenty, or thirty times a day, not for the sake of meeting a specific call, but in order to maintain that inner communion constantly. Then the calls can come thick and fast, and no specific meditation is necessary because you are living in that *I* which has been lifted up in you, the *I* which is the healer.

But I warn you: if your patients are not getting the results that they should get, it is because you are not meditating often or deeply enough to bring forth that depth of realization of God that is necessary. There is no such thing in this work as merely saying piously, "Oh, let God do it." There is no God on the field until you have brought God on to the field by this inner realization.

Do not forget that there would be no sickness in the world if God were on the field. There would be no sin or death on earth if God were on the field. It is only when you bring God to the scene by raising up the *I* within you that you wipe out the discords of sense and bring forth divine harmony.

It is possible to bring the very presence of God to earth if you will meditate, make contact with your Center, and let that Presence be released into the world.

From

BEYOND WORDS
AND THOUGHTS

Truth Unveiled

Every book of spiritual wisdom you have read has brought about a greater spiritualization of your consciousness, what might be called the peeling off of the onion skin, or the refining of consciousness. Each book, each class, and each principle taken into consciousness has prepared you for the one ahead, leading to greater unfoldment and toward that "act of Grace bestowed on individuals at a certain time in their unfoldment, lifting them into the master-state of consciousness."[1]

Always, since my first spiritual experience, living in two worlds has been difficult for me—living in that higher Consciousness and then coming down to earth, going back into that Consciousness and coming back down to earth—but never was it as difficult as in 1963. That year marked another period of initiation for me, but, even though in 1962 I knew it was to be, I had no knowledge of

[1]Joel S. Goldsmith. *A Parenthesis in Eternity* (New York: Harper and Row, 1963) P. 224.

its intensity, its length, or the nature of the message that would be revealed.

It is not unnatural, therefore, that that year should have revealed the higher unfoldment, the higher Consciousness. This you will understand as you study the work that came through during this period. With each successive unfoldment, something was breaking through, leading to the teaching of going beyond words and thoughts, of going beyond the mind. This idea you will find in all the 1963 work,[2] revealing the nature of life as it is lived when you go beyond the mind and beyond thoughts: beyond taking thought, beyond reasoning. This is the revelation of the nature of Sabbath and of Grace.

A work of this kind leads to the highest point in consciousness that has yet been revealed in The Infinite Way, and it would seem that it is the high point in the revelation of both Moses and Jesus, and probably also that of Buddha.

THE MIDDLE PATH

The fleshly sense of man cannot enter the kingdom of heaven, Spirit. The healthy fleshly sense is as illusory as the sickly sense, and the sense of good man is as illusory as the sense of bad man. The Middle Path, or spiritual consciousness, does not engage in exchanging the sense of erroneous man for the sense of correct man, but knows only spiritual man, or the son of God.

In healing work as understood in The Infinite Way, we are unseeing and unknowing the corporeal or physical sense of man: well or sick, rich or poor, good or bad. We are not unseeing or unknowing a corporeal man or a physical man for there is none, but we are unknowing or unseeing the corporeal or physical *sense* of man. The corporeal sense is the tempter. The healing truth is our consciousness of incorporeal man and the universe.

Melchizedek, or the Christ, who was never born and will never die, is the true man, and that which we see, hear, taste, touch, and

[2]EDITOR'S NOTE: Lectures and classes given by Mr. Goldsmith during 1963 were tape-recorded and are available to students.

smell is our false sense of that man. There is not a false man, a fallen man, or a physical man, but there is a false sense of man which we entertain.

THE MEANING OF ASCENSION

On the spiritual path, we begin our journey by studying the truth, learning and practicing the truth. We never attain the goal of realization, however, until we reach beyond the mind and its knowing of the truth to our becoming Truth: "That which I am seeking, I am!"[3]

On the Mount, in a high state of consciousness, Moses realized *I AM*, and thereby became *I AM*. Yet, there remained still a sense of Moses as is evidenced by the fact that he spoke of himself as being slow of speech. The realization of *I AM* prevailed, however, and with that great illumination came such a height of consciousness that he was able to lead the Hebrews out of slavery to the Promised Land. Had Moses been able to crucify or relinquish completely the mortal sense of himself which still remained, he would have been able to enter the Promised Land, or heaven. But he was bound by a finite sense of himself.

Jesus, however, not only knew the truth but *realized* and *became* the Truth: "I am the way, the truth, and the life."[4] Nevertheless, a sense of Jesus, the man, remained, because he said, "I can of mine own self do nothing. ... If I bear witness of myself, my witness is not true."[5] This personal sense of self had to be crucified, as eventually it must be in all of us, or we will not ascend to the Promised Land, the realization of our spiritual identity.

Jesus' realization of the need to crucify, or rise above, the seeming mortal sense of self, enabled him to make the ascension. The ascension is always the same: a rising above mind, above knowing the truth, to Truth Itself.

[3]Joel S. Goldsmith. *The Infinite Way*. (San Gabriel, Calif.: Willing Publishing Company, 1960). P. 107.
[4]John 14:6.
[5]John 5:30, 31.

In many classes and even in some of the Writings, I have said that I did not understand the reason for the crucifixion of Jesus: why it took place or why it had to take place if it had to. It puzzled me, and I have frankly admitted this. It was not until the year 1963, when I myself went through the experience, that the reason and need for the crucifixion of Christ Jesus was revealed to me. Somehow, after that experience, the memory of it passed from me, and I could not bring it to conscious recollection, until later the entire scene was revealed to me again when I went through the experience of ascension: that rising above mind to Truth Itself.

THE SIGNIFICANCE OF JESUS' EXPERIENCE
ON THE MOUNT OF TRANSFIGURATION

This is what I saw: In Jesus' statement, "He that seeth me seeth him that me,"[6] he revealed that he had attained the goal of *I AM*. " 'I *am the way*'—thou seest me, thou seest God, for I and God are one." And there is an experience in which he proved this: he took three disciples to what is called the Mount of Transfiguration, which again is high consciousness, and he revealed to them the Hebrew prophets who were supposed to be dead.

But, to his enlightened sense, they were not dead, and he proved to his disciples that they were alive, and that they were with them there in form. Whether he translated them into visible form or whether he translated himself and the disciples into invisible form makes no difference because it is the same experience. He translated: he demonstrated to his disciples the truth he later proved: " 'I lay down my life, that I might take it again'[7]—*I* can walk into the invisible realm and *I* can walk out again, for *I* am Spirit, *I* am the way."

Because of Jesus' experience on the Mount of Transfiguration, I understand now that crucifixion was not necessary for him, and that he could have avoided it. Enoch was translated without knowing death; Elijah was translated without knowing death; Isaiah, also,

[6]John 12:45.
[7]John 10:17.

may have been translated. Therefore, it was shown to me through Jesus' experience on the Mount of Transfiguration that he could have been translated without knowing death, but when he became aware of the Betrayal, the Trial, and the threatened Crucifixion, he chose to accept corporeal death in order to reveal to his disciples that death is not an experience, but an illusory sense that must be understood and seen through.

Death is not a condition that a person actually goes through. There is no death; no one has ever died. God has no pleasure in our dying. Death is an experience only of corporeal sense, the sense that testifies that we are physical, mortal, finite, but death itself is never an experience of our true being.

By permitting himself to experience corporeal death, Jesus revealed that there is no death, and he revealed himself in what appeared to be the same corporeal form with all its wounds. Then, having served this purpose, he had no other function here on earth. His continued presence would only have been an embarrassment to the disciples, to Rome, and probably to himself.

Jesus ascended out of corporeal form: he was translated. This can be interpreted to mean that he rose beyond the mind; he rose above his own mind because it is only in the mind that the corporeal sense can be entertained, not in the spiritual faculties.

In our Soul-faculties, we are Spirit; we see each other spiritually, whether we are here on this plane, or whether we are looking at those who have gone to another plane, or to those who are not yet born.

NOT KNOWING THE TRUTH, BUT BEING THE TRUTH

This revelation is the proof of the message that there must come a rest to *My*[8] people. There must come a rest from the activity of the mind: taking thought for our life, fearing for our life, constantly knowing the truth in order to avoid some experience. There must come a Sabbath, and in this Sabbath we live by Grace, because then

[8]The word "My," capitalized, refers to God.

we do not know the truth, but Truth reveals Itself to us, and we become the Truth. It is not an activity of the mind: it is Soul revealing Itself.

When you reach that place where, instead of searching for a truth, feverishly reading or studying to latch on to some truth, you can relax and rest in the Truth—without taking thought, without speaking or thinking—you can be a state of awareness, and then you understand the meaning of "Man shall not live by bread alone, but by every word that proceedeth out of the mouth of God."[9] You will then discover that every word, every feeling, every emotion, and every thought that comes to you from the deep Withinness of you is what you now live by. The Spirit within guides, It directs, It sustains, It protects, It goes before you to "make the crooked places straight."[10]

Our ultimate goal must be to live in, through, and as God. If we are not to do this, why did the Master teach, "Take no thought for your life"?[11] Life is meant to be lived by Grace, without might, without power. It is meant to be lived by every word of God that we receive in our consciousness. In The Infinite Way, students are being fed with the words of God that have been revealed by prophets, saints, and seers. These, the students take into their mind and bury deep in their consciousness until they, too, rise above the level of the mind to where they can live without taking thought.

Be receptive to the still small voice, for God is not in the whirlwind, God is not in your problems, God is not in your thinking, God is not in books: God is in the still small voice. How quietly and peacefully is it necessary to live within in order to hear that Voice, to receive Its impartations, and to partake of Its grace!

There is always a sufficiency of God's grace present for this moment, and therefore, we have only to be still in this moment in order to receive a sufficiency of Grace, but only for this moment.

The teaching of The Infinite Way is that the goal toward which we are working is the attainment of the realization that that which

[9]Matthew 4:4.
[10]Isaiah 45:2.
[11]Matthew 6:25.

I am seeking I am. The goal is a rising above the mind. I personally did not invent or create this message: it was received. And always it has been received through listening: sometimes in moments of deep meditation, sometimes in periods of initiation, sometimes on the platform while giving lectures and classes, but always while in a state of receptivity. That state of receptivity has been my hidden manna. It is that which has produced all that appears as this message, and all that has taken this message around the world.

As you have learned to work hard and long with the principles of The Infinite Way, so you must learn to stop doing this occasionally, sometimes for a day or two, and say to yourself, "Let me not trust in my mind. Let me relax in God."

When these principles are embodied in you, your Soul begins to feed you. Until you really have that hidden manna, however, keep working with all the principles that are emphasized on every page of the Writings, but do not make this an "eight-hour-day." Take time out to work in the garden, read a good solid book, or perhaps an entertaining novel. Never believe that The Infinite Way is trying to teach you to "mentalize." Mental activity is necessary only when you are learning the truth, when you are feeding consciousness with the letter of truth. We want no Infinite Way student to live by affirmations and denials because that is not living by the grace of God. Invite the Soul! Your Soul overshadows you as you sit, walk, or sleep. Relax in It, without words and without thoughts.

THE SPIRITUAL SABBATH

The fruitage of abiding in these principles is a period of rest, and this is the true meaning of the Sabbath. The Sabbath Moses commanded the Hebrews to observe was a period of rest forever. Labor for six days; yes, labor to know these principles; but after the six days of labor you come to a place of Sabbath, which means that for the rest of your days you live by the grace of God, by *My* Spirit. Eventually you come to a place where you realize that *I* is God, and the Word that It imparts to you is your bread, meat, wine, and water. When you have attained a quietness and confidence, you may be sure you have entered the Sabbath.

See what happens on the seventh day: "In the mean while his disciples prayed him, saying, Master, eat. But he said unto them, I have meat to eat that ye know not of"[12] He was telling them not to go out to get meat; but to rest in the Sabbath of I have: no words, no thoughts, no might, no power.

You students who are ready for the Sabbath must prepare for it by learning to rest back in this realization: "Let my Soul take over instead of my mind." Then every time you go within, something new and fresh will come forth.

In the consciousness of Sabbath, you need not go out and get meat, for you have it. By what right? By your recognition that you and the Father are one. For six days you have labored to study and to train yourself, and those "six days," remember, are for most of you many, many years. But there comes a rest to *My* people; there comes a Sabbath; and that is when you stop all your metaphysical struggling, relax, and *let* Grace live your life.

When you come to the "sixth day" of your practice, just smile: "I do not have to pray for anything. I already have hidden manna the world knows not of." Do you see how the teaching in the Bible is veiled, and how it takes a transcendental consciousness to unveil it? The mystics did not hide it: words hide it.

Those few students who have been listening and studying with the inner ear must now be entering that period of Sabbath when they can feel within themselves: "I do not know any truth. I cannot live on the quotations of yesterday. The only truth I know is what is coming through today. As far as I am concerned, I am living in the period of unknowing, in which every day I go within to receive the manna for that day, to listen for Thy voice."

A person who is in the Sabbath-consciousness realizes, "Thy grace is my sufficiency for this moment," and he is satisfied. He is resting, not only in the assurance that God's grace is his sufficiency, but that there is a sufficiency of God's grace. In that awareness

[12]John 4:31, 32.

of Grace, he settles into a consciousness of peace. The "six days" of struggle are over, and today he refuses to labor. Then, whatever is to come through comes through.

The truth found in The Infinite Way is Scripture spiritually interpreted. Because of this, you can go back into your own consciousness and draw out the spiritual interpretation of the passages that come to you. The interpretation may come in a different form from what I have given you, but the principle will be the same.

The Infinite Way takes you through the "six days" of labor—the thinking and knowing of the truth, the searching for truth, pondering truth, meditating on truth—until you go beyond the activity of the mind or intellect. Finally, you come to a place where you can rest in quietness and in confidence because you are now no longer living your own life. Every word that flows from God into your awareness becomes the bread, the wine, and the water. It becomes your health, strength, vitality, and all those things that are necessary for your experience.

"MY DOCTRINE IS NOT MINE"

We are on earth but for the one reason of showing forth God's glory, not our own. It was never meant that we should glory in our wisdom, our gifts, or in our skill; but rather that we should recognize that what appears to the world as these are not really ours, but His. "My doctrine is not mine, but his that sent me."[13] So, too, all that the Father has is mine, and I am showing forth God's glory, not mine. In the message of The Infinite Way, I am speaking God's message, not mine. Whatever shows forth as the prosperity or success of The Infinite Way is not my prosperity or success, but His glory, His grace.

Up until this year, I have never spoken openly of my own spiritual experiences, my initiations, or my contacts with the Infinite Invisible because I know that in the Occident there is no preparation for an understanding of such things. This year, however, I

[13]John 7:16.

have made no secret of the fact that for eight months I have been under an inner initiation by means of which a higher unfoldment of the Message has been coming through.

Part of my function during this time has been to lift The Infinite Way message itself out of metaphysical language into mystical language, so that our students begin to live only in mystical language, even as we all are trying to live only the mystical life, and yet, not separating ourselves from the everyday business of living because there must always be constructive activity. There must always be business; there must always be all the activities that are going on in the world of a human nature, but they must be lifted up into a higher consciousness. Even though some medium of exchange, such as money, may always be necessary, there can be a greater degree of love and grace in the sharing of its activity. It need not be what is called "cold, hard cash." It can be warm, spiritual cash.

This is written only so that you may know that in your life, in your activity, your business, or your profession, you, too, must realize that the nature of your experience is that God may be glorified, that God may speak through you, sing through you, play through you, or that God may do business through you; but always it is God functioning through and as your individual being.

CRUCIFYING PERSONAL SENSE

In all of us, none the less, there remains a finite sense of self, which in the last analysis must be crucified. Moses had it in his feeling of his unworthiness. Jesus had it for a great while in his feeling of "I can of mine own self do nothing." I had it definitely in this knowledge that I could not bring forth or carry on the message of The Infinite Way. And each of you has it in the measure that you believe you have a skill, a wisdom, or a talent. In that degree, you still have it, and in the degree that you continue to have it, ultimately that personal sense will have to be crucified, until in the end you can realize, "I do not have any truth; I do not know any truth; I do not have any skill; I do not have any talent: *I* am the truth; *I* am the talent; *I* am the skill." In that moment, humanhood has "died," Christhood has been "born" and revealed in its fullness, and the ascension or transition can take place.

This is repeated in the message of The Infinite Way over and over again in the passages that remind us that it is the personal sense of "I" that must "die," the personal sense of "I" that must be crucified. All our study, all our knowing of the truth, all our healing ministry must eventually lead to the period of Sabbath or Grace, which is the full and complete surrender of self, to the end that God may live on earth as He is living in heaven.

There is then no longer a man in heaven *and* a man on earth; the man who came down and the man who went up are one and the same; the two have become one. There is no longer a kingdom of heaven *and* a kingdom of earth; but the kingdom of heaven is made manifest on earth in oneness. In the realization that *I*, God, is individual consciousness, mine and yours, I turn within so that *I*, God, may reveal Itself through the Word to "I," Joel, as long as there remains an *I*, God and an "I," Joel. When *I*, God, and "I," Joel, can sit in the same chair and commune with each other, this is getting very close to oneness. It is not as close as it will be some day when I ascend unto the Father and thereby become the Father.

Those students who realize that The Infinite Way is a relevation of God Himself appearing on earth, will, of course, understand that the purpose of that revelation is that they may go and do likewise, for "if I go not away, the Comforter will not come unto you."[14] If you keep thinking of this as the demonstration of Moses, Isaiah, Jesus, John, Paul, Joel, or anybody else, you will miss the truth that each one has demonstrated in order to reveal the universal nature of Truth.

HOW TRUTH BECOMES "VEILED"

What always puts the veil back on the truth that "I AM THAT I AM"[15] is that those who have not yet attained, those who have not yet come into spiritual awareness or the demonstration of their spiritual Selfhood, always love the message so much that they

[14]John 16:7.
[15]Exodus 3:14.

become do-gooders and go out in the world to try to spread it around the world, and they do not have it. Then it becomes lost, because truth can be revealed only by Truth, not by a human being. Truth can be revealed only through the Soul-faculties, not through the mind. Whenever well-meaning persons go out and begin to teach truth through the mind, they are preparing the generation for another period of the absence of God on earth. It is always the do-gooder who gets in the way of spiritual demonstration—the do-gooder or the egotist.

When there is an organization, there are a certain number of persons serving as teachers, and because the demands of organization do not make it possible to wait for those who are spiritually attuned, those closest to that state take over the work. Because The Infinite Way is not organized, that is not necessary. We can be satisfied if we find one, two, three, four, five, or six illumined ones to teach. And if we never have more, it would make no difference, because one, two, three, four, five, or six can do more for the world than ten thousand unillumined.

Therefore, let those who would seek to teach be watchful, and let each person exercise spiritual discernment or discrimination when he seeks to be taught, so he is sure that those who teach are showing forth the fourth-dimensional Consciousness, and not merely some knowledge picked up out of a book. Then we can prevent what has always happened before: the loss of Truth through the ministry of those who have not attained spiritual illumination.

Remember that this rising above the mind, above words and thoughts, does not eliminate the mind, words, or thoughts, but it does eliminate living by them. For example, was there not a day in our metaphysical experience when we lived primarily by affirmations, thereby hoping to bring out harmony? It is true that by our words, by our thoughts of truth, our statements of truth, and our remembrance of truth, we did bring out a measure of harmony; but in the days of the Sabbath and Grace, this is no longer true. We do not live by words or thoughts: we live by Grace.

True, the activity of Grace can come to me as words and

thoughts, and then it can be imparted to you in words and thoughts. But I am not living by those words or thoughts, and you are not living by them: we are living by the Grace that produced the words and thoughts. I am living in the Sabbath of resting from declaring words and thoughts to receiving words and thoughts, and letting them flow, filled with the Spirit of God. The Holy Ghost is in them because I did not make them up, I did not arrange them: I let them flow through me. Such words and thoughts are with power. These are the thoughts of God that make the earth melt; these are the words of God that are "quick, and powerful, and sharper than any twoedged sword,"[16] even though they still come through the teacher.

But all you have to do, really, is to remember how many times you affirmed statements of truth because you thought they were going to remove some error or bring forth some harmony, and how many times you have pondered the truth for that same reason, and you will know then that you were living by words and thoughts, sometimes words and thoughts out of books. But not now! Now you live by Grace, and that Grace appears as the message which you may speak or write, and because it is a message of Grace, persons hearing or reading it are healed, and have their lives transformed.

[16]Hebrews 4:12.

The Way of Grace

In the metaphysical world, the attention given the subject of supply is almost equal to the attention given the subject of health. Sometimes, however, spiritual freedom in the area of supply is not as easily attained as is freedom in the area of health. But because the basic truth about health is also the truth about supply, there should be no difference in attaining the consciousness of either supply or health. Nevertheless there seems to be; and often it is not easy to convince the human mind of the ever-availability of supply. A person may have been on the metaphysical path ten, twenty, or thirty years, but when the thought of supply comes to his mind, with it comes the thought of money, also, because to him supply and money are synonymous. Of course, they are not the same at all, but because they seem to be the same to the human mind, it is difficult to separate the one from the other.

Contrary to all human belief, supply is the word of God, and unless we are receiving the word of God, we are not receiving supply. "Man shall not live by bread alone, but by every word that proceedeth out of the mouth of God."[1] Bread alone does not suffice. No, we live by every word that proceeds out of the mouth of God. Daily we pray for bread, but not for baker's bread. We pray for the bread that is the word of God, and they way in which we receive it is to open our consciousness to receive that Word which is the bread of life, the meat, the wine, and the water.

Anyone who believes that he is going to be fed permanently and abundantly by any other means than by receiving the word of God has entirely missed the way. No matter how much money a person might temporarily have, without the word of God he does not have supply: he merely has money, and it has been truly said that money has wings.

RECEPTIVITY TO GOD'S GRACE, ESSENTIAL

We do not live by money but by the grace of God, and that Grace is already within our consciousness because God constitutes our consciousness. Therefore, we are never separate or apart from our supply, but when we speak of supply, we are not speaking of money. In the whole kingdom of God, there is no money, there are no houses, and there are no automobiles. God knows nothing of food, clothing, and housing, so praying to God for such things is a waste of time. It is a form of paganism. It goes back to the ancient days when people thought of God as the source of gold and silver, and all material things. God is not the source of material things, but God is the source of the substance that appears outwardly as gold, silver, trees, and all the good of this universe.

In the kingdom of God, there is only life and love. These are the two great qualities of God: life and love—just life and love, and such additional facets as wisdom and intelligence, which are offshoots of the two great qualities, life and love. But unless we have God's love, which is the substance of all form, we will never have the form.

[1]Matthew 4:4.

Therefore, when we open our consciousness to God as love, love is the substance or fulfillment of supply. It is love that puts leaves and fruit on trees; it is love that gives us divine Grace; it is the love of God that appears outwardly as what we call food, clothing, and housing. We open our consciousness to God's grace, God's love, to the substance of all form, the Spirit of God. "Where the Spirit of the Lord is, there is liberty"[2]—freedom from lack and limitation, from sin and disease. To go to God for anything but the Spirit of God is to pray amiss.

Our first act, our repeated act throughout the day, and our final act at night, therefore, is closing our eyes and opening our ears consciously to realize that the kingdom of God, the allness of God, is within us. It does not come to us because we earn it; it does not come to us because of somebody's good will; it does not even come to us because we deserve it.

God's grace is omnipresent, and not only is it omnipresent, it is infinite. But it is not available except as we specifically open our consciousness to receive it. God's grace falls alike on the just and the unjust, and we do not have to be what the world calls good to receive that Grace. As a matter of fact, very often the prodigal receives a little bit more than the humanly virtuous person. The one requirement is opening consciousness to receive It. That is the price God has placed on the infinity of supply: opening consciousness; and it is not that God put that price on it: it is that through the closing of our consciousness we have shut out God's grace. God makes no distinction between the good and the bad. God's abundance is never withheld from anyone, regardless of his sins, nor is it ever given to anyone because of his virtue. All this is a part of human superstition.

Lack and limitation and every other ill that man seems heir to come about through our failure to keep our consciousness active, alert, alive, and above all, receptive. All that is necessary, therefore, to enjoy the infinity of God's supply without limitation is to rec-

[2]II Corinthians 3:17.

ognize that supply is not material, and then to open consciousness to receive it.

God's supply and God's grace are not received in the pocket-book: they are received in consciousness, and when they are received in our consciousness it does not take very long for them to translate themselves into the pocketbook. But we have nothing to do, at the moment, with a pocketbook: we have to do with receiving God's grace.

Our whole experience after we come into The Infinite Way should be lived from the standpoint of the truth that we are the offspring of God, that is, that we are spiritual, heirs of God and joint-heirs to all the heavenly riches. And yet, if we have been trained in metaphysics, we try to turn those heavenly riches into houses, automobiles, and dollars. But we cannot approach the subject of supply from the orthodox metaphysical idea of demonstrating effects because this attempt usually ends in failure. The fact of the matter is that students have sometimes demonstrated effects and then have been very sorry later.

"My grace is sufficient for thee"[3] does not mean that God's grace gives us dollars, automobiles, and houses. It plainly states that "My grace is sufficient." As spiritual beings, we have to be satisfied with that promise, and all we must seek is Grace.

Grace always interprets itself at the level of the experience of the moment in which we are living. As we realize the sufficiency of God's grace, It will appear to us as air to breathe, transportation, dollars, or whatever our life may require, and It can very well appear in forms that we could not possibly expect. Our idea of what constitutes supply, of where we would like to live, or what work we would like to do may differ entirely from God's idea for us.

LET THE DIVINE DESTINY BE REVEALED IN US

As offspring of God, we must remember that being His children is far different from being children of human parents. When parents

[3]II Corinthians 12:9.

have children, they do not know what purpose they have been brought to earth to fulfill. They bring them into the world, try to give them some kind of guidance, and hope for the best. But how can parents guide their children except in accord with their own concept of what is right?

In my case, my father, who was a businessman, thought that the highest right was to make a businessman of me, and yet all the time the divine plan was that I should be in religious work. Because of that, I had to fight my way out of the business world, not because my father did not love me, but because my father's idea of what was good and right for me was what was good and right for him.

But this is not true of God. God is omniscience, and when God has a child, it is for a specific purpose. There is something definite in mind with every individual offspring, something that he was actually sent into expression to do.

As human beings, we have completely missed the mark because most of the activities of human beings were not intended for us, and in our ignorance of our divine destiny, we went into something quite unrelated to that destiny.

So when we say, "Thy grace is my sufficiency in all things," we have to turn within with an open mind, and stand on that word "Grace," and let It assume the form necessary. If It shocks us out of our skins, we have to be willing to be shocked. If It makes us leave mother, father, brother, and sister, we leave mother, father, brother, and sister. If It makes us leave our homeland to go to a distant country to carry the message, we leave our homes and go where It takes us. Saul of Tarsus humanly never intended to be a carrier of the Christian message to Europe and Asia, but that is what he became the moment he came under Grace.

We have no right to outline the form Grace is to take in our experience. But if we keep ourselves open to God's gift of Grace, we can very well be more surprised at the form It takes than a child going to the Christmas tree on Christmas morning and finding the things he does not expect. What he receives is his parents' sense of love. They are giving their child, not necessarily what the child wants, but what the parents feel is for his good.

This is much more true when we go to the Father for divine Grace. It is utterly useless to have an idea of what gifts we would like, what form Grace should assume, or what form supply should take. Omniscience knows all, and It knows all about every individual because Omniscience is the allness of every individual. Therefore, Omniscience operates within us to reveal Its plan for us. "Nevertheless not my will, but thine, be done."[4]

GOD TRANSLATES ITSELF IN TERMS OF HUMAN NEEDS

As we take no thought for what we shall eat, what we shall drink, or wherewithal we shall be clothed, this Grace translates Itself into terms of food, clothing, housing, transportation, and all those things needful for our human experience. But if we insist on taking thought for these things, we lose our entire spiritual demonstration of peace and harmony because God knows nothing of food, clothing, housing, on transportation. God knows no more about how our ancestors transported themselves on donkeys than He does about the increasing mobility that has come to us through the use of automobiles or airplanes. God knows no more about the unleavened bread of our ancestors than he does about the overly refined nutritionless bread that we buy in our supermarkets of today.

God's grace! God feeds, clothes, houses, maintains, and sustains His image and likeness, not by any act of yours or mine, but by an act of divine Grace. Our only activity is receptivity, but we cannot stand with a begging bowl and be receptive, nor can we stand with an open pocketbook and be receptive. We must open the only thing through and as which God appears: our consciousness. God appears and acts in, and through, and as consciousness.

It is as if we were opening our ears to the realization of the truth

[4]Luke 22:42.

that God's grace is our sufficiency. In such receptivity, God's grace is pouring through to us. Then all that we have to do is to be about our business, whatever it may be, taking no thought for the morrow, just doing those things which are necessary for us to do, returning half a dozen or a dozen times a day to the opening of the inner ear to God's grace, to God's supply, and then going about our business.

We have nothing to do with the way in which supply reaches us. All we have to do is to recognize that God is Spirit, and therefore supply is spiritual. We have to open our consciousness to receive it, and then, in whatever way is natural for us, the heavens open, figuratively speaking, and our supply appears. We are not to take thought as to how that is to be. We are merely to do that which is at hand for us to do, leaving the means with the Father within.

In all the miraculous ways which God has, supply always appears. It appeared to the Hebrews when they were fleeing from Egypt. It appeared: it fell right out of the sky, and let no one every doubt that it did.

GOD'S GRACE IS NOT THE PREROGATIVE OF ONE SEX

It is true that some of us have been business men and women and have thought that our supply must come through business, and then some of us have had the joy of witnessing how we were removed from the business world, and supply still came in. Others have thought that because they were housewives their supply had to come from their husbands, only to find suddenly that they were painting, writing, or doing something else equally creative, sometimes even engaging in healing work. So they discovered that God never decreed that their support should come from, or be dependent upon, their husbands. That is just a man-made custom, and some day we are all going to be sufficiently awake to realize that each one of us derives his supply from the same God. Then, if we wish to share it voluntarily with husband or wife, we will. It never was spiritually meant that God's grace should fall only on one sex, the male. God's grace also falls on the female sex, and the day must come when it is recognized that it does so equally.

The point that I am making is that God's grace is an act of consciousness—of the male consciousness and of the female consciousness—and it is only as we, male and female, open our consciousness to that fact that we discover the spiritual source of supply and realize that there is just as much of it in the female consciousness as in the male, with or without the help of the other.

That does not mean that each one must earn a separate livelihood. It means that each one is going to realize that as he or she receives Grace from God, he or she will contribute to the other, probably one in one form and one in another.

Witness that in our modern world more women are working and earning money than ever before. But this is really only a prelude to a great experience that is coming when neither male nor female will have to struggle for a living. Evidently that day can be ushered in only when it has been proved to the women of the world that they have as much access to supply as the men have, and that God's grace is a universal and an equal experience.

As we are receptive to the grace of God, It will appear as supply. More and more the truth will be revealed that one sex is not dependent on another for supply, but that both sexes are dependent on the kingdom of God that is established within them. Then they can share with one another, and that day will come.

So let us never forget that when we open our ears and minds in receptivity, we are not going to God for material supply—for money, automobiles, houses, or clothing: we are realizing that God's grace is "closer . . . than breathing, and nearer than hands and feet."[5] The ears are open to hear; the mind is open to receive; and what we receive is the Spirit of God, the awareness and the feeling of the Presence. This is God's supply. When we receive This, It, in a way unknown to us, is translated in our human picture as food, clothing, housing, money, or whatever form it is that the supply must take.

The reason that the world as a whole does not receive God's supply is that it is turning to God for those material things of which God has no awareness, when the truth is that it is legitimate

[5]Alfred, Lord Tennyson. *The Higher Pantheism*, Stanza 6.

to turn to God only for His grace, His love, His peace, and to know His will. God is Spirit, and to go to God for anything but spiritual awareness is like going to a pauper for money, like going to somebody for something that he does not have.

God does not have money. God does not have gold, silver, or diamonds. God does not have meat, potatoes, fish, or vegetables. God knows nothing of those things. All that God knows is the Spirit which, through God's grace, is upon us. We translate This into food, clothing, and housing in terms of our particular conditioning. For example, two thousand years ago donkeys were considered an adequate form of transportation; today we are satisfied with nothing less than jet planes flying a thousand miles an hour, and upwards.

PRAYER, AN OPENING OF CONSCIOUSNESS

Prayer is effective only in the measure that we go to God without a desire because otherwise we are holding a mold up to God and arbitrarily saying, "Fill it for me. Here is the mold of my wish, of my desire. Become my servant and do what I would like." The Infinite Way knows no such form of prayer.

We cannot ask God for anything. If we did, we would be dishonoring God. We would virtually by saying, "God, I know what I need, but You do not, so I will tell You." Remember, we are saying this to the infinite Intelligence that created the whole universe, including us. How stupid it must seem—not to God, because He would not know how stupid we can be. But think how stupid it is to plead, "Give me food," and "Give me clothing," and "Give me housing."

It is the same in our healing work. There is no use in going to God with the desire that God heal us of our diseases or that God heal this inharmony or that lack. Real prayer is an opening of consciousness to God, and then a communing within.

The fruitage of this kind of prayer is that sooner or later the revelation is given to us from within, "Do not look to *Me* because you are ever with *Me*, and all that *I* have is already yours. It was incorporated in you in the beginning, 'before Abraham was.'[6]"

TEACHING GIVINGNESS

In the beginning, because of our oneness with God, He incorporated into us His life, His mind, His soul, His Spirit, His substance, His supply, and His infinity. He can add nothing to us now, nor are there any powers on earth to take anything from us as long as we live in the realization that infinity, Grace, and the gift of God are ours by virtue of our relationship to God, that oneness that was established within in the beginning. When this is revealed to us and perceived by us, we can understand why we must open out a way for "the imprisoned splendour"[7] to escape. Since infinity is the measure of our supply and since nothing can be added to it, we must begin to pour; we must start the outflow.

In every department of life, we must constantly search, not to see how we can get something, or what we can get, but in what way we can pour. The damming up of supply results from our failure to pour in some manner.

There are times when we may find it difficult to impart this to students because an embarrassment arises. Some students may get the impression that we want them to give something to us and that we are using this gentle way of hinting. But when they are further enlightened, they will know that a teacher must already have reached that stage where he understands that he is spiritually fed and has gone beyond the point of looking to students or patients for his supply.

No thought of gain ever enters the spiritual teacher's consciousness, because the spiritual teacher does not go into this kind of a ministry until he has demonstrated that he is living by God's grace. Then, when he has demonstrated that, he can freely teach that the secret of supply is in giving, in pouring.

[6]John 8:58.
[7]Robert Browning.

We are not concerning ourselves at the moment merely with money, although sharing in this concrete way is a kind of giving-ness that cannot be ignored. However, important as this form of sharing is, money is the least of the pouring and the givingness of which we are talking. The real givingness is the sharing of the spiritual treasures that have been given so freely and so abundantly to us. The kingdom of God is full of spiritual treasures, and since that Kingdom is within us, we are a storehouse of spiritual reaches, but we are not a storehouse in the sense of withholding them: we are storing up these treasures by distributing or sharing them, because it is only in the spending of them that we really store them up.

To the human sense this is, of course, a contradiction, but any-one who has ever had any teaching experience must know that the more he teaches a subject, whether he is teaching bookkeeping, architecture, language, science, or art, the greater knowledge and understanding of it he himself has. The more he imparts, the greater is his own unfoldment.

GOD'S GRACE, THE GIFT OF HIMSELF

God's grace is the gift of Himself appearing on earth as us. God, the Father, is appearing on earth as God, the son; and these are one, not two. Therefore, all that the Father has is ours; all that God is, we are, once we have overcome our religious superstition and ignorance.

"He that seeth me seeth him that sent me[8] . . . [for] I and my father are one."[9] There is lack and limitation in the world because the people of the world have forgotten this. They have set them-selves apart as if there were a God up there and they were down here. They believe that God has lost sight of them, and through their many petitions, they are trying to remind God that they are down here in lack, forgetting that the kingdom of God is within them, not up there, and that God is omniscience, the all-knowing.

[8]John 12:45.
[9]John 10:30.

In trying to tell God anything regarding your needs or my needs or the world's needs, how clear it is that if God could be insulted, we would be insulting Deity. Fortunately, just as a little child cannot insult its parents because the parents understand the child's ignorance, so God cannot be insulted by us. God is Spirit; we are spiritual; our needs are spiritual; our supply is spiritual; and because of our oneness with God, it is all omnipresent where we are. If we were separated from God, we might have to do something about it; but all we have to do is to recognize:

"I and my Father are one," and where the kingdom of God is, I am, for we are one.

Then we turn within in that oneness, not for money, not for food, not for clothing, not for housing, but for His grace:

Thy grace is my sufficiency; the will of God is my sufficiency; the love of God is my sufficiency.

GOD'S GRACE IS DEPENDENT ON THE AWARENESS OF OUR RELATIONSHIP OF ONENESS WITH HIM

Within ourselves, we are receptive, not to money: to love. We are receptive to the love of God that is within us; we are receptive to the grace of God that is always upon us. In our stillness, we develop a sense of receptivity: the ears are open, the mind is awake, and we are receiving. What are we receiving? The grace of God which is the word of God and which is spiritual. Then we go about our business. If we are in the wrong business, it will not be long before we will be moved into the right business.

Years ago, a man who came to me for help had just such an experience. He was working for a brewery, doing window dressing of signs in beer saloons and, as part of his work, buying beer for whoever was in the place. This man was ill, and he had tried to get spiritual help from several metaphysicians, but they would not give it to him because he was working for a brewery, and that was the wrong business. Eventually he was sent to me. I told him that he did not have to give up his position and that God's grace was not dependent on something he did or did not do, but that God's grace was dependent on what he was, an offspring of God. That is the only qualification for receiving God's good.

It makes no difference if a person is dressing windows in a saloon or if he is the thief on the cross. It has nothing to do with God. God's grace is dependent on a person's relationship to Him, and that relationship is oneness. The truth of "I and my Father are one" stands whether we are saints or sinners, whether we are good or evil. Our relationship to God cannot be changed; and in any instant in which we realize our divine sonship, God's grace is upon us.

This Grace will take care of our supply and our health. It will even change our natures. But if God's grace was dependent on our first being virtuous, I am afraid that none of us would make the grade. If God's grace were dependent on our being good first, we would still be outside the kingdom of heaven begging; but it is not that way at all, I can assure you.

The adulteress, the thief on the cross, the syphilitic, all received God's grace. When? In the moment that they opened themselves to it, not by being reformed first. No, there are many things we ourselves cannot really do much about, and unless we receive the grace of God we are not going to be reformed. There are things that are wrong with many of us that none of the ministers and none of the doctors can cure, so if God is going to withhold His grace until those things are healed, it is going to be too late for most of us.

The truth is that God's grace falls on the saint and the sinner alike, the minute an individual opens himself to that Grace. We must open ourselves to God in our sins as well as in our saintliness, and discover that it is by opening consciousness to God's grace that the sins and the desire for sin disappear. Trying to be good before we go to God is putting the cart before the horse. Let us go to

God before we are good and find that this going to God provides the goodness.

Let us forget for a moment that we are male or female; let us forget that we are saint or sinner; let us forget that we have or have not arrived at some degree of spirituality. Let us forget all that, and let us just be receptive to divine Grace.

Thy grace, omnipresent, is my sufficiency in sickness and in health. Thy grace is my sufficiency whether or not I humanly deserve it. Spiritually, I am the child of God, and God has never disinherited any of His children, whatever their human faults.

Regardless of what we humanly may be or may have been, in that moment when we open our consciousness to the nature of the Divine, though our sins were scarlet, we are white as snow. It does not make any difference if those sins continue to persist for a while because sometimes just the tenacity of habit makes them continue in effect, even after they have inwardly been forsaken. But pay no attention to that; ignore that.

Only one thing matters. From the moment that our consciousness is opened to receive an inner Grace, our sins begin to be dissolved. With some persons, it is an instantaneous process; in some, the faults and sins drag on a while. But from the time that we wholeheartedly turn in a spiritual direction, these sins are dissolved, the penalties for them begin to disappear, and we are on the way to living under Grace.

Outwardly, nothing may seem to happen, and in other cases, something very dramatic happens, and sometimes we are more puzzled about that because we do not know what it is that has happened. The point is that we live by Grace, and in the moment that we recognize this and abide in this truth, we live "not by might, nor by power."[10] We do not then live by our brains or by our virtues: we live by divine Grace.

[10]Zachariah 4:6.

From that moment on, the new way opens, not always as quickly as we would like; not even all of our bad traits disappear as quickly as we would hope for, nor our lacks and limitations. But be assured that from the moment we have recognized our oneness with the Father, the sins, the sinful thoughts, the false appetites, and the bad habits begin to disappear, and we are living a life by Grace.

From

God the Substance of All Form

Developing a Healing Consciousness

Remember that the treatment is not the healing agency. The healing agency is the consciousness that is developed through the realization of the treatment. It is the Christ-consciousness of the practitioner that is the healing agency. Everyone has that Christ-consciousness as a potential, but it has to be developed, and its development is begun by overcoming in some degree the fear of disease and the fear or love of sin. Only that consciousness which has, in a measure, been purged of its hates and fears is a healing agency. People are drawn to the practitioner who has a realized Christ-consciousness, and that is why such a practitioner is so busy.

Therefore, in the earlier stages of your work, treatment is necessary, or at least helpful, to lift consciousness up to the point of realization. By treatment, I do not mean any formula, any special words, but I mean realizing, no matter what the claim is that is brought to you, that right there is the wholeness, harmony, dominion, and perfection of the one God, and that harmony is, therefore, universal, impersonal, and impartial.

God, the Only Activity

When called upon for help where the substance of the human body seems to be involved, it must be clear that Spirit, being the only substance, must be the substance and the form of the body, and Spirit, being omnipresent, the perfect form also must always be present, regardless of the appearance. Spirit in all Its infinite form and variety is omnipresent. While the senses say that the power or substance is in the form, spiritual illumination reveals that the power, substance, and law are ever in Spirit.

Let us assume that the claim is one of inaction or underaction. The bowels, the blood, or some other part of the body may be affected. Your first realization would be that all action is the activity of consciousness, that it would be an impossibility for the body to have either good or bad action because all action is the activity of consciousness, and this activity expresses as body-action. The body has no action of its own at all.

So every time there is a claim or belief of discordant activity in the body, whether inaction, underaction, or overaction, there is only one answer: All action is God-action. Mind, as an instrument of God, is the only actor, the only action, and body merely reflects that action. Therefore, for anyone to attempt to treat a hand, an arm, or a foot, or some organ or function of the body, would be like trying to treat the walls to change their color or form or texture. It cannot be done. Remember, mind is the only instrument of action, and, therefore, we do not treat the action, itself. Our treatment is the realization of the truth that all action is the activity of consciousness.

Only One Life

Sometimes claims are presented where the fear of death is involved. It is then that we turn to the realization of life. What is life? There is only one Life, and that Life is God. The Life which is God cannot die; neither can the Life which is God pass on. Let us not fool ourselves by the use of the expression: "There is no death; he passed on." God cannot pass on and God is the only life. There is only one answer to any claim that relates to the fear of death, and that is that Life has no opposite for Life is infinite. Life, the Life which is God, is universal; it is the life of all being whether the life of man, woman, child, animal, or plant. Life is always God; there is no other life. Whatever you know about the Life which is God is the truth about the individual life which is appearing as you and as me.

Agelessness

The treatment for the claim of age is the realization that you are as young or you are as old as God. And how old is that? How young is that? The moment you think of your age, you are thinking of a selfhood apart from God and then you are trying to treat the illusion. Do not do that.

There is a great need for the realization of agelessness and timelessness in our experience, only we should have begun it much earlier—about the time we were under the belief of being seven or eight years of age. What a bad one that is! Then there was the belief of being twelve or thirteen, which is a little bit worse, and after that along comes the belief of being sixteen, seventeen, or eighteen, which is even worse. Probably the most trying age-belief of all is that period between eighteen and the early twenties. That is the point at which we know all there is to be known. No one can tell us anything; we have become men and women! That is the age-belief that really needs a good treatment once in a while. Then comes that period described as "change of life," and what a nightmare that is! This is followed by the last and final stage—old age.

The best time to begin treatment for age is when a person is around seven or eight. If we successfully handle that age, probably by the time we become twelve or thirteen, we shall have solved the whole problem of age and obviate the need of treatment for the other age-beliefs. However, for most of us, the age-belief was not met at seven or eight, or twelve or thirteen, and so we are having to meet it now. This is the moment to begin to realize that since God is our individual life, we are the same age as God. As we learn that, we learn further that that life never had a beginning and will, therefore, never have an ending.

In the same way, we handle the beliefs pertaining to body. God, Spirit, being the only substance, there is no reason for the body to be less vital or powerful at ninety than at nineteen. The body itself does not know its age; it cannot read the calendar. It is only we who know that and it is we who accept the belief of age which outwardly reflects itself upon the body.

On the other hand, if we realize our true identity to be Spirit, then the body is spiritual, and the body is as ageless as we ourselves are. The body should show forth the fullness of maturity at all times. It should never show forth that which we know as childhood or youth or middle age or old age. It should show forth the fullness and ripeness of maturity, and it would—had we known this truth in time. Had we early enough understood our true identity to be Spirit, we could have avoided many of the changes in physical structure that take place. But it is not too late: Now is the only time there is, and we can begin this moment. Then, ten years from now, we may look ten years younger than we do now. But we shall have to know this truth consciously.

Never think for a moment that just because you are reading metaphysical books or attending metaphysical lectures or classes, that you are demonstrating truth. *This truth has to be demonstrated by you individually through the conscious activity of your own consciousness.* It is not something you can take for granted. You cannot declare, "Oh, God is my life," and have that take care of everything. No, not at all. This is a *conscious* activity of individual consciousness, a conscious activity of awareness, until it becomes so much a part of our nature that we no longer have to give thought to it. But, for a long, long time, it is necessary for us to remind ourselves when we get up in the morning:

I am the same age I was yesterday; I am the same life, the same mind,

*the same Spirit, the same body. All that the Father has is mine—all that
the Father has of agelessness, changelessness; all that the Father has of
intelligence, wisdom, guidance, and direction—all is mine.*

Business as an Activity of Consciousness

At certain seasons or periods, the world comes under beliefs of
unemployment and depression. There again our realization must
be that God is the only being. God is not employed, except that
He is employed in being God. How could God be unemployed?
He would have to cease being God. God, employing Its own qualities and action and intelligence and service, individually as you and
as me, is the only employment there is. It is not you and I who
work or are employed. God is the only employer and God is the
only employee, and furthermore God is always employed in great
action, in great works, in great ideas. God cannot become the victim of mortal or material conditions, whether God is appearing as
you or as me; but to be unaffected by such conditions, it is necessary to realize this treatment which is that it is God, always and
only God.

The same thing applies to our business. Do you think it is possible to be engaged in any business in the world and just trust some
"unknown God" to save it from the ravages of present world conditions? It will not work. Business is an activity of Spirit, and, since
that Spirit is your Spirit, business is an activity of your Spirit.
Therefore, your business will reflect the condition of your consciousness on the subject of business. You must *consciously* realize
each day that business is an activity of God operating through the
instrument of the one mind and is, therefore, an ever present activity of my mind. As the activity of my mind, it is not subject to the
vagaries, the changes or whims, of men or of government, but is
spiritual and under the jurisdiction of the most High. My business,
being God's business, is God-governed.

Merely repeating these statements as affirmations and denials
will not do anything for you. Only when these truths about busi-

ness so permeate your consciousness that you have the full realization of them, will they become a reality in your experience. Just making statements will do nothing. I have known too many people who have walked around declaring, "My business is good; my business is good," when all the time they were going into bankruptcy. It is not *my* business that is good. It is *business* that is good—business, the activity of divine Wisdom. But, since that is the activity of my mind, that makes my business good. However, only as I associate my business with God's business, does it become individually expressed, harmoniously and joyously evident.

Consciously Realize the Truth

The same thing applies to family relationships. We have all seen families split on the rack of incompatibility, sin, disease, or some other condition of human experience. Do you think there is some mysterious God who is watching over your family relationships? Do not ever believe that. If your home becomes a divided home, if your family is separated, it is because you are not consciously doing something about it; it is because you are not *consciously* treating; it is because you are not consciously taking the subject of family, husband, wife, and child into your consciousness, asking the Father for light, for guidance, for help, and for inner wisdom.

In the same way, we go out and drive our car, and sometimes we think, "Mind is the driver and sits at the wheel of my automobile, so everything will be all right." But, do we remember to include the whole world in that? Do we realize that God is the mind of every individual on the road? No, instead we are likely to complain about the driving of the other person on the highway at the same time that we are claiming God as our individual mind. That is where the trouble comes in. There is no justification for our believing that because we are metaphysicians we have some kind of divine protection which the other person does not have. We have divine protection only in proportion to our utilization of these laws of truth, bringing them into our conscious awareness until they become part and parcel of our being.

Do you see how necessary treatment is? If you do not know this truth, you have nothing with which to heal because all healing is based on a consciousness of truth, and before you can gain the consciousness of truth, you must at least know the correct letter of truth. In living with this correct letter of truth, ultimately your consciousness is filled with truth and, then, when you are faced with any claim, you do not have to go through the process of thinking about truth or repeating it. There is the awareness of Omnipresence, and it is enough just to say, "Thank you, Father." It is like being able to say one hundred forty-four when someone says twelve times twelve. Do not hesitate to use treatment. Do not hesitate to ponder spiritual truths regarding any claim that might arise.

So, for several years to come, you will find that you will have a very active time treating. Never let treating, however, become a routine procedure—a ritual or a rite. Never let treatment become a habit. Never let it become so much a habit that you go through it sluggishly. Never do that. Such treatment will not help because it would be a formula and would be only suggestion. *A treatment must be a conscious realization of the truth.*

The Last Enemy

Everyone is interested in the subject of immortality—immortality here and now, in this body, not merely an immortality to be attained after death. It is in this very body that immortality must be experienced—this very body which we are now using as our instrument. We shall not lose our body, but we will lose our false sense of body and come into the realization of the true nature of body.

By losing the sense of disease, accident, and old age, and coming into a higher realization of perfect body, there is no loss of body: There is just the loss of a false sense of body and the realization of the true nature of body. In the same way, experiencing immortality here and now involves no loss of body, but only the loss of a false sense of body. In our daily meditation, let us realize immortality here and now—the immortality of this body and this universe—in order that we may lose the false sense the world entertains of the body and of the universe.

"The last enemy that shall be destroyed is death."[1] That may seem very discouraging to many people. Of this we can be sure, however, whether or not it is the last enemy to be overcome, it will never be overcome until *we* begin the overcoming, until *we* begin to do something about it. Just going on from one year to another, aimlessly saying, "Oh, well, death will be the last thing to be overcome," is not going to postpone it. If we want to postpone death and finally overcome it, we must begin now.

What is death? Death appears to be a momentary cessation of consciousness. But consciousness cannot be or remain unconscious. In fact, consciousness can never become totally unconscious. What we call death is but an apparent lapse into deep unconsciousness, from which we become conscious again, usually upon the same level as that upon which we fell asleep.

Body Expresses the Activity of Consciousness

The first step in beginning the overcoming of death is the realization that the body does not have any intelligence with which to live or die. Just as the body does not have the intelligence with which to catch cold, and we have to catch the cold for the body through the activity of the fleshly mind by accepting the beliefs of human thought; so, in the same way, we have to contract disease of any nature for the body. Disease is never contracted through or by the body. The body has no intelligence: It cannot move itself; it is inert; and, like a shadow, it reflects our own state of consciousness. *Any disease, therefore, appearing to be of the body is contracted through the activity of the human mind because of its acceptance of universal beliefs.* The first point then in overcoming death is overcoming the belief that the body of itself can either live or die and realizing that the body can only reflect, or express, the activity of our own state of consciousness.

When we accept in consciousness the thought or belief of death,

[1] I Corinthians 15:26.

that is when the body succumbs to it. It has been said over and over again, not only by metaphysicians, but by physicians as well, that people die only when they give their consent. In one way or another that is true. Consciously or unconsciously, consent is given to the experience of death. If you understand this point clearly enough, you may not only postpone and probably overcome death, but you will have a workable truth with which to meet the claim of disease and age.

The fact that an individual on the spiritual path goes through the experience of death, or of passing on, does not necessarily mean that he has died. Please remember this: What I have to tell you is not the product of guesswork, nor something I have read in a book. What I am going to tell you is from actual experience in interior revelation.

Progression or Retrogression

When people in the ordinary run of human existence die, or pass on, there is only a momentary lapse of consciousness from which they awaken in practically the same degree of mortality or material sense. They have not advanced or been made spiritual through the act of passing on; they have not been released from materiality into spirituality. True, they may have been released from the immediate pain or the immediate disease, but such release is similar to the release brought about by materia medica. Medical aid might release them from their pain or disease but it would never advance them spiritually. In the same way, even though the experience of death may relieve them of the particular disease or the particular distressing sense under which they labor, it does not change their level of consciousness; and they continue on the same mortal, material level, with the same opportunity at any moment to turn to the spiritual path and advance upon it or with the opportunity to retrograde. The choice is theirs either here or hereafter. All of this, of course, applies to those on the ordinary level of human existence who die, or pass on, from accident or disease, or from what is commonly termed "normal death."

Those who leave this plane of existence while on the downward spiral of life, that is, as an alcoholic or drug addict, as a criminal, or in any state of dense materiality, continue on that downward spiral immediately after their passing. Their materiality becomes even more dense, although at any time, awakening to their true identity, they can change their course and begin their spiritual ascent.

The student of religion or metaphysics who experiences death, or passing, while on the spiritual ascent, while on the upward path, not only awakens well advanced on the path; but in many cases, if his closeness to spiritual truth is sufficiently great, his passing may be the means of complete liberation from physical or mortal experience. That is the liberation which followers of certain Eastern religions have in mind when, in connection with their teaching of reincarnation, they refer to that state which they hope to attain when they no longer have to return to earth. In other words, some individuals reach such a level of spiritual consciousness that they are in full awareness of their true identity and understand that the physical body, so-called, is not they, is not of itself a living intelligence, but that it is a vehicle or an instrument through which they appear as form. To such, the experience of passing may completely end their experience with mortal or material sense-consciousness, and they go on in the fullness of spiritual living.

Overcoming the World

We have the opportunity of completely overcoming death in the sense of remaining right here on earth in our present form and in a continuing and progressive appearance of that form. I do not know whether or not it has ever been done, but there is the opportunity. However, that is not the important point. It is not of any more importance whether we stay here for two hundred years or two thousand years than it is important whether we go to New York or California or Europe. There is nothing important about where we live. The important thing is *how* we live and *why* we live. The important point is on what level of consciousness we are living. Are we living so that wherever we live, on whatever plane of existence, we are overcoming the body, we are overcoming the drag of morality and materiality?

One of the last statements Jesus made was, "I have overcome the world."[1] *But it was still Jesus saying it, while he was in the same body.* "I have overcome the world." We, too, overcome the world in proportion as we realize:

This body is not a power over me. I am the life and the mind, the intelligence and the directing power of this body. Not I, a human being, but I, the divine consciousness of Being, govern this body, this business, this home, this teaching, and this anything that comes within range of my consciousness.

In the degree in which we realize that divine Consciousness is governing us, in that degree have we overcome the world. Then we can walk through the waters or we can walk through germs or we can walk through war or we can walk through panic, and none of these things can have too great an effect or power over us because within every one of us is *I*, and *I* am the power that goes through every experience with us. Wherever we are and whatever the conditions around us, we find ourselves being daily fed and clothed and housed. If necessary, we find manna coming from the sky; if necessary, we find gold in the fish's mouth; if necessary, we find the loaves and fishes multiplied. In one form or another, we find ourselves supplied daily with all that we need, whether appearing as person, place, thing, circumstance, or condition. But this is our experience only as we overcome the world.

Overcoming the world begins with our understanding of oneness, of our unity with God, with the realization that, inasmuch as "I can of mine own self do nothing,"[2] all that is pouring through me is the life, the health, and the wholeness which is God.

[1] John 16:33.
[2] John 5:30.

Thus saith the Lord, Let not the wise man glory in his wisdom, neither let the mighty man glory in his might, let not the rich man glory in his riches:

But let him that glorieth glory in this, that he understandeth and knoweth me, that I am the Lord which exercise lovingkindness, judgment, and righteousness, in the earth.

JEREMIAH 9:23, 24

The moment we begin to realize that all that we have is of the Father, that it is universal, impersonal, impartial and, therefore, we have no copyrights or patents on it, we have opened our consciousness to its flow; and then that government takes over in our body, our business, our home, wherever we may be.

Resurrection and Ascension

In the consciousness of God, there is no death. God cannot die. God is eternal life, and infinite Consciousness cannot die or become unconscious. God, the divine Consciousness, is forever unfolding, disclosing, revealing, manifesting, and expressing Itself as individual consciousness.[1] God is your individual consciousness, and that consciousness cannot die. If God could die or become unconscious, then, and only then, could you die, or pass on. Since God is individual life, your life, can that life die? And can that life appearing as your form or body disappear from the earth? No, it can only rise through the process of ascension out of sight of morality.

When we, ourselves, lift up consciousness from the belief that life is in the body and that the body controls life, we experience resurrection; we gain the realization Jesus had when he said, "Destroy this temple [body], and in three days I will raise it up."[2] When we are imbued with the understanding that the divine Consciousness, which is individual consciousness, governs and controls

[1]This is the theme of the author's book, *Consciousness Unfolding* (New York: Julian Press, 1962).
[2]John 2:19.

our body, and as we individually perceive the truth that our own consciousness is the power of resurrection, of rebuilding, that becomes our experience of resurrection. Then comes the ascension.

The ascension comes with the realization that God is forever revealing Itself as our individual being, and because Spirit must appear or manifest as form, then this body is as spiritual and immortal and eternal as the Spirit-substance of which it is formed. With the light of this realization comes our ascension.

There is a spiritual meaning brought out for us in the birth, crucifixion, and ascension of the Master: If there is a progressive unfoldment of consciousness until the birth and the crucifixion have been fulfilled in us and we come to the ascension, no longer *in* the body but a law *unto* the body, we shall never again have to go back to those experiences. The ascension is that state of consciousness which knows that the body does not control life, but that life controls the body. The Master proved that he had achieved that state of consciousness when, in referring to his body, he said, "I have power to lay it down, and I have power to take it again,"[1] and also, "Destroy this temple [body], and in three days I will raise it up";[2] or in other words, "*I*, Consciousness, control this body." Consciousness controls body by letting the Consciousness of the *I Am* form Itself into the wonders and beauties which we call *here and now*.

[1] John 10:18.
[2] John 2:19.

Gaining the Consciousness of God

Consciousness is the real secret of the world. When you think you are searching for God, what you are really searching for is an understanding of Consciousness, because Consciousness *is* God; God *is* consciousness. These are interchangeable. Consciousness is God, and God is consciousness. When you have found the inner meaning of Consciousness, you will have found God. When you find God, you will have discovered your own consciousness.

You can now more nearly understand what I meant when I said, and have repeated several times, that the purpose of this work is not to give you more truths that you already know. I am sure that you already know all of the letter of truth there is to be known. It is so easily available, not only in my writings, but in many others. So I repeat: The purpose of this work is not to add one iota to your intellectual knowledge of truth, but to quicken the unfolding of consciousness—the unfolding of the divine Consciousness as your individual consciousness.

The key to what we call "demonstration," that is, to a successful and happy life, a joyous and complete existence, is consciousness, gaining the consciousness of good in one form or another.

If we were asked what the object of our work is, I suppose we might say, "We are searching for God." To most people God is a vague term. Would you know what to do with God after you found Him? Actually, if we were honest with ourselves, we would say, "I am seeking a sense of peace, a consciousness of harmony, a consciousness of health, a consciousness of the wholeness of being." We can sum that up, too, in the phrase, "a consciousness of happiness." If we are happy, we have all these things, and our happiness is all inclusive.

Someone has said that happiness is a butterfly, which when pursued, is always just beyond your grasp, but, which, if you will sit down quietly, may alight on you. If it is true that the kingdom of God is within you, happiness cannot be found outside. Happiness is that which flows from within your own being. So, the state of consciousness which is always pursuing happiness must be given up, and the consciousness of sitting quietly and letting joy come must be attained.

Happiness in this world, when it comes, comes incidentally. Make it the object of pursuit, and it leads us a wild-goose chase, and is never attained. Follow some other object, and very possibly we may find that we have caught happiness without dreaming of it.[1]

To attain happiness or peace, to attain peace of mind, or a sense of wholeness and harmony means, first of all, to stop running around, stop trying to get something, and rather learn to sit quietly, to meditate, and to ponder within yourself the realities of Being, and then *let* this happiness come. It has been said that happiness is a perfume you cannot pour on others without getting a few drops on yourself. So before this perfume of happiness can come to us, we have to begin pouring it upon others.

[1]Nathaniel Hawthorne, *American Note-books*, November, 1852.

Nothing Can Be Added to You; Nothing Can Be Taken from You

All this goes back to the teaching of the Master: "The kingdom of God is within you";[2] it must well out from you. Nothing can be added to you; nothing can be taken from you: You are eternally complete and whole. Whenever we attempt to meditate, let us remember this: There is nothing "out there" separate from us to be attained. We have only to gain the consciousness of that for which we are seeking, and we shall find that we have it. And let us never forget that in bringing about a sense of improvement in our affairs, we begin where we are at the moment. We do not dream about what will happen after we get more understanding or after we have been another year on this path.

For example, if the problem is one of health, we sit down and right where we are we begin to realize whatever truth we know about God and God's infinite spiritual creation. We do not wait until tomorrow, we do not wait until we know more truth, or until we are more spiritual, or until we are more deserving. We sit right down now and use the one grain of truth that we know. If we do not know more than a grain, we put that one grain to work. We take whatever of truth we have and utilize it. We sit down and ponder the truth of God, the wholeness of spiritual Being, the nature of the spiritual universe, the truth that error is not power, disease is not power, sin is not power and, therefore, cannot cause anything. That is the way we begin to build this new consciousness of the allness of God, which includes the allness of health, the allness harmony, the allness of abundance, and the consequent nothingness of any power to obstruct the operation of this Allness.

If the problem is one of supply, we would immediately utilize all the truth that we know and put it into operation by doing whatever there is to do at the moment. It might be that we would have to begin with the most menial job in the world, but that would make no difference—even if we did not get paid for it. The

[2]Luke 17:21.

thing to do is to get busy with it, knowing that little grain of truth and continuing in it. Thereby you build a new consciousness of activity, of employment, of income, in fact, of everything there is.

In the same way, if we want our bodies to be vital, if we want them to be useful and remain active with the passing of years, we do not accomplish this just by gaining a better body. Humanly, we can gain a better body: We can go to a gymnasium; we can take exercises; we can diet and build ourselves a good physical body, and we might even bring about a measure of longevity, adding five, ten, or fifteen years to our human span. But, in spiritual work, that is not our aim. Our aim is to attain a spiritual sense of body, a spiritual consciousness of body, so that that consciousness maintains the body, infinitely and eternally and harmoniously. Therefore, we have to gain a consciousness of immortality; we have to gain a consciousness of eternality; we have to gain a consciousness of bodily perfection. The secret of gaining health or of gaining supply is not in gaining health or in gaining supply, but rather in gaining the *consciousness* of health and the *consciousness* of supply.

Your Consciousness of Truth Becomes the Substance of Your Demonstration

Do you realize now how important consciousness is? To learn to change our consciousness is really and truly the purpose of our work because whatever is discordant in our experience is but our erroneous consciousness of that which is appearing, and it is not going to do any good merely to achieve a better appearance. For example, if you are in a home you do not like, it will not be of any permanent value to you to get a better home. That is not the solution. The solution is to gain, first, a better consciousness of home; then the better home will follow.

The same principle applies if you are dissatisfied with your business, if you are dissatisfied with your practice or with your profession. You must gain a freer or better consciousness of that with which you are not satisfied before you can experience the desired good itself.

If that clear? You may as well being right here and now by realizing that the secret of having anything is first attaining the consciousness of it: Why is that? Because consciousness is God, and the moment you have the consciousness of a thing, consciousness creates it, whatever the "it" may be—home, companionship, supply, employment, health, eternality, immortality. Your consciousness of it builds it. "With all thy getting get understanding."[1] With all thy getting, get a consciousness of good, and then the good will follow.

As you gain the consciousness of anything, this consciousness produces it: Consciousness becomes the substance of your demonstration. If we should tell you that what you looked like and that what you were when you were born were the direct result of your own state of consciousness, you might think that incredible and that you had nothing to do with it. But that is only because you may believe that you began at the moment of your birth or a few months before. That is not true. You have coexisted with God since "before Abraham was,"[2] and therefore, the state of consciousness that you were prior to birth is the cause of what you were when you were born. In the same way, whatever state of consciousness you are now is the cause of what you now demonstrate, and the state of consciousness that you attain next year or ten years from now will be the cause of the appearance of your body, of your business, of your home and home relationships, or of your national and international relationships.

Do you really and truly believe that your own consciousness governs your life? Can anyone doubt it? The whole teaching of The Infinite Way is based on the premise that Consciousness is God, and that Consciousness, being universal Consciousness, is your

[1]Proverbs 4:7.
[2]John 8:58.

individual consciousness. From that standpoint, you should have a perfect body, a perfect business, a perfect home.

As you, yourself, become more and more aware of the infinite nature of your own consciousness, the effect begins to appear in your experience in infinite form. The more the mesmeric suggestion or universal belief of a selfhood apart from God grips you, the more will your demonstration be governed by world-consciousness, instead of your own infinite consciousness. If there is a depression and you find yourself out of a job, you will have become the victim of a world-belief, instead of demonstrating that world-beliefs have no power over you and that your consciousness of being is the law unto you.

This in no way denies scriptural teaching. In Genesis, we were given dominion over everything in this universe from under the sea to above the stars. And certainly the teaching of the Master does not make us the victim even of a tyrant or a dictator. His teaching was that nothing could in any wise have power over us, unless it came from the Father, but we must have the consciousness of that truth in order to demonstrate it. The fact that truth is true will not do the work: *It is your consciousness of truth that does the work.*

From

Living Now

The Power of Resurrection

History is filled with accounts of man's attempts to find a power that will be stronger than his fears, and with which he can surmount the fears that make of his life one long nightmare. Every nation has sought to free itself from fear by amassing tremendous concentrations of armaments, but what has been the result of this attempt to settle the world's fears by the use of more and more power? The fear remains, and the enemies!

Practically all fears that ever touch an individual, as well as the fears that touch the life of his nation, are related in some way and to some extent to the one word "power": the dreaded power of bombs, the hated power of dictators, or the frightening power inherent in economic cycles. Always there is some power to be feared.

Let us suppose right now that we were to withdraw power from the things or persons that we fear, or suppose that we were to withdraw fear from the powers that we fear. Suppose that for just a single moment we could give up the word "power" in thinking of our personal, national, and international relationships.

To make this concrete, let us bring it down to ourselves and consider what would happen if you and I determined to live in a relationship in which we never used the word "power," never thought of any power that we have over one another, or of using a power to get our way or to enforce our will. Under such a relationship, I would want to live in harmony with you, and you would want to live in harmony with me, but we would no longer have access to any power. In other words, we would have no way of enforcing our will, desire, or hopes. Where would we be then in relationship to one another, with each of us desiring harmony, peace, joy, and friendship, and yet no longer being able to promise or threaten each other? By withdrawing the word "power" from our experience, and all that it implies, it would seem that we have placed ourselves in an absolutely defenseless position.

To continue such philosophic conjecture and speculation does not lead us up a dead-end street, but rather to the realization that the powers that we have been fearing are not really powers, not those that were going to do either such terrible things to us or such wonderful things for us. These powers are not powers at all: they operate as power only in the consciousness that accepts them as power; and for this reason, therefore, any power they may seem to have is only of a temporary nature, and it is a temporary sense of power that causes all our fears. The ultimate of this unfoldment is that power does not exist in that which has form or effect: power is in the consciousness that produces the form or the effect.

Gaining a Release from Fear

The result of a spiritual unfoldment of this nature is to lift the individual above the realm of fear. This release from fear, however, is not achieved instantaneously. There are few of us who can rise immediately to the point of saying, "I do not fear an atomic bomb." We have to begin with things which seem less powerful, perhaps with the weather or climate, with food or germs, and withdraw power from these by understanding that, in and of themselves, they cannot have power because all power is in the consciousness that produces the form, not in the form.

To attain this state of consciousness, it is helpful in our medication to practice beholding effects, looking out at the weather, the climate, food, germs, and perceiving that they of themselves have no power except the power with which we imbue them. The power is within our consciousness. Shakespeare expressed it succinctly when he said, "There is nothing either good or bad, but thinking makes it so."[1] In other words, the evil is not in the thing, nor is it in the effect. Whatever evil there is, is in our sense of what we are beholding, or in the power with which we imbue an individual, a condition, or a circumstance.

Most of us have already demonstrated this in some degree, and have proved that many of the so-called powers of the world have been rendered powerless by our spiritual awareness. We have experienced, some in small degree and some in very great degree, the operation of this principle in our life, but until we consciously take it into our Self, into our inner sanctuary, and abide in it, we cannot make it practical in our daily experience. True, we can receive benefit from those who have attained the consciousness of non-power, but this is of only temporary help to us.

Eventually we must take this subject into meditation, let our thought wander across the whole span of our human life, and make a mental check of those things, persons, or conditions we have feared, and begin to silence those fears by withdrawing power from things, persons, or conditions, realizing:

> *God is infinite consciousness, the consciousness of the entire universe. It is out of that Consciousness, which is God, that the whole world has become manifest. God looked upon His universe and saw that it was all good. God, as Consciousness, the Substance of the entire spiritual*

[1] *Hamlet.* Act II.

creation, could create and manifest a world only in the image and like-
ness of Himself. Therefore, this spiritual universe is inbued with the
qualities of God, and with no other qualities. Only God entered His
own universe—only the qualities and the activities of God—and there-
fore, all that exists is in and of God.

There is no evil power in the spiritual creation because there is
no evil power in God. "In him is no darkness at all."[2] Nothing
could ever enter the consciousness of God "that defileth ... or
maketh a lie."[3] God is too pure to behold iniquity. The consciousness of God is absolute purity, life eternal, immortality itself.

Life Is the Eternal Reality

"For I have no pleasure in the death of him and dieth ... wherefore turn yourselves, and live ye."[4] God has not created death or
anything that could cause death. God is pure, undefiled Spirit, life
eternal; and God, functioning as the consciousness of Christ Jesus,
says, "I am come that they might have life, and that they might
have it more abundantly[5]—not "I have come that they might have
death," or not "I have come that they might have life until they are
threescore years and ten," but "I am come that they might have life
more abundantly." Furthermore, the voice of God, again speaking
as the consciousness of Christ Jesus, says, "I am the resurrection,
and the life."[6] Always God is voicing the eternality and immortality of man. Nothing was ever created by God that is empowered to
cause the distress of man. There is no room in the lift more abundant for death or for anything that would cause death.

As we go back into the original spiritual creation as revealed in
the first chapter of Genesis, there is not only single sign of discord
or of anything that has power to destroy God's universe. If there

[2]I John 1:5.
[3]Revelation 21:27.
[4]Ezekiel 18:32.
[5]John 10:10.
[6]John 11:25.

were, we would be admitting that God, the Creator, is also God, the Destroyer; that God at the time of creation also made something to destroy His own creation. There is only one sense in which the Oriental teaching of God as both Creator and Destroyer can be accepted, and that is that God as Creator of the universe must automatically be the destroyer of anything that is contrary to the spiritual creation. That, however, would never mean the destroyer of anything real.

Since God is the Self-created, Self-maintaining, Self-sustaining principle of this universe, the responsibility for our immortality and eternality rests with God, not with man, not with bombs, not with germs, and not with the upswings or downswings of Wall Street. The fate of man is not in effect, but in Consciousness, the Consciousness which is God, the infinite, the divine, the pure. Actually, this Consciousness is the consciousness of man, and in its unconditioned state leaves man, as it did Melchizedek, spiritual, untouched by mortal conditions, material circumstances, or human beliefs.

Attaining the Unconditioned Consciousness

The evils that befall us are not in God or in man, but rather in the conditioning that we have received through the ignorance that has been foisted upon us from time immemorial. In other words, every time that we give power to a person, a thing, or a condition, our consciousness is showing forth its conditioning, and to that extent we become victims of it.

It might come as a surprise to see how easy it would be for some person, either for a specific purpose or just as an experiment, show us how quickly we could be made to distrust one another, and then in the end, fear one another. It has been done over, and over, and over again. It is a very simple thing to condition the minds of persons who are not alert so that they unthinkingly accept the opinions, thoughts, and beliefs of others and respond robotlike to individual suggestion or mass hysteria. If we listened to all the propaganda and the opinions of others, very soon we would be fighting not only with our families, but with our neighbors and the whole world.

The question is this: To whom do we give allegiance? To whom do we surrender our minds and our thoughts? It is very difficult for persons who have not been taught the value of meditation to turn within to the Presence for Its guidance, instruction, and wisdom. Instead, they rely on opinions gathered from newspapers, magazines, television broadcasts, and thereby fear every headline, as if it could be a threat to the life which is God.

If it is true that the kingdom of God is within us, then the kingdom of power is within us because God is power, and not only is God power, but God is all the power there is. God is omnipotence. If we can accept God as All-power, and if we can accept the presence of God, the power of God, and the kingdom of God as being within us, then we can understand that the place whereon we stand is holy ground. Why? Because we are inseparable and indivisible from our Father, for the kingdom of our Father is within us. The kingdom of Omnipotence is within us, but only as we meditate upon this can we look out and state with conviction: "I will not fear what mortal man or mortal conditions can do to me. I will not fear what mortality can do; I will not fear what germs or bombs can do because the kingdom of God, Omnipotence, is within me. All-power is within me."

Ordinarily, God is accepted, not as Omnipotence, but merely as a great Power to be invoked over whatever the enemy may seem to be. It could be sin, disease, or death; it could be war; it could be anything. Regardless of all our prayers for health, safety, and peace, these are still absent from the world. And why? Have not our prayers been unsuccessful because God is not a great power over lesser powers? God is omnipotence, and these other powers are not powers, except in proportion as we are conditioned to accept them.

One has only to travel the world to witness the fears that are hammering at the consciousness of men. Is there any hope for freedom in the world until there is a release from fear? Is not fear at the root of all problems; national, and international? Is not fear the real bugaboo?

Holdups have been committed with toy pistols even though there is no power in a toy. Was not the power in the acceptance of it as a real weapon? How many persons have died through the diabolic suggestions of the kahunas of ancient times! How any persons have been made miserable through witchcraft! Was there ever any real power in kahunas or in witches or witchcraft? Was not the power in the fear that these were a power, a fear that took possession of the victim?

Recently, experiments have been conducted whereby one half of a group of persons were fed cold germs, and the other half capsules of water. They all believed that they were being given cold germs, and about the same percentage in each group caught cold; but when the procedure was reversed, the same results were obtained. The power was not in the capsules: it was the minds of those participating in the experiment that gave the capsules the only power they had.

In our unconditioned state, we are immortal and eternal, and nothing external to us and nobody external to us have power, jurisdiction, or control over us. We are individuals, yet one with God. All the Omnipotence, all the divine Grace, all the divine Love, all the divine Power are ours. Therefore, nothing external to us can act upon us.

If we permit ourselves to be conditioned through an acceptance of universal beliefs and universal fears, however, then they act upon us in the same way as they act upon the rest of the human race, and we make ourselves victims of them. We do not fear ghosts, but there are some persons who do. Is there any power in ghosts, or is the power in the fear of them?

There are today perhaps millions of persons in the world virtually untouched by harmful germs and practically immune to germ-diseases. Why? Is this because there are fewer germs in their systems than in anybody else's? Or is it because they have accepted Omnipotence, because they have agreed that all the power of God is given unto them, not unto germs, weather, or climate? God has endowed every one of us with His power; God has given us dominion over all that exists on the earth, under the earth, and above the earth. This dominion we have surrendered by permitting ourselves to be conditioned by the world's ignorance and the world's fears.

Resurrection Here and Now

In our oneness with the Father, we find not only spiritual power but food, water, inspiration, and even resurrection. how often we hear the questions: "Do you believe in resurrection? Did Jesus rise from a tomb? Did anyone see the risen Jesus? Did he walk the earth?"

Those who do not believe that Jesus was crucified and entombed, that he rose from the tomb and walked the earth, do not have the spiritual vision that would enable them to see that which the eyes cannot see, and hear that which the ears cannot hear. The truth is that Jesus was crucified; he was entombed; he rose from the tomb; he walked the earth, and was seen by at least five hundred persons who bore witness to that fact.

This was the truth about Jesus beyond all question of doubt, but this is also the truth about all of us. We, too, will walk freely on the earth after our so-called burial. The only difference is that there will not be five hundred persons to identify us because we have not told them to expect us or to believe in our powers of resurrection. So our friends will turn away from our funeral with grief, believing we have gone somewhere, and according to their belief so will it be until them.

The dead are never entombed in the grave, and they are never cremated. That happens only to the shell, the body. I know this to be true because I have actually seen those who have passed away standing in my presence, and in some cases have heard them speaking to me.

Each of us, in his time, will pass from visible sight, and this is in accord with divine Wisdom, which enables us to outgrow the form of an infant and become a child, then to outgrow the form of a child to become a mature person, and to continue maturing until we have outgrown the need for this particular form or body, and are enabled to make a transition so that we may function in still another form.

If everyone remained on this earth forever, there would be no opportunity for the coming generations, nor would there be any activity for the older citizens who have outgrown their ability to serve the world. Provision must, therefore, be made for continued growth and unfoldment, and after a certain length of time on this earth, these cannot come to us here.

I am sure that there are many who make the transitions before their time, many who are forced out by disease or poverty, and this will change only as the world becomes more spiritually minded. But when we see those of mature years go forward to a new experience, we should rejoice in the greater opportunity that is now being given them to function usefully, harmoniously, and joyously.

It is destined that we be immortal, for the offspring of God cannot be less immortal than God. We are immortal, temporarily clothed upon with a belief that we are mortal. We are clothed upon with mortality, but the Christ-message is that we must be unclothed; we must remove from ourselves this false concept of self, which claims that we are mortal, and we must be clothed upon with immortality. We must "die daily" to our mortality and be reborn into our immortality.

From beginning to end, Scripture reveals that there is a power that restores to us "the years that the locust hath eaten."[7] There is a power or resurrection, a power of restoration, regeneration, and renewal, and it is this power within us that the Master came to reveal. He restored to full and complete dignity the woman taken in adultery; he restored to heaven the thief on the cross. What was that restoration and regeneration but a resurrection?

[7]Joel 2:25.

Love Is the Power of Resurrection

The power of resurrection lies in love, but it is difficult to understand what love is. Everybody wants to be loved, but so few want to love and it is only in loving that resurrection can come, not in being loved. We could be loved by millions, and still die miserably. The power of resurrection is not in the love that is given to us: the power of resurrection is in the love that flows through us and out from us. In other words, the "imprisoned splendor" must be permitted to escape, and that imprisoned splendor is our life eternal. But life is love, and there is no life separate and apart from love.

So many persons find life to be futile, not really worthwhile, and when we come to know them, we see why. The power of loving has left them—not the power of being loved. They spend most of their life seeking for companionship and understanding, which they never quite succeed in finding because they are not to be found: they are to be expressed.

If we want life—and I mean life harmonious, not just an existence from morning to night, and night to morning; real life, a life abundant in every way, physically, mentally, morally, financially—we do not go around looking for life: we live, we live! A man who has attained a hundred years and was asked how he had reached such an advanced age wisely answered, "I just kept on living." Of course that was the answer, but we cannot just keep on living unless we have something to live for. The moment a reason for living disappears, life disappears.

The only reason there is for living is to love. It sounds strange, but it is true. There is no other reason for staying on earth than the opportunity to love, and anybody who has experienced this knows that there is no joy like loving: no joy like sharing, bestowing, understanding, an giving, all of which are but other names for love.

It is difficult to make this clear to those who are living entirely from the standpoint of getting, wanting, and desiring. On the other hand, it is simple to explain this to a person who has within himself some touch of the Spirit of God. Unfortunately, there are some devoid of this Spirit of God; and these, the Master referred to as barren and rocky soil. One thing is missing in them, one thing only: love, love. The love they are seeking is the love they must give. Once that love is there, once that nature that wants to give, share, and understand is there, the nature that wants to meet this world halfway, the next step is easy: it is gaining the understanding that the real power of this world is in consciousness, not something external to it.

This is our great lesson: God is the infinite, divine consciousness, the consciousness of which this universe is formed, and God has given Himself to us so that the life and consciousness of God may be ours. The whole, immortal life of God is ours; the whole divine consciousness of God is ours—all this divine Consciousness.

Learning to Release the Gift of God

Since we are already infinite, there is no need for us to seek good, love, companionship, or supply: we are already one with the Father, and all that the Father has is already ours. In order to enjoy our spiritual heritage, we must learn how to let this gift of God escape.

One way of doing this is by living constantly in the awareness that dominion has been given to us—God-dominion, spiritual dominion—and therefore we need not fear anything or anyone external to ourselves. The second way is to open up ways for a greater expression of love to flow out from us. The Master has pointed out how this love can be expressed: we can visit the prisoner in prison; we can comfort the widow and the orphan; we can heal the sick; we can feed the hungry; we can clothe the naked; we can pray; we can pray for our enemies; we can forgive seventy times seven. All this is loving, all this is letting love flow out.

In one way or another, we must ask ourselves the question, "What have I in my house?" The moment we say, "I," that brings

us right back to "I and my Father are one."[8]   All that the Father
has is ours to share: all the love, all the life, all the dominion, all
the Grace, all the supply. Even is we only share the few drops of
oil that may be immediately available, or the little meal, or if we
begin with that old pair of shoes in the closet—no matter where
we begin—if we begin to pour out what we have in the house, it
increases, and the more it is used, the more it increases.

It is like teaching. No student has ever learned as much from a
teacher as the teacher learns from teaching the student because it
is in the teaching that the flow begins, and the more the teacher
pours out, the more is pouring in. Whether it is teaching on the
spiritual level or on the human level, the more experience or practice a teacher has in his particular field, the greater his own knowledge becomes because the flow is from the infinite Source that is
within each one of us. Infinity is within us; the kingdom of God is
within us; and we draw from this infinite source of Withinness the
moment we acknowledge, "I and my Father are one."

All Power Is Within Us

As we seat ourselves comfortably for our meditation, with our eyes
closed, we are looking into darkness, and we can see the infinite
nature of this darkness which is our Withinness, full and complete.
All this darkness is within us, all this space is within us, all this
world that we are confronting is within us:

> Now, here where I am, within me, within this very darkness, is the
> kingdom of God. The kingdom of Allness, of Omnipotence, of divine
> Grace is stored up here within me.

If we were sitting alone in a rubber boat in the middle of the
ocean, this realization would bring us protection, safety, food,
water, or whatever we needed. If we were lost in the desert, this
realization would lead us, even with our eyes closed, out of the

[8]John 10:30.

desert into safety and security, or would lead others to us, since right where we are, God is: the fullness of God, the allness of God, the omnipotence of God, the grace of God.

When we know this, we have no fear of any circumstance or condition in the outer world because all dominion is within us. A thousand of those who do not know this truth may fall at our left hand, and ten thousand at our right, but it will not come nigh our dwelling place. As we realize the very presence of this Omnipotence within us, God is abiding in us, and we bear fruit richly.

Through practicing this one principle of the nature of spiritual power, we are living the Christ-life. The Master feared no disease, no death; he feared no Pilate. "Thou couldest have no power at all against me, except it were given thee from above."[9] Pilate is only another name for the particular tyrant seeming to operate in our experience.

Because of his realization of Omnipotence, Jesus feared nothing external to him; but at the same time he was not fearing external powers, he was pouring forth to the world his love, his healing consciousness, his sharing consciousness, his forgiving consciousness, and not only pouring forth to the saints but to the sinners as well.

We must do likewise that we may be disciples, that we may be the sons of God. We are not fulfilling ourselves as children of God unless, first of all, we are acknowledging Omnipotence within ourselves, and thereby fearing nothing external, and secondly, letting the Christ-love pour forth in infinite abundance. Then we shall witness the resurrection taking place within us here and now.

ACROSS THE DESK

Consciousness is the most important word in the entire vocabulary of The Infinite Way. Nothing we can think of can ever take the place of the word "Consciousness~" In Its pure state, Consciousness is God; and in Its pure state, It constitutes our being. As human beings, we live as states and stages of consciousness, degrees

[9]John 19:11.

consciousness. In fact, the moment we are conceived humanly, the consciousness by all that our parents think: the fears and the hopes they entertain are transferred to us. Then we enter school and are conditioned by schoolteachers, schoolmates, and parents of schoolmates, always picking up more conditioning so that by the time we go out into the world 90 per cent of the things we are convinced are true are in reality untrue. Out in the world on our own, the conditioning continues.

From the moment we touch a metaphysical teaching, however, we begin to condition ourselves along other lines. For example, if we pondered the statement, "Call no man your father upon the earth: for one is your Father, which is in heaven,"[10] and if the truth of that principle ever registered in our consciousness, we would soon be able to look around and say, "Oh, then there is only one Creator, and we are all children of that One; we are all equal in the sight of God."

That alone would wipe out of us our prejudices and early conditioning toward other persons. On this point, we would have a new consciousness. We would have "died" to the state of consciousness which had been filled with biases and prejudices and we would have become one with our fellow man universally. On this one point, we would have become a new man.

If this kind of conditioning continued, eventually we would come to another extension of that same idea and would realize that if this is true, we then derive our qualities and inheritances from that One. It was Emerson who said, "There is but one universal Mind, and all men are inlets to, and outlets from, that One." Once we begin to perceive that we are inlets to and outlets from that one God-consciousness, we perceive that we are inlets to and outlets for Its qualities, and we are not limited as we thought we were; we are not dependent on what our human parents were: now we are dependent on our Source. It might take months of pondering, but eventually it would sink in, and we could then say that whereas we were blind, now we see.

[10]Matthew 23:9.

Through a realization of this one truth, we begin to draw on Infinity; we are in a new consciousness in which two things have happened: we have lost our bias and our bigotry and have thrown off some of the handicaps and limitations of our ancestors. No longer is it true that the sins of the fathers shall be visited "upon the children unto the third and fourth generation."[11] Once we take this one principle and work with it, we are a freer state of consciousness; we are not the same person; we have thrown off our dependency on others and have learned to go within to the Source.

Every one of us from childhood has been told to fear external powers, whether in the form of germs, infection, contagion, or weather. But what if we were to catch a glimpse of the metaphysical principle, "Pilate, you have no power over me. 'I and my Father are one.' God gave me dominion, and because of that dominion, there is no power in the external world"? Would not the acceptance of this principle and the conviction of its truth set us free from 70 to 80 per cent of the world's fears? We would no longer fear the power of anything external to us, and again on this one point, we would be a different state of consciousness: we would have "died" to our fears.

We have not yet "died" to the greatest fear of all, the fear of death. It is this fear that makes illnesses so frightening. If there is such a thing as becoming immune to the fear of death, then we would have demonstrated living eternally, and I do not mean by that staying on earth forever.

We all have to make a transition, but the time for that transition is when we have served our purpose on earth, and while we might look forward to the transition, we no longer look forward to death. In losing the fear of death, we are set free from most of the diseases of this world, and with even a partial movement into that state, we are not the same person we were before. No longer are we fearing outer conditions and circumstances. We have moved into still another degree of consciousness.

By this time in our spiritual life, we are in a state of conscious-

[11]Exodus 20:5.

ness entirely different from what we were the day we found ourselves on the spiritual path. We are no longer giving power to the
external; we have fewer superstitious beliefs; and we have lost some
of our ignorance. This progress is made only as we take one spiritual principle after another and work with it until each one "rings
a bell" and registers within.

As consciousness is purified, that is, as we rid ourselves of erroneous conditioning, more and more do we approach the pure Consciousness, God-given life and immortality. Now, as always, our
prayer should be, "Father, give me the pure Consciousness I had
with Thee before the world began."

The basic principle emphasized in The Infinite Way is that there
is neither good nor evil but thinking makes it so. We neither look
to external good nor evil but thinking makes it so. Nothing—no
thing—has been empowered with evil. God has given us His own
Spirit, His own consciousness. The degree of our failure can be
measured by the degree of which we have picked up man's universal consciousness.

Each one has within himself his own degree of realization of that
mind which was also in Christ Jesus. When we consciously know
the truth, we are attaining that mind. In proportion as we give no
power to the external, we will understand that eventually the lamb
will lie down with the lion, and as we adopt his principle in our
life, we will find that we are affected less and less by the external.
The closer we come to the principle, the closer we come to a consciousness of good.

This becomes more and more true as our consciousness can
accept the revelation that there is neither good nor evil, that it is
only the universal sense that makes it seem so. There is just *IS*.
The grass *IS*, the weather *IS*, the water *IS*. The only power there
is, is Being. The close we live to the consciousness that all is Being,
God created and God endowed, the more we find ourselves
attuned to the love of God and the grace of God. This then
changes our consciousness because a life free of some of the old
fears is a whole new consciousness.

Every time we receive an inner impartation, it knocks out some external fear, and to a degree we are freed from our early outside conditioning. If we could look back ten years and see ourselves as we were then, we would say, "Why, I am not that person."

The reason the word "consciousness" is so important is because we know that the goal of our work is to change our consciousness. In accomplishing this, we have to leave the world alone. Any change that takes place has to come from within our own consciousness. Let us ask ourselves: What is our reaction to persons, weather, theories? What is our reaction to death? We do not know what special conditioning of mind is our particular barrier, and it is because we do not know what is limiting us that we need frequent periods of mediation.

Eventually, we come into an awareness that our consciousness determines the nature of our life, but it is only as we accept a change of consciousness that the change can come. No teacher or practitioner brings about a change in a student: he is only the instrument through which the student himself makes the change. The thing to be grateful for is the inner God that prepared us for the change. Whatever degree of changed consciousness comes to us depends upon our devotion to that end. A teacher or practitioner is only the means to the end. He has the power to bring out what is in us and no more, and that only in proportion to our humility and willingness to pitch in and work.

There is something inside that is pushing us toward attaining a pure consciousness. Somewhere in a past incarnation or in the present one, something happened to spark our spiritual center, and as each one of these specific principles becomes illumined in us, we get closer to the pure state of consciousness. Then as we make each of the principles our own, we have taken one step out of human bondage, and we are tied less to human limitation.

In proportion to our ability to grasp and become convinced of the truth that there is neither good nor evil, we become pure Consciousness. Pure Consciousness is that of which we are composed: the states of consciousness we express are superimposed by the beliefs of the world. To attain pure Consciousness involves a process of "dying daily." Every time we drop a theory, every time we drop an anxiety or a superstition, to that extent we have "died" to this world.

When the Master said that he had overcome the world, he had overcome these temptations, but when he had overcome death he had really overcome the world. Personally, I do not think he overcome the world until he was in the Garden of Gethsemane. There he faced death. There he left his human sense of life. No one fully "dies" until he faces death; then he is in the Fourth Dimension. He is then alive not in the human sense but in the spiritual sense.

God-Endowed Dominion

The healing principles of The Infinite Way differ so radically from those found in other teachings that students who want to be successful in the practice of Infinite Way healing should work only from the standpoint of what has been given to them in this work.

There are some teachings in which the practitioner endeavors to find the error that is causing the trouble and identify it with the patient. This practice is called "uncovering the error," and assumes that there is some erroneous thought in the patient, which is producing his particular disease.

Early in my practice I discovered that this was not true. Evil does not originate in the patient's thought, although he may permit himself to become an outlet for it. All evil of any nature, whether it is sin, false appetite, disease, lack, or limitation, has its origin in the universal or carnal mind. The moment a practitioner knows this, he begins to set his patient free. Instead of pinning some error on to him and fastening it to him, he immediately realizes, "This does not have its origin in a person: it has its origin in the universal or carnal mind."

Recognize the God in Everyone

If I sit on a class or lecture platform in front of an audience, thinking that everyone in that group is the child of God with the mind of God and the Soul of God and that only God lives and works in and through him, what happens? Even though the members of the class or audience do not know that this silent realization of their true spiritual nature and origin is going on, they begin to respond to the truth about them. They do not know why, but they rejoice inwardly because I am seeing them as they are in their real nature, seeing their real Self, seeing behind the human masquerade.

If, on the other hand, I were to sit on that platform and criticize the persons in the audience, resent or judge them after human standards, they would begin to twist and squirm and feel uncomfortable. Why? Because I would be malpracticing them, and even though they did not know what I was doing, they would feel the effect of it.

This same thing happens in the healing practice. If I try to find the error in a patient, he begins to feel my malpractice, and instead of being free and happy and joyous, he is uncomfortable under my censure and judgment. That is no way to set anyone free.

It is possible to experiment with this principle in dealing with cats, dogs, birds, or little children. Instead of saying, "You bad dog," "You naughty cat," or, "You impudent child," we should realize: "God made individual being, and that being possesses all the qualities of God. The mind and the intelligence of individual being spring from God. Life is of God, and God governs even the sparrow's fall." When this is known, the animal's or the child's behavior changes because condemnation has been removed.

If you would heal, you must remember to remove the original sin from mankind, the belief that man was created in sin and brought forth in iniquity. That is not the truth about anybody.

"Call no man your father upon the earth: for one is your Father, which is in heaven."[1] And what does this mean except that you are to recognize the spiritual origin of every man?

Although scientists may trace man back to a seed, the question remains: Where did the seed originate? Was not the seed created by God? Man is not a creator: God is the creator. Man is only the instrument through which creation appears, but behind man is God that created the seed. Everything that is visible, everything that is made, is made of a substance that is invisible.

The Universal Impersonal Nature of Evil

The minute I recognize that God constitutes individual being, I must also recognize that no person contains within himself the source of any evil. There is no evil in anyone, no God-constituted evil and no self-created evil. Any evil that is manifesting through a person has its origin in what for lack of a better name may be called the universal carnal mind. To so dispose of it immediately separates it from the person, and leaves him as he originally was, the image and likeness of God, God Himself in expression, Life expressing Itself as individual being. There is then no evil in him: the only evil there is, is the impersonal evil inherent in the universal carnal mind.

Whenever there is an outbreak of colds, influenza, or other diseases of that nature, there is the belief that weather, climate, or germs are the cause, but can you not see that this belief did not originate in the person? He did not originate the idea of colds or flu; he did not originate the idea of germs. This is some kind of a belief out in the atmosphere, which he has picked up because of his ignorance of the truth.

In working with such cases, there is no point in treating a person, because the average practitioner might have a hundred persons with colds or the flu calling for help, and he would have a hard

[1]Matthew 23:9.

time trying to give each one of them a treatment every day. Fortunately, this is not necessary because there is only one problem, and that problem has nothing to do with a person. It is a universal belief of weather, infection, contagion, or of germs, and when it is handled in this way, if there are a hundred sick, a hundred are healed as each one brings himself to, and touches, the consciousness of the practitioner. Yet there has been only one treatment because there is only one belief: a universal belief in a selfhood apart from God, a power apart from God, or a presence apart from God.

When you experiment with this principle and prove conclusively to yourself that a cold, flu, or pneumonia is not caused by a person's erroneous thinking, you will then be able to apply this principle to other diseases, to sin, and to false appetites. In each case, you will observe that the origin of the problem is not in the person and that you cannot uncover the error in him because it is not there.

The error is in a universal belief that there is a mortal man or that there is a condition or a creation apart from God. It is a *universal* belief, not your belief and not my belief. In The Infinite Way, this is called "impersonalization," and this principle is of primary importance in Infinite Way healing. No matter what the problem is, from corns to cancers, from an empty pocketbook to an empty relationship, it is not a person, and it is not in a person: it is a universal belief of a selfhood and a power apart from God. It is not the person because the person is God made manifest: he is Life expressed; he is Spirit revealed; he is the Soul of God incarnate. The very breath he breathes is the breath of God. He is really God-Selfhood. There is no evil in him, and there is no sin.

Was it not at the trial of Jesus that Pilate said, "I find in him no fault at all:?[2] That is exactly what our practitioners must say to every case, "I find no fault in this patient, no fault at all, no evil. I find only that he is the Holy One of Israel, the child of God, the

[2]John 18:38.

offspring of Spirit, the very life of God expressed." This is impersonalizing the appearance.

"Nothingizing" the Problem

After the error has been impersonalized, there is a second step, and this is called "nothingizing," making nothing of it, in other words, realizing that God did not create the evil condition:

> Thou art of purer eyes than to behold evil, and canst not look on iniquity.
>
> Habakkuk 1:13

> For I have no pleasure in the death of him that dieth ... wherefore turn yourselves, and live ye.
>
> Ezekiel 18:32

The Master said, "I came down from heaven, not to do mine own will, but the will of him that sent me."[3] The will of the Father is that we be healed of disease, that we be freed of lack, that we be forgiven our sins. Can these errors, then, be of God, and if they are not of God, do they have any power? If they are not of God, can they have any real existence? "And God saw every thing that he had made, and, behold, it was very good."[4] He found no evil in His creation.

This brings us to something you already know, but which you may not have accepted as an absolute principle. You may have declared that God is the only power, but have you accepted this truth as an absolute principle, or do you continue to accept two powers, a good power and a power of evil? do you look upon germs as an evil power? Do you look upon dictators as evil men? Do you look upon disease and sin as evil conditions? If you do, you are not accepting God as Omnipotence.

[3]John 6:38.
[4]Genesis 1:31.

If you would practice spiritual healing, you must accept God as Omnipotence and you must be able to look at sin, false appetite, disease, or any other condition without fear or horror, realizing: "If you are not a part of the omnipotence of God, you can exist only in man's belief." A person can believe that there are ghosts in a room, but the ghosts do not have reality.

You cannot say that evil does not exist as a belief in the mind of men: it does, or else there would be no need for a teaching based on the nonpower of evil because you would not be experiencing any evil. You experience evil only because there is a universal belief in its reality and power. In proportion as you can accept God as Omnipotence does evil lose its seeming power, its power in belief.

There Is No Law of Disease

Some years ago, a physician came to me with a presumably incurable disease. Now, one cannot very well explain the nothingness of disease or its unreal nature to a doctor because he is devoting his life to trying to cure disease. Nevertheless, I could say to him, "this disease has no law to support it. If it had a law, you could not cure it because you cannot break a law. You cannot break the law of two times two is four; you cannot break the law that H_2O is water; you cannot break anything that has a law. And so if a disease had a law to support it, it would be an eternal disease because it would be perpetuated by its law.

"If disease had a law, would not that law have come from God? Is not God the one and only law-giver? If disease had a law of God governing it, could anybody stop the disease? Or can disease be healed only because it has no law of God to support it?"

Because in his own mind this physician was able to accept the truth that if anything has a law, it has immortality, he had a very beautiful healing.

If you can grasp the principle that disease has no law, it will fall by the very fact that you have recognized its nothingness. If you can comprehend and really understand this truth, the appearance will be dissolved. If you can recognize the truth that God is not responsible for disease and death, you will destroy them both. This is the truth that makes you free.

One Power

Every time you realize the spiritual nature of any person and the universal nature of human beliefs, you are helping to free him from disease, sin, fear, or lack. All these have their basis in the belief of original sin as related in the Bible in the allegory of Adam and Eve. They ate of the tree of the knowledge of good and evil, and it was their acceptance of these two powers that sent them out of the Garden of Eden. Ever since that time, we too have been eating of that tree, thereby keeping ourselves out of Eden.

But we can return to Eden the instant that we realize that God never created two powers. God is the only power, and besides God, there is no other power. Because God is Spirit, the only power there is, is spiritual power, and nothing else is power. Material power is not power; mental power is not power: only Spirit is power.

As you cling to this: "I acknowledge only God as Spirit, God as Law, God as Power; and all else I recognize to be a universal belief of the carnal mind," you find yourself healing because you are not fighting a belief of disease, sin, or lack any more than you would fight the belief that two times two is five. Once you have recognized and realized that evil is not personal, that it has nothing to do with the person who is suffering from it except that temporarily he has accepted it, but otherwise it does not have its rise or origin in him and is no part of his nature, you have won a victory over the error, regardless of what its name or what its nature may be.

Remove Malpractice by Impersonalizing the Error

You must be firm in impersonalizing error. In one breath, you cannot lay the blame for evil at a person's door, and then in the next breath call evil impersonal. You must be absolutely universal in accepting this principle. At first, this is hard to do because there are many persons you might feel are to blame for some of your troubles. I am sure you all believe someone else has caused trouble for you when he really did not. The truth of the matter is that the trouble arose out of your acceptance of the universal belief which made you see the other person as less than the child of God. In that failure, you malpracticed him, and the malpractice came back upon you.

It is literally true that you must call no man on earth your father because you have a spiritual origin. You are the spiritual manifestation of the divine Spirit, the eternal and immortal expression of God Itself. You are not physical; you are not mortal; you are not material; you are really not even human: you are divine. The only part of you that even seems to be mortal arises out of the belief that there are two powers.

When you accept one power, it is easy to understand why the Master did not react to the appearance of disease and sin. He just looked at them and said, "Neither do I condemn thee.[5] ... Today shalt thou be with me in paradise."[6] In other words, as you reach out to the Christ, recognizing that sin and disease do not have their origin in a person and that he is not responsible for them, he is absolved.

This takes the burden of malpractice off your patient, your student, and off your neighbor. It takes the burden of malpractice away from everybody, even your pets. You do not ask your pets to be spiritual, to read so many pages of so many books, to be more loving, more generous, more kind, or more patient. When your cat, your dog, or your bird is suffering, you know the truth of God as Life, as the only Power and the only Presence. You know that none of these evils belongs to the cat or the dog, that they are just part of a universal mortal belief, and thus you free it. That is the same way you should act toward your patient.

[5]John 8:11.
[6]Luke 23:43.

Teaching is quite a different thing. In teaching, students are given instruction and directed to books and to passages in books which will further enlighten them. All the Writings present specific principles for students to learn. This is not so that they may be healed: this is that they may learn the principles which transform consciousness from a material to a spiritual basis.

When someone asks you for help, this must be your response: "Of course, I will give you help at once." It is not necessary to know the nature of the problem or the name of the person who is seeking healing. Nobody has ever told me the names of the cats and dogs for whom help was asked, and yet they were healed without my knowing their names. I have learned that nobody has to tell me the name of the patient who wants to be healed because, as far as I am concerned, he is the same spiritual offspring of God that I am.

What difference whether a flower is called a rose, an orchid, or a violet? It is still a flower. And so, whether a person is called Bill, Jim, or Henry, he is still the spiritual offspring of God. I am not transferring any truth to his mind, nor am I communicating any truth to him. I am knowing the truth within me, and the only truth there is about him, or about any "him" it happens to be, is the truth about God. I do not specifically have to know the truth about Mary Jones or Bill Smith: I know the truth about God. I do not believe that God knows the names of those who ask for help any more than I do.

When a problem is presented to you, first of all, you must realize that this is not only not of man, but that it has no real existence: it exists only as an illusory appearance. Look at the difference between a condition and an illusory appearance: a condition, you have to fight; an illusory appearance, you dismiss. If you were treating conditions, you would have to study for years, be licensed, and be a part of the practice of *materia medica*. But you are not treating conditions; you are not treating disease; you are not treating diseased people: you are knowing the truth of man's identity and of the illusory nature of the appearance, thereby dismissing the problem.

You, yourself, however, must be firmly grounded in these principles. You cannot waver between hope one minute, faith the next minute, and doubt another minute. It is for this reason that it is always better to begin the practice of healing with the lesser claims of the human world and build a consciousness of the nonpower of any appearance, although this is not necessary. You can begin with any problem that touches your consciousness if you have learned to impersonalize and to realize instantly that this has nothing to do with a person: this is an impersonal belief in two powers, the Adamic belief, a universal error. In this way, you have taken it away from your patient and immediately placed it where it belongs, as a part of the vast mental illusion. It is an illusory appearance, a false belief of the universal carnal mind.

The Immortality and Eternality of Life

When you have thus separated error from a person, ask yourself: "Is it of God? Did God create this?" No, God could not have created it because God could never have created anything destructive to Himself. Your life is God's life. If anything is happening to your life, it is happening to God's life. Certainly, God who is infinite wisdom and divine love has never made any provision for destroying His own life, and His life is the only life you will ever have. This is why you can know beyond all question that you are immortal: you did not begin on the day that is called your birthday, and your life will not come to an end on the day that is called your death-day. The only life that you live is God's life. It is not really you living: it is God living His own life as you. Therefore, since God is the only life you have, you can be assured that He did not create any disease to destroy it.

The Christ has "come that they might have life, and that they might have it more abundantly."[7] When? "Before Abraham was."[8]

7John 10:10.
8John 8:58.

For how long? "Unto the end of the world,"[9] Always remember that the Christ has been with you since God began; the Christ will be with you unto the end of the world: "I will never leave thee, nor forsake thee."[10] So there cannot be any provision for your aging or dying.

As was pointed out in the preceding chapter, you are an unfolding consciousness, and you will continue to unfold unto infinity. There is a time provided for everyone to pass from visibility, but no one should have to be pushed out of that visibility through a disease: he should make the transition in some normal and natural way.

God's life is the only life you are living, or that is living you. God is the only mind you have. God is the only Soul you have, and even your body is the temple of God. Can there, then, be any error in you? Regardless of what the appearance may be, the error is not in you. When you have realized that, you have impersonalized the error, and you have placed it out in universal mortal consciousness where it always was. There, you make it nothing by realizing that God did not create it, that it has no part in God, and that the Christ is present to nullify it.

Error exists only as an illusory appearance. Just as the sky appears to sit on a mountain, so all false appetites, all disease, all lack, and all limitation exist only as illusory appearances. The moment you impersonalize and "nothingize" them, you are well on the way to their destruction, so much so that in some cases, you will have instantaneous healings through this realization.

In other cases, it may take time because there is another element with which you are dealing, and that is the receptivity of the person. That is why it is much easier for cats and dogs to be healed than for human beings. The cats and dogs are not trying to hold on to something, whereas human beings usually are. And the very things they are trying to hold on to are the things that are most harmful to them.

[9]Matthew 28:20.
[10]Hebrews 13:5.

ACROSS THE DESK

As human beings we find our supply in money, and our health in the body. If our assimilation and elimination function according to what is considered normal, then we believe we are healthy. We believe that life is dependent on breathing and on the functioning of the heart, and that intelligence is associated with the brain. What we are doing in The Infinite Way, however, is making a transition from this material sense of life to the spiritual.

Our healing work, therefore, is never an attempt to correct what is wrong in the body, the mind, or the pocketbook. "We cannot meet a problem on the level of the problem."[11] If we should try to do something about any inharmonious or discordant condition, we would not succeed. First, we have to move outside the realm of the problem before harmony can be revealed.

We find our harmony in Spirit, in Consciousness. Since God is Consciousness, and since God is supply, we find our health in God or in Consciousness. Even the prophets of the Old Testament knew that God is the health of our countenance. Health and supply must be found not in the body and the pocketbook, but in Consciousness, and then the body expresses health and the purse abundance. Even our longevity must be found in Consciousness.

If we try to perpetuate ourselves by patching up the body, the results will be temporary. Medically, it is possible to change sickness to health and, if that is all a person is seeking, he can find it in *materia medica* because today there are not many incurable diseases.

But if we are seeking a principle of life whereby we hope to find our immortality in the fullness of our being, then we have to leave the realm of mind and body and find our good in Consciousness. But since the realm of Consciousness is invisible, no proof or sign that this is true can be given in advance.

So, we start at some particular time in our spiritual journey: it

[11]Joel S. Goldsmith. *The Infinite Way* (San Gabriel, Calif.: Willing Publishing Company), p. 62.

could be today for some, and next year for others. But one day we have to make a transition from looking to our bank account for our supply, looking to our body for our health, or to human beings for our happiness, and realize that wholeness in every department of our life is embodied in the God-consciousness which is our individual consciousness.

This may seem to leave us hanging in space, as it were, but just as Scripture says, "He ... hangeth the earth upon nothing,"[12] so in making this particular transition, we, too, have nothing to cling to because we are no longer looking to the body, the pocketbook, or the brain; and we cannot see, hear, taste, touch, or smell Consciousness. We do not even know what Consciousness is, yet we are putting our complete reliance and our complete dependence on It.

At this point, even though we know the truth, we may still find ourselves hanging in space because we do not know what is to come next. We are transferring our faith to Consciousness, but we have no way of knowing what Consciousness is. All we can do is continue to hang in space until Consciousness comes through with a demonstration which convinces us beyond all doubt that we are on holy ground.

There is no real limitation anywhere in the world except the limitation we place on ourselves. Everyone on the face of the globe can experience the allness of God because Consciousness is indivisible. So it is that any person can have an infinity of supply, and there will still be enough left over so that everyone else can also have an infinity of supply.

When we make this transition, our whole state of consciousness undergoes a change because now, instead of looking to the body for health, our vision is on Consciousness. Consciousness is not encased in the body. Consciousness is actually Omnipresence, never confined to time or space. Therefore, the moment we are called upon for help from any part of the world and close our eyes to realize Omnipresence, we can be certain that our patient will

[12]Job 26:7.

receive the benefit of the treatment. There is but one Being, and
God is that Being.

The more we live with that, the less we look to the body, and
the fewer fears we have of our aches and pains. We are never really separated from our health, our supply, or our happiness, completeness, and perfection.

We can enjoy human relationships, certainly, but we must never
be so dependent on them that an absence of them breaks our heart.
Once a person makes the transition to a point where he finds his
completeness in Consciousness, the whole nature of his life
changes. There are no vacuums in Consciousness: there is only the
going and coming of the human scene as the fulfillment of the
activity of Consciousness. When our home experience is the activity of Consciousness unfolding, we will find a complete continuity
of harmony.

Until we are ready for it, this transition of finding our allness in
Consciousness rather than in man, body, or purse is difficult. It
must be continuously remembered:

> *I find the harmony of being in my consciousness, and it is the har-
> mony of my body and of my human relationships.*

This should become a matter of hourly practice until that
moment of transition from one state of consciousness to another
when we can say, "Whereas I was blind, now I see."[13]
To be able to close our eyes, shut out all persons, and realize that
our good and our companionship are in Consciousness would mean
that on opening the eyes we would find ourselves in the presence
of those necessary to our experience. Since God constitutes our
consciousness, and God constitutes the consciousness of every individual on the face of the earth, we are one with everybody. But first
the human experience must be blotted out. We cannot meet a
problem on the level of the problem.

[13]John 9:25.

To find our good in the Consciousness which we are is to bring such a change in individual consciousness that bit by bit over a period of time we would find ourselves in a whole new consciousness, and would see our life transformed and on higher ground.

All that God is, I am. All that God has is mine, for I and the Father are one. All this universe is embodied in my consciousness—the skies above, the earth beneath, the waters and all that is in them— because God constitutes my individual consciousness.

My consciousness embodies the fullness of the Godhead. My consciousness is the law unto my health and my supply. My consciousness embodies every activity of intelligence, guidance, and direction.

The infinite allness of God is mine. In my oneness with God, I am all.

This realization of oneness is our assurance of completeness and perfection, and it acts to break the human ties of dependence on person, place, or thing. In one experience after another, we transfer our allegiance or faith from effect back to Cause. We break our dependency on "man, whose breath is in his nostrils."[14]

With every appearance of discord, we lift our thought immediately in meditation:

I find my oneness in Consciousness which is Cause, not in matter or effect. I look to Cause for my peace, my wholeness, my satisfaction, and my joy, and these become manifest in tangible form.

Every day, we make the decision to live in Consciousness, to find our health and our supply in Consciousness, and in Consciousness alone. After that, we drop it and let it rest, but sometime later in the day we will again remember that we are seeking our good in omnipresent Consciousness. As we persist in that, we bring the day closer when the transition in consciousness takes place. Then there

[14]Isaiah 2:22.

are no more statements or declarations: there is just the living of it.

This cannot be explained to anyone, and moreover, we have no right to try to explain it. This is an experience to be lived, but never talked about because the human mind could never understand what we mean by a transition of consciousness.

From

The Contemplative Life

Conscious Awareness

Many persons who are seeking for truth or striving to find a way that will lead them out of the inharmonies and discords of life gather the impression that there is some quick or short way of overcoming all their problems; that there is some kind of a message that they can read in books or hear from the lips of a teacher or lecturer, that will quickly take them away from the troubles of a material way of living into the harmonies of the spiritual life. This is the mistake that is made in every one of the Western countries.

It is not so in the East, where the relative unimportance of time is better understood and where it is realized that an evolution of consciousness can take place only over a span of years. But in the

AUTHOR'S NOTE: The material in *The Contemplative Life* first appeared in the form of letters sent to students of The Infinitive Way throughout the world in the hope that they would aid in the revelation and unfoldment of the transcendental consciousness through a deeper understanding of Scripture and the practice of meditation.

West, where in one short life-cycle we have gone from lamplight to modern electric lighting and from the horse and buggy era to automobiles and airplanes, where there has been an increase in the speed of travel from 100 miles an hour to thousands of miles, we do not seem to have sufficient time or sufficient interest to take the time for the development of spiritual consciousness. Because of this unbelievably rapid progress, materially and mechanically, which has set the tempo of our times, many think that it is possible to apply this same accelerated speed to the spiritual life.

But when it comes to spiritual unfoldment and spiritual progress, it is quite a different story. There, an element of time enters into the situation, and it is this element of time that our Western world seems unwilling to accept, or may not be able or prepared to accept.

It is often possible for those of us who come to a spiritual teaching to have our problems quickly met—physical, mental, moral, or financial—but, of course, even if all our major problems were quickly met, we still would be no better off than we were before, except for a little temporary relief from the world's discords, because regardless of what freedom we attain through the help of a practitioner or a teacher, we still have to evolve in our own consciousness in order to maintain and sustain that freedom.

The Function of the Transcendental Consciousness

Although work such as that of The Infinite Way does help students to overcome their present physical, mental, moral, or financial difficulties, this is not its primary function. The goal of this particular Message is the spiritualization of consciousness which, in the Western world, is described as the attainment of that mind which was in Christ Jesus: Christ-consciousness or the transcendental consciousness. In the East, this same goal is called the attainment of Buddahood, or the Buddha-mind, or Buddhi, but all those terms mean the same thing, because whether one receives enlightenment in the East or in the West, the result is precisely the same.

The point that I would like you to see at this moment is that the goal of all religious work should be spiritual enlightenment, that is, the attainment of spiritual light. When this light comes, it comes as a transcendental state of consciousness, and it is the attainment of this transcendental state of consciousness that really constitutes the activity of The Infinite Way, and is basic to its teaching.

The first question that would naturally arise in any seeker's mind is: What is the transcendental state of consciousness and what function does it perform in my experience? My answer to that is that the transcendental or spiritual consciousness is a state of consciousness which instantaneously releases an individual from all material concern. That, I believe, is its first and greatest function in our lives. It releases us from fear and doubt; it releases us from concern over what we shall eat, or what we shall drink, or wherewithal we shall be clothed. Most important of all, it releases us from the fear of death.

Whether we have ever consciously thought about it or not, all of us on the human plane of life fear death. In fact, the one reason we fear disease is because the natural consequence of disease is death. We also fear age because age carries with it the connotation of coming death. Death, because of its inevitability, is that which is feared, and the fear of death is often the very cause of our diseases.

With the first touch of spiritual light, however, all fear of death disappears, because that light reveals that there is no death and that the experience of passing from this plane of life to what is called the next is not really a death: it is just another experience like our birth; it is a passing from one phase of life to another. In other words, life never had a beginning; therefore our coming into this world was but a coming forth from another phase of life.

Some of those who have attained a certain degree of illumination are able to go back and see different aspects of their life prior to their present earth experience. Although that may not always be possible, nevertheless, with the first taste of spiritual light, we do realize that, since there is no death, there need be no fear of it, and once that fear is eliminated, the body seems to adjust itself, and health begins to manifest instead of disease and the signs of age.

The Transcendental Consciousness Brings a Release from Concern for Persons or Things

Furthermore, when spiritual light has once touched the soul or consciousness of an individual, never again can there be concern about what we call supply: what we shall eat or drink, wherewithal we shall be clothed, or how much money we shall or shall not have. The reason for this lack of concern constitutes the sum and substance of what must be our goal if we are to attain the spiritual way of life.

In the ordinary human sense of life, concern is nearly always for things, persons, or conditions. If at this very moment we were to think about what it is that worries us most we would in all probability find that our fear is undoubtedly about something in the form of an effect: a person, a condition, a thing, an amount, a body, a bit of money, or a piece of property. Always it is about an effect, and what concerns us is always in the realm of an effect.

As human beings, are we not always striving for some thing, some person, or some condition? It may be for a living, for fame, or for wealth; it may be for an education; it may be for health—but nearly always our life is centered on the attainment of something or other.

Most human beings fail during their lifetime to attain what they have been seeking and pass out of this life frustrated without ever having achieved their goals. Those who do reach their goals find that this achievement brings little permanent satisfaction. Some attain temporarily the perfect body, only later on to witness its disintegration; some attain the wealth that they have sought, and then after they have it, find that when they have eaten three times a day and have an ample wardrobe of clothing, all the rest of their money is of so little use that their efforts to attain it seem almost foolish in retrospect. Rarely does money ever give a person the satisfaction that he thought it would when he was struggling and striving for it. And I do not have to remind you that fame gives back even less of satisfaction and is even more of an empty bauble than is wealth.

This does not mean that there is anything wrong about the attainment of fame or wealth or health or a perfect body. On the contrary, all these are the added things that inevitably come when the spiritual way of life becomes our first and major concern. In the spiritual way of life, our first step is to disregard temporarily our concern for things, persons, and conditions, and center our attention on attaining a conscious realization of our Source.

Becoming One with Our Source

It is a part of the Christian teaching, as given in the fifteenth chapter of John, that when we are one with our Source, we bear fruit richly, but when we are separated from that Source, we are as a branch of a tree that is cut off and withereth. The Ninety-first Psalm also promises that none of the evils of this world will come nigh the dwelling place of those who have made God their dwelling place, again indicating to us that our oneness with our Source is what separates us from the evils of this world and maintains in our experience the harmonies of heaven.

The revelation was given to me that in my conscious oneness with God, in being consciously one with my Source, the good things of life were added unto me, that is, I was at-one with all good: with every form of good that might ever be necessary in my experience. The Master said, "Take no thought for your life, what ye shall eat, or what ye shall drink; nor yet for your body, what ye shall put on ... But seek ye first the kingdom of God, and his righteousness; and all these things shall be added unto you."[1] And so it was that this very same consciousness revealed to me that when I am consciously one with God, I am instantaneously one with all the good necessary for my experience. Therefore, I must stop taking thought about my supply, my health, or my home. I must stop taking anxious thought or concern for the things of this

[1] Matthew 6:25, 33.

world, and I must make every effort to abide *consciously* in my one-ness with God.

The vital part and the heart of that revelation is that we are *already* one with God. We are already one with our Lifestream, or the Source of our life. As a matter of fact, "I and my Father are one"[2] is a relationship that is indivisible and indestructible. It is an impossibility for my Father and me to become separate because we are not two: we are one! We are and always have been one with our Source, one with God.

The reason that the harmonies of heaven and the blessings of divine Grace do not come into our experience as they should lies in the one word *consciously*. Nothing can enter your life or mine except as it enters through our consciousness. This is the greatest law, the greatest discovery, unfoldment, or revelation that has ever come into my experience: *nothing can come into your or my experience except through our own consciousness.*

In other words, you consciously brought yourself to the reading of this book. There are millions of people not reading it and, there-fore, not a spark of this message has entered their consciousness, so that they are not even aware that anything of this sort exists in the world, but even you who are reading these words could, if you so desired, shut out of your consciousness the message that is being brought to you. You could sit where you are, completely unaware of the import of these words, reading them with your eyes only, and they would make no impression upon you; they would not enter the depths, the realm, of your consciousness. If you are to benefit by this message, there must be a responsive activity within your consciousness. Later, as you go deeper into the study of The Infinite Way, you will discover how you have admitted the inhar-monies and the discords of life into your experience through your own consciousness and how you can eliminate them after they are there or how you can prevent their taking root there, because noth-ing can transpire in your experience except as an activity of your own consciousness.

Although you and I are one with God, although we are one with

[2]John 10:30.

our Source, one with the Fount of everlasting life, one with the Source of infinite abundance, these can come into our experience only through our acceptance of them in our own consciousness. In other words, when we begin to declare within ourselves that there is a Source of life, then it must be true that that Source forever governs Its creation and forever maintains and sustains that which It has brought forth into expression.[3]

And so from the moment that we consciously perceive that we are always in the bosom of our Father and always one with our Source, indivisible and inseparable from that Source, it becomes clear to us that all that is flowing forth from that Lifestream, all that emanates from that infinite Source, is pouring Itself into, through, and from our individual consciousness.

Gaining the Consciousness of the Presence

As we abide in this, that is, *if* we abide in this Word, if we let this Word abide in us, we shall bear fruit richly. The secret of the spiritual life is to recognize consciously—consciously realize, accept, and declare—our oneness with our infinite, immortal, eternal Source, and accept the spiritual statement that all that the Father has is ours and that the place whereon we stand is holy ground. Not only must we accept it, but we must abide in it every single day of the week, bringing to conscious remembrance the truth:

"I and my Father are one."[4] *I am one with my Source, and all that is flowing forth from God is flowing into my experience.*[5]

---

[3]In the spiritual literature of the world, the varying concepts of God are indicated by the use of such words as "Father," "Mother," "Soul," "Spirit," "Principle," "Love," or "Life." Therefore, in this book the author has used the pronouns "He" and "It," or "Himself" and "Itself," interchangeably in referring to God.
[4]John 10:30.
[5]The italicized portions of this book are spontaneous meditations that have come to the author during periods of uplifted consciousness and are not in any sense intended to be used as affirmations, denials, or formulas. They have been inserted in this book from time to time to serve as examples of the free flowing of the Spirit. As the reader practices the Presence, he, too, in his exalted moments, will receive ever new and fresh inspiration as the outpouring of the Spirit.

When we perceive that this is true and are willing to make it a part of our *conscious* experience, we are engaging in a form of contemplative meditation. This contemplative meditation, which should take place either before we get out of bed in the morning or a few moments later, might begin with a conscious remembrance of the invisible Presence and Power operating in this universe.

How did this day come to be? Surely, there must be a tremendous Force, Power, Being, or Presence, which has brought forth the sunlight, the rain, or the snow of this day. There is a Something operating invisibly in this universe, sending forth all this glory into expression, a glory of which I am a part, for I, too, have been sent into expression by That which sent forth the flowers and the trees, the birds, and all that is.

I am one with all life. And just as this invisible Force is pouring sunshine into the room, so it is pouring life and being into me, and through me: intelligence, wisdom, guidance, direction, love, care, and protection. All of these are flowing in and through me from the infinite invisible Source.

And so we go through this period of contemplative meditation at least three or four times a day, each time taking some other subject. For the moment, however, we are considering our major theme, which is that we are consciously one with God; we are consciously one with our Creator. We are consciously one with the Source of life, but until we make it a conscious activity, until we consciously realize that we are one with our Source, that we are inseparable and indivisible from infinity and eternality, and that all these qualities and activities are pouring themselves through us— until we *consciously* do this we are not experiencing that which is our birthright. We are children of God, and as children heirs to all the heavenly riches. But let us not think that we are going to come into our heritage without consciously bringing our heritage into expression. It has to be a conscious activity.

Whatever of harmony, joy, or success is to come into our experience must first all be brought there through some conscious activity of our mind or through a conscious activity of a meditative nature. Some day, the Western world will understand this subject of meditation better than it does today, and even the Eastern countries will have restored to them the knowledge of meditation which has largely been lost in that part of the world. It is not that those of the East have not meditated, but, because they have not known the real secret of meditation, they have not meditated correctly, even though it is in the East that meditation was discovered and has been practiced most widely. With the loss of the art of meditation comes the loss of all that is really worthwhile in life, because this lack of communion with the Father removes us from that conscious oneness with our infinite Source, and when that happens, we are no longer one with our good.

It takes only a very few weeks of devoting a few moments a day to a quiet meditation in which we recognize our oneness with the Source and realize that our oneness with that Source constitutes our oneness with all our good before we begin to perceive in our outer and daily experience the fruitage of that meditation.

Every moment of meditation rewards us richly. Far more will come forth from it than we put into it. One the other hand, nothing will come forth except what we do put into it. For example, the presence of God is closer to us than our own breathing, and this has always been true. If we try to visualize something closer than our own breathing, we shall understand that actually the very presence of God is where we are. When we are in the depths of disease, sin, or lack, at that very second, the presence of God is as available to us as it was to Moses when he was leading the Hebrews out of slavery, or as it was to Elijah when he was finding cakes baked on the stones or a widow supplying him with food. The presence of God is as present with us as it was with Jesus Christ when he healed the sick or when he multiplied the loaves and fishes or forgave sinners, but even so, that presence of God may be doing absolutely nothing for us because the responsibility for bringing it into active expression in our lives rests with us.

The presence of God is on the gallows; the presence of God is on the battlefront where death and destruction are imminent; the presence of God is where every accident occurs anywhere in the world. The presence of God is in all those places and circumstances, but the presence of God is of no avail to anyone except to those who are dwelling in the conscious awareness of this truth. We must abide from morning to night and night to morning in this realization:

> *Where I am, God is. The presence of God is closer to me than breathing; I and my Father are inseparable and indivisible because we are one. If I mount up to heaven, I will find God, not that I will find God in heaven, but I will take God up to heaven. If I make my bed in hell, I will find God, not because God is in hell, but because I will take God with me; and if I walk through the valley of the shadow of death, I will find God because where I am, God is, and where God is, I am: we are inseparably and indivisibly one.*

Those who abide in this realization consciously find that when any form of evil comes into their experience, it dissolves and disappears. This is the secret of the mystical life; this is the secret of the spiritual life. It is all embodied in the one word *consciously*. Those who consciously know the truth are those who experience truth because truth is present, whether or not they know it. Two times two is four, even in the presence of those who do not know it; but to be of any benefit, two times two must be consciously known.

Gratitude and the Contemplative Life

Gratitude is one of the most powerful forces in the life of any individual because it is one of the many facets of love. If we understand the nature of gratitude, we shall find that it will play a far greater part in our experience than we can possibly realize. The mistake of most of the people in the world is that they are grateful for the good that comes to *them*. They are grateful for the bread on *their* table. They say grace, little realizing how much time they are wasting as long as their grace is only a gratitude for the bread on *their* own table.

Gratitude has nothing to do with gratefulness for the good that comes to us. Like everything else in the spiritual life, God is not only universal, but impersonal, in the sense that God is no respecter of persons and never has sent anything to you or to me or given anything to you or to me. All that God has is ours, but if we were to claim that for ourselves alone, we would perhaps lose it. When I say, "All that the Father has is mine," I mean that that same allness is yours and everyone else's. The fact that all the people in the world are not recipients of that good is because of their unawareness—their lack of conscious recognition—of this truth.

In other words, be assured that God has never singled out Joel or anyone else to whom to give anything: not even the message of The Infinite Way. The Infinite Way is an activity of consciousness, and anyone who opens his consciousness to it can experience it, because God is no respecter of persons. God does not set a table for you or for me; God has set a table for this whole universe. God has not put anyone's name tag on the cattle on a thousand hills, the crops in the ground, the pearls in the sea, or the diamonds in the earth. God has not put anyone's name on anything that He has given to this universe: God has expressed Himself universally; God has shown forth His glory universally.

The moment we begin to be grateful just for the fact that God is in His heaven, our lives begin to change. Therefore, let us stop thinking in terms of "me" and "mine" and begin to be grateful for all the good that God has provided in this universe: grateful that crops are in the ground and that the bowels of the earth are filled with His riches, rejoicing in the universality of God's good, rejoicing and being grateful for the riches that are upon the face of this earth, rejoicing that everyone who opens his consciousness to them receives them, not because God sends these things to him but because God sends them out into the world as His presence made manifest.

The presence of God appears as food, clothing, housing, and raiment. All that is, is the presence of God made manifest, and when we begin to express gratitude for the presence of God appearing as the good in this world, our souls, our minds, and our hearts are filled with love. When we personalize and believe that for some reason God has given to one person and is withholding from another, we dishonor God.

Let it be clear, then, that to our meditation and our practicing of the Presence, we must add the all-important ingredient of gratitude. As we walk in the park, let us be grateful for all the beauty that is on every hand to gladden the heart. If we look up into the sky when the stars are shining, let us be grateful that they are there—but let us be equally careful not to claim the stars for our own!

What concerned me in my earlier years was that so much of God's abundance and love were in evidence and yet that there was so much of poverty, sin, and disease among men. And for me, the burning question was why this was true, and how it could be eliminated. The answer that came was that only through our conscious awareness and acceptance of God's grace, through consciously living in the realization of God's grace, through consciously living in the realization of God's presence could those things that do not belong in our experience be eliminated and be repealed by those things that are ours by divine right.

For this reason, the two books *Practicing the Presence*[6] and *The Art of Meditation*[7] have been provided as the foundational studies in our work because all our work must necessarily be founded on the ability to mediate consciously and to practice consciously the presence of God until we reach the point where we never go to sleep at night without God in our thought, nor awaken in the morning without God as our first thought. We go forth from our home with God in our thought. We live constantly with God in our thought.

This is the way, then, that the blessings of God reach man:

[6]Joel S. Goldsmith (New York: Harper and Row, 1958).
[7]Joel S. Goldsmith (New York: Harper and Row, 1956).

through an activity of our own consciousness, through our consciously knowing the truth and praying without ceasing. And these blessings are all by-products of the one great goal of conscious awareness of the presence of God.

Everything visible, audible, touchable, smellable, and thinkable is the external expression of something in the realm of the real—even the superstitious, myths, and so-called pagan practices.

As visitors from the Occident go to the Orient and observe the unusually large number of temples, shrines, religious statues, and prayer groups, they often speak of these as the paganism of the Orient. When they return home and in the churches on nearly every corner of every town find even a greater number of prayer groups, many stained glass windows, religious figures, and statues of Jesus in different forms and positions from that of prayer to crucifixion, statues and paintings of saints and sages, I wonder how many of them perceive that all these outward symbols stem from the same source.

Let us be very clear on this point: Behind all the seemingly paganistic practices of the East and the West, there is spiritual truth. First of all, the very existence of a prayer group in a church, temple, or garden is an acknowledgment of a supreme Being or Deity. Whether sitting, standing, or on the knees, through prayer one acknowledges a divine Presence. On this point both East and West are in agreement.

The statues and carvings of religious leaders in the East are a recognition of those whose lives have revealed their attainment of some measure of divine consciousness. The paintings, the stained glass, and the figures in Western churches are but the recognition of the attained measure of spiritual light of the Western Saviour, his disciples and apostles, and of other religious lights. Here, too, the East and the West are in agreement, and rightly so, because all religious symbolism in ritual, rite, or ceremony is the attempt to use such means to attain an elevated state of consciousness.

Behind all *forms* of worship, it must be recognized that there is a divine, infinite, universal principle of law, life, or being, and in such recognition it becomes clear that *the Lord He is One*. To the discerning person there is, therefore, no paganism in any religion, and no one can correctly claim that there is a right or a wrong religion. The paganism exists in the form of men's worship and in their differing beliefs about religion. For example, to believe that man can influence God by words, thoughts, or deeds is a form of paganism; whereas to realize God as Omniscience, Omnipotence, and Omnipresence is true religious worship.

To believe that God has finite form, emotions, or responses is a form of paganism; whereas to understand God as the Life, Law, Being, Substance, and Activity of all spiritual form is true worship. To tell God, to advise, inform, or beseech God is a form of paganism; whereas to love and trust God and to listen for His voice is the higher worship.

To have an inner experience of the outer forms of worship such as is carried on in church services or in celebrating religious holidays, feast or fast days, is true worship, and the true worshiper can participate in the services of the Hebrew synagogue, the Protestant or Catholic church, or the Moslem or Buddhist temple with equal devotion, because behind this worship, whatever its form, he recognizes and acknowledges the One "appearing as many."

With equal dedication, I have spoken to Christian groups and non-Christian groups in the Orient, and all of them have listened to me with equal interest and attention. Thus, The Infinite Way bears witness to the divine Spirit in man, the divine Spark which is without race, religion, nationality, creed, or political affiliation, yet is the one animating Principle, Life, Soul, and Spirit of all. In this oneness, there is a spiritual bond uniting us in His grace.

Beginning the Contemplative Life

In the Orient, as many of you know, those who are interested in attaining spiritual illumination go to a teacher and, as a rule, live with or near the teacher for a period of six, seven, or eight years, and by means of meditation with as well as without the teacher, meditation with other students, and spiritual instruction, eventually attain their illumination: *satori*, enlightenment, or the fourth dimensional consciousness.

Mankind as a whole, however, is not geared for this kind of teaching, nor do many desire, need, or even have the capacity for full enlightenment. This is attested by the fact that some students and disciples who have lived in close association with their teachers even for many years could not or did not reach the heights, whereas others may have received it in two or three years.

The question, then, for the young student at first is not one of attaining that degree of illumination which would set him up as a spiritual teacher or healer, but primarily how to attain sufficient illumination or enlightenment to be able to free himself from the discords and inharmonies of daily living and build up within himself a spiritual sense that would not only lift him above the world's troubles—his family or community troubles—but would enable him to live a normal family, business, or professional life, and yet be inspired, fed, and supported by an inner experience and contact.

Recognize the Universality of God

It is well known that all people of a religious turn of mind—whatever their religion may be—can attain some measure of inner harmony and peace and find themselves in possession of an inner grace that eventually lives their lives for them. It makes no difference what a person's religion is because there is only one God, only one Spirit; and that Spirit knows no difference between a Jew and a Gentile, a Protestant and a Catholic, and Oriental and an Occidental. The Spirit is beyond and above any denominational beliefs or convictions, free to all and independent of ceremonies, rites, creeds, or forms for Its worship, just as the life that permeates a blade of grass is the same life that permeates an orchid, a daisy, or a violet. The Spirit recognizes no difference. The same Life animates all life, whether that of a mongrel dog or a pedigreed one.

In Scripture, we are told that His rain falls on the just and the unjust. As far as God is concerned, there is neither Greek nor Jew, neither bond nor free. The Master made that very clear when he said, "Call no man your father upon the earth: for one is your Father, which is in heaven."[1] If Jesus had meant that this applied only to the people who were listening to him, then, of course, according to that, God is the Father only of the Hebrews because Jesus was talking to his fellow Hebrews. In his day there was no Christian church, nor were there any Christians: there were only Jews, and Jesus was one of them, a rabbi in their midst; and if he had intended these words only for those to whom he was speaking,

[1]Matthew 23:9.

we would have to admit, then, that the Jews are the only ones who can claim God as their Father.

As a matter of fact, however, anyone with even a smattering of spiritual insight knows from the import of Jesus' teaching that he was not speaking of cabbages, but not meaning that only two times two cabbages is four, but meaning two times two is four, whether applied to cabbages or kings. And so, when he tells us to "call no man your father upon the earth," he is not addressing you who are reading this, nor was he addressing those who were sitting before him listening to him: he was speaking to the world, proclaiming a message that had been given to him of God.

Years later, Paul carried that same message to the pagans, the Europeans—even to the atheists—and always he was voicing a spiritual truth which was not meant to apply to any specific group of people, but was a spiritual truth which has always been, is, and always will be—a universal truth. Therefore, it must be the truth about Greek and Jew; it must be the truth about you and me; it must be the truth about white and black: there is but one Father, but one God.

No person can ever hope for spiritual enlightenment unless he can first of all recognize that there is only one creative Principle in this world, whether It creates cabbages or kings, whether It creates the Greek or the Jew. There is only one creative Principle, and It is located, not in holy mountains, nor yet in the temple of Jerusalem. Its location is neither "Lo here! or, Lo there!"[2] but within you, and it makes no difference who the *you* may be. It makes no difference if it is you in a hospital, the you in a prison, the you in business, or the you in some art or profession: the kingdom of God is within *you*, and the kingdom of God is a Spirit— not a superhuman being, but a Spirit.

To recognize this truth constitutes the very first step in attaining spiritual light, the first step in attaining an awareness of the presence of God. If you cannot accept this, then you will have to

[2]Luke 17:21.

believe that God is a respecter of persons and that only Jews have the presence of God, or only Baptists, or Buddhists. This is the rankest kind of nonsense.

The presence of God is within *you*, whoever the you may be.

Your Givingness of Yourself Brings the Givingness of the Universe to You

When you have come to the place where you actually feel the truth of this, where you feel the presence of God in the air, in your body, in your business, in your home, in your competitor, or in the enemy across the sea or across the street—when you begin to perceive that, you are ready for the next step which everyone must take before enlightenment can come, and that is the realization that inasmuch as the kingdom of God is within you, it must be permitted to flow out from you. It cannot come to you, and you must, at some stage in your unfoldment, stop looking for it to come to you.

An illustration of this can be found in the area of companionship. Many, many persons are seeking companionship, but when they come to me with that problem, asking for a demonstration of companionship, my reply always is: "It's no use, because I know you don't want companionship. If I could show you how to attain it, you would refuse it. What you want is a companion, and probably he has to be five foot eleven to six feet, and weigh one hundred eighty pounds, and have nice blue eyes. You have it all decided in advance. But companionship, you don't want." No one who ever asks for a demonstration of companionship—not anyone I have ever known—has really wanted it. They have merely wanted a companion, and that I cannot get for anybody.

It is so simple to have companionship. All it requires is that you be a companion. That's all! Once you become a companion, once you find something or somebody to companion with—it does not have to be a human being at first, or a member of the opposite sex, or a stranger—you have companionship. You can begin to find companionship with some members of your own family, or with the birds that come to your lawn, or with the stars. The point is

that companionship is a sharing of one's self. That is what constitutes companionship—the sharing of one's self. It could be at the
level of neighborliness; it could be at the level of friendliness; it
could be at the level of husband, wife, brother, or sister; but companionship means a sharing of one's self with someone else.

Companionship is always available to you, because it is within
you: it is the gift of God, and you are the one who determines
whether you will keep it locked up within you, or whether you will
let it loose and be a companion. And the moment you decide to be
a companion, you have companionship.

Of course, the wonderful part of it is that when you begin to be a
companion, you find those who are also desirous of being companions, of sharing, and then it is not a question of give and take, it is
a question of both giving. There is no taking: there is just giving.

The kingdom of God is locked up within you. There is no way
for one person to demonstrate supply for another because everyone, everywhere, has all that the Father has—infinity—and to try
to get something out here, when there is nothing out here but
space, is folly. Supply is demonstrated, not in the getting, but in
opening out a way for the supply already within you to flow out
from its Source, which is the kingdom of God within you.

Illumination can come only to those who realize that the kingdom of God—Light, Truth, Wisdom, Love—is within. All that the
Father has is yours, and then just as you have to find a way to
express companionship, so do you have to find a way to express
supply.

This we can do in many ways. The Master has indicated in the
Sermon on the Mount that we should give, but be sure that no one
but God knows about our giving; pray, but be sure that no one but
God knows about our praying; forgive; pray for our enemies. All
this he gives as an activity that takes place within ourselves and
flows from within us to the without.

The entire secret of spiritual illumination is bound up in the
realization that the kingdom of God is within and that we must
find a way to let this "imprisoned splendor" escape. Therefore,
whatever it is we are seeking, we must find a way to give it out, so

that even if we are seeking spiritual light, the way to gain it is to give it.

Many teachers have discovered that by the end of the school term, they have learned more about the subjects they have taught through the teaching of them than have the pupils in the classroom. Always a person learns more by teaching than anyone ever learns by being taught.

So it is in a spiritual teaching. Those who teach learn far more than any student or group of students, because in the very act of giving out, there is a constant inflow—and really not in: it is only that the infinite Source is within, but It cannot flow out if we do not let It out. The moment we being letting out a little of what we know, all the rest begins to flow, more than we ever were aware that we knew.

There is no way to gain love from the world or from the people of the world. Many have tried it, but everyone fails. It cannot be accomplished. The only way is the way of spiritual light. By loving, we become loved. There is no other way. Waiting to be loved is like waiting for someone to come from the blankness of space. Before love can flow to us, we first must put it out here. We must first put the bread on the water, before the bread can return to us. Only that which we put forth finds its way back to us, because, in and of itself, a blank space has nothing to give—nothing! But in proportion as we put something out into space, in that proportion is a way made for it to find its way back to us, pressed down and running over.

So is the whole goodness and infinity of this universe flowing back to us as we let it flow out from us. It is the givingness of ourselves that brings the givingness of the universe to us.

Man Cannot Influence God

Spiritual illumination begins with the realization of as simple a thing as that the whole kingdom of God is already established within you, and for you to enjoy its blessings you have to find a way to bring it forth into expression.

As you meditate and ponder on these things, you come to a place where there is nothing more to think about. You have thought it all; you have said it all; you have declared or affirmed it, and you have come to the end of all that. Now, since there is not anything more to say, you come to a place where you are still, and you find that in the very moment that you achieve stillness, something jumps up here from within you—something of a transcendental nature, something of a not human nature. Something jumps up into your awareness that you yourself have not been declaring, affirming, or stating, but which you are now hearing and receiving from the depths of your withinness. You yourself have created the circumstance by means of which this transcendental hearing can take place: you have known the truth, declared it, felt it, stated it, and then been still, thereby creating a vacuum, and now up into that, the Voice announces Itself, bringing with It illumination.

The first step is always consciously knowing the truth, intellectually knowing the truth, and then, though this constant pondering, meditating, and cogitating, you bring yourself to the place where you are completely still, and into that stillness and up from that stillness comes the very light that you have been seeking.

But do you think that that light is given only to one person or one group of persons? Do you not see how important it is, first, to divest yourself of every bit of belief that God is a respecter of persons, of religions, or of churches, or a respecter of races, and come to see clearly that God is a Spirit, that God is life, that God is love, that actually the presence of God is within you?

The very place whereon you stand is holy ground because the presence of God is there. But when you are declaring that about yourself, look up, look around you, and see all the hundreds of people in your neighborhood, and then remember that whether or not they know this truth, you must know that it is the truth about them, because if you are not knowing this truth as a universal truth, you are again trying to pinch a little of it off for yourself, to make it finite or limit it, and God cannot be limited.

The next step is easier now than it would have been but for the two previous steps, namely, (1) knowing the truth, and (2) realizing that God is no respecter of persons. Now you are better able to recognize that man cannot influence God, that man has no power over God's creation, man has no jurisdiction over God's world, man has no jurisdiction over God, period. Man cannot have his way with God; man cannot get God to do his will or his way; and therefore, the next need is to become a beholder because, since you cannot influence God, you can at least watch what God is doing. You can become a witness to the activity of God in your life and everybody else's life because, remember, when the sun comes up in the morning, it comes up for Jew and Gentile, white and black, Oriental and Occidental: it has no favorites; and you have to be willing to recognize that just as the sun rises for everybody in the whole world, so is God's grace available to everybody in the world.

When you watch sugar cane or pineapples growing, it is foolish to think that God is growing them for you or for me. God is just growing them. God's grace falls on the just and the unjust.

Always there must be the remembrance, then, that what God is doing, God is doing, and He does not need your help; and furthermore He cannot be controlled by you or me or by anybody else. God's grace cannot be stopped. Even if you think that you are acting in disobedience to His laws, God's grace is still flowing, even though you may not get the benefit of it because you have cut yourself off from it.

"Whatsoever a man soweth, that shall he also reap."[3] God has nothing to do with your sowing or your reaping. It is as *you* sow: "He that soweth to his flesh shall of the flesh reap corruption; but he that soweth to the Spirit shall of the Spirit reap life everlast-

[3]Galatians 6:7.

ing."[4] It is always what *you* do. By your thoughts and actions of today, you determine your reaping of tomorrow.

So therefore, even if by some act of your own—whether it is a disobedience to one or more of the Ten Commandments, or whether it is a violation of the second great commandment of the Master to love your neighbor as yourself, or whatever it is—if you have shut off health, safety, security, and inner peace, do not blame God for it, for God neither gives you peace nor takes it from you; God neither gives you health nor takes it from you; God neither gives you supply no takes it from you. God's grace is as free as sunshine. If you like, you can pull down the shades and never see the sun, and never feel it, but that is because of your action, not God's. As far as God is concerned, the sunshine is always there.

So it is, then, that in the moment when you realize that God's grace is very much like the sun hanging in the sky, it is there; it is available for everyone, even though, temporarily, there may be clouds hiding it, but nevertheless, it is there. Your very recognition of this and your refusal to try to get God to do something, your ability to refrain from entreating or begging God, from attempting to influence or bribe Him, the very act itself of refraining from doing these things brings the activity of God into your experience.

When you can sit back and realize that God is—not because of you, but that actually in spite of you, still God is closer to you than breathing, the place whereon you stand is holy ground, and where the presence of the Lord is, there is freedom and fulfillment—when you learn to refrain from attempting to take heaven by storm, and when you are able to sit back in the realization, "Where I am, God is," and be still, you have opened the way in your own consciousness for the Omnipresence which is already there to make Itself manifest and evident in your experience.

The great error has always been trying to influence God: "God, go out there and destroy my enemies! God, go out there and bring

[4]Galatians 6:8.

my enemies' possessions to me!" This attempt to personalize God or to get God to do something for some specific person and not for everybody indicates a lack of understanding of God as Spirit.

The very statement that God is Spirit is in itself a freeing and a healing one. No one can do anything about moving or changing Spirit, influencing It or bribing It. There is nothing to do but *let* It envelop you, *let* It pick you up, *let* It dominate you, *let* Its will be done in you, and then you make of yourself a transparency through which the light that is already present within you can shine: not a light that is gained from books or from some form of worship, or from teachers, but a light that books or worship or teachers can reveal to you as already having existence within you.

The teacher's function is to unveil the light that already constitutes your innermost being, self, or identity. The function of the teacher and the teaching is to unveil the presence of the Spirit of God that is within you, so that you can eventually live in this conviction, "Thank You, Father; You and I are one."

What the Master has said is true: "I will never leave thee, not forsake thee.[5] ... Lo, I am with you always, even unto the end of the world,"[6] but the teacher unveils and reveals to you the Presence that is saying this to you from within your own being and reminding you that the Father knows your need before you do. It is His good pleasure to give you the Kingdom. Therefore, you can rest in this realization: *The Father is within me. The kingdom of God is within me.*

The Indwelling Presence

There is a divine Presence within you, and it is the function of this Presence to heal the sick, raise the dead, preach the Gospel, feed the hungry, and forgive sinners: this is Its function. It has never left you—It will never leave you! You could change your religion seven times over, but that Presence would still be with you. You could

[5]Hebrews 13:5.
[6]Matthew 28:20.

live in a place where no one had ever heard of a church, and the Presence would still be with you. It will *never* leave you, nor forsake you. And remember this: It is not dependent upon anything. It is not even dependent upon your having a right thought. It is always there, but your enjoying the benefits of It is dependent upon your knowing the truth of its omnipresence.

Gradually, as you receive confirmation from within yourself that it is true that there is a Presence, the Voice speaks to you. Whether It speaks audibly or not is of no importance, as long as in one way or another you feel that you are living by Grace, not by might, not by power, not by force, but by Grace, by a divine Grace that operates just as freely as the incoming and outgoing tides or the rising and the setting of the sun, and just as painlessly. It is not a matter of earning or deserving it.

As human beings, we can never earn or deserve the grace of God, and that is why we are told that we must *die daily* and that we must be reborn of the Spirit. The truth is that as children of God we are heirs to God's grace, and all we have to do is to recognize our sonship.

And so as we ponder these basic truths, as we learn to come into a state of mind, a state of consciousness, that is filled with an assurance that there is an inner Presence, and learn to relax in It, we find that It does our thinking for us; It corrects and enlightens us; It goes before us to make the crooked places straight; It is a healing influence in mind and body; It is a supplying presence. But It does all this without any help from us, except for our ability to relax in It.

"He maketh me to lie down in green pastures: he leadeth me beside the still waters"[7]—it is always *He*. "He performeth the thing that is appointed for me"[8]—not the little "I," but *He*. "The Lord will perfect that which concerneth me."[9] But do you not see that He cannot do it if we take hold of the reins and do all the driving?

[7]Psalm 23:2.
[8]Job 23:14.
[9]Psalm 138:8.

If we take thought for what we shall eat, or what we shall drink, or wherewithal we shall be clothed, we are leaving no room for any *He*: it is all that little "I," the very "I" that should be *dying daily* in order that that *I* which is our spiritual identity can be reborn.

If you have grasped what I have said up to this point, you should be able to understand the passage, "In quietness and in confidence shall be your strength"[10]—in quietness and in confidence. How can you be quiet, how can you have confidence unless you have this awareness of an inner Grace? And you can only have this awareness of an inner Grace when you begin to recognize Its universal nature, recognize that It belongs to all men.

Those who are not recognizing this inner Grace, we are told, are the thousand that fall at our left and the ten thousand at our right, those, as the Master tells us, who are not abiding in the Word nor letting the Word abide in them and who, therefore, are as a branch of a tree that is cut off and withereth.

So it is that not everybody will benefit by this truth just because it is the truth. No! Only "ye" who know the truth permit the truth to make you free—you who abide in this Word of an indwelling Presence. Those of you who stop—I was going to say stop annoying God, but I am sure that God cannot be annoyed—those of you who stop going through the motions that would annoy God, if God could be annoyed, that is, trying to influence Him, trying to bribe Him, trying to promise Him something in the future, instead of realizing that God is Spirit, God is life, God is love, and that you have to find a way to let all of this flow out from you, will come into an actual awareness of the presence of God.

The Contemplative Life Develops a Sense of Universality

This really constitutes a way of life. True, it is a religious way of life, except that if you use such a term, it would seem to denote some particular religion with special rituals and ceremonies, and it is not that kind of life at all. It is a religious life in the sense that

[10]Isaiah 30:15.

this teaching develops a conscious awareness of God, but to avoid giving the impression that we have found some particular religion through which God is blessing us, we should rightly call this the contemplative way of life because it is a way of life that can be lived by all people regardless of any personal or denominational persuasion.

The contemplative way of life recognizes God as Spirit, and that Spirit as Omnipresence—the Spirit within one's own being. Therefore, it is an absolutely unrestricted way of life, available to anyone of any faith or no faith, as long as he can recognize that God is Spirit, recognize God as its central theme—not your God or my God, just God—and a God that belongs to nobody, a God that just is, and is universal.

That is why the contemplative life can flourish in every country on the globe where there is freedom and where people are not compelled to worship in a specific way. Even where there is no freedom, this way of life can be followed because it does not build a fence around God or lay down specific rules: it just recognizes God as the Principle of life, the Grand Architect of the whole universe.

For this reason, then, the contemplative life is the way for any person who can recognize that wherever or however God is worshiped, it is the same God, that there cannot be more than one God. Whether as Hebrews we go into a temple with hats on, or as Christians with hats off, as Orientals with our shoes off or as Christians with shoes on, it must be understood that these outward forms can make no difference, that all we are doing is worshiping in whatever way means dedication or sacredness to us.

What represents sacredness to an individual determines his worship. If an individual feels that he is honoring God by keeping his hat on, that is merely his idea of worship and sanctity, but the act of wearing or not wearing a head covering does not change God. If another individual feels that he is honoring God with his shoes off, that very act is an evidence of the sincerity of that individual's worship. Therefore, when you live the contemplative life, you will respect the Moslem who takes off his shoes and sits on the ground, and you will respect those who have other ceremonial forms of worship, and you will also respect those who have no form of worship at all, because you will know that each in his own way is dedicating himself to God, and not his God because God is not the possession of any one person: there is only God, and God is Spirit.

The contemplative, then, is actually paving the way for world peace, because he is recognizing that there is only one Father, one God, equally of all, and that all men everywhere are brothers and sisters; and therefore, the only relationship that is essential is that we treat each other as members of one united household.

To do this is to love the one and only God supremely, but it is also to love your neighbor as yourself. When you acknowledge one God as Father and all men as brothers, you wipe out one of the most important causes of war, and when you love your neighbor as yourself and wipe out the other, because controversies over religion and commercial rivalry have always been recognized as the two major causes of all war and discord.

Another important result of learning to love God supremely and your neighbor as yourself is not immediately apparent. If you can accept God as Spirit, you can never again fear. You can never fear what form of government we have or any other country has. You can never fear what anyone does. God is then animating human consciousness, and because there is only the power of God, there is nothing left to fear, and when fear is gone, the final cause of our discords is gone.

When we learn to love one another, which means not to fear one another, we have set the pattern for individual and world harmony. We could all live in eternal harmony and world harmony. We could all live in eternal harmony if we did not fear, but just let fear creep into any group of people and there can easily be a first-class war, and then there would be sides taken: your side and my side. But as long as there is a realization of God as Spirit, no one has anything to fear, for Spirit fills all space, and where the Spirit of the Lord is, there is nothing to fear: no danger, no insecurity, no powers apart from God. Therefore, just to realize that God is Spirit begins to free this whole universe of fear.

ACROSS THE DESK

Much of the world belief about God is the truth about the karmic law of cause and effect. It is this general misconception that makes ineffectual so much prayer. Prayer is answered *only* as we come to "know Him aright."

Do you really grasp the significance of *law* and *Grace*? Do you actually discern that God is not responsible for the rewards and punishments we experience? Can you realize that we ourselves set in motion the evil and good influences that touch our lives by our ignorance or by our awareness of the nature of God? Do you understand how the belief in two powers binds us, and how we can release ourselves from the law of cause and effect, at least in a measure, and come under Grace?

Our students should feel a deep sense of responsibility to continue daily specific work for the realization of spiritual government universally expressed. We need to feel God's government as a universal law of peace, justice, life, and love—not that mortals can express these qualities, but that God expresses them as individual being.

From

Conscious Union With God

Teaching the Message

For the benefit of those who are having patients or students coming to them and who are not only trying to bring about healing for them, but at the same time introduce them to the subject of spiritual truth, let me point out that one of the first things that must be taught to the person who either has had little or no experience in metaphysics or to the one who is coming from some other school of metaphysics into The Infinite Way is the meaning of terms like Soul, Consciousness, and the Christ.

Rarely do you meet a lay person in this work—I don't mean practitioners, I mean an average patient or student—who has caught the vision of the word, "Soul." It is one of the most misunderstood words in metaphysics and is so important that, without an understanding of it, the spiritual vision of this message cannot be perceived.

The Soul-Faculties and Consciousness

Soul, or Consciousness, is the seat of those faculties which we interpret as physical organs and functions and physical faculties or physical senses. The day will come when, if you know enough about Consciousness, you can leave everything else alone, for in the word, "Consciousness," and the spiritual understanding of it, is contained all the knowledge that is to be known about God, man, and the universe. As a matter of fact, the five senses—sight, hearing, taste, touch, and smell—sometimes metaphysically called "the unreal senses," are but our misinterpretation of Consciousness.

For example, if I see you, I am conscious of your presence through the faculty of sight; if I hear you, I am conscious of your presence through the organs of hearing; and, of course, I can also become conscious of you through my sense of smell or taste. But what is happening is that I am conscious of you. Therefore, the five senses are really just five different facets of the activity of Consciousness, which is the one real faculty and is spiritual; they are but the finite sense of that one spiritual activity, Consciousness.

Inasmuch as we do not deny the body and do not deny the senses, we have to account for them; and as has been previously explained, it is through right identification and reinterpretation that we find we really have these activities of Consciousness which are called sight, hearing, taste, touch, and smell—only instead of five, there are seven.

There is the faculty of intuition, and there is also the faculty of Consciousness which is without any thought process or any outer process—it is actually a silence. In that silence, which is the ultimate, we are alive in God, experiencing only God acting through, or as, individual you and me.

However, the activity of Consciousness can be called the Soul-sense, in contradistinction to the five physical senses. Without eyes, it is possible to see, and this I have done repeatedly and can do at will through inner vision, but this inner vision involves the development of the Soul-sense. For example, years ago in experimenting with the development of that sense, I found that the time came when I could be in a dark room in the country at midnight, with no lights at all, blindfold myself, and in a few minutes I could see every detail of the room and see even outside the room. That was because consciousness was operating without the limitation of physical eyes.

Seeing without eyes is similar to hearing "the still small voice" which is just another facet of the same thing. If you skeptically doubt or deny the possibility of such an experience, the next time you hear "the still small voice" you will have to deny that too, because you are hearing without ears, that is, without using the organs of hearing.

I know that this is possible because of the experience of a member of my family, who was a musician and who through an illness became stone deaf. It was discovered upon examination that both eardrums were broken, and he was told that never again would he hear. One of his relatives who was just becoming interested in spiritual healing asked him to have treatments, and because of this insistence he had one treatment, and from that day to this his hearing has been perfect—but he still has no eardrums. Because of his work—he is no longer a musician but an engineer—he has been required to have many physical examinations, especially during the war. Each time the physician has declared that it is impossible for him to hear—but he does, and without any hearing aid. Undoubtedly, the practitioner who opened up the Soul-sense of hearing for him must have reached an exceptionally high state of consciousness to bring about such a healing.

Life as Consciousness

Another example of life as Consciousness is that of Brown Landone who, in 1931 at the age of about eighty years, collapsed in The Pennsylvania Hotel in New York City. Physicians who were called in while he was still unconscious stated that he could not live more than two hours. When x-rays were taken, the verdict was that no one could possibly live even minutes, certainly not over two hours, with a heart in the condition his was.

When Mr. Landone became conscious, he was told that he had but a short time left and that he should get his affairs in order, if he could, as quickly as possible. To this he replied, "If I have only two hours, I am going to spend them at my desk finishing important work."

With that he got up, and the next day he was still at his desk, working. Several times the doctors came in to examine him, and each time they said it was a miracle, but certainly he could not go on for another two hours. In spite of their prognosis, however, he lived and continued to work for about twenty years more, never again knowing a sick moment. His was a case of a man who lived and worked without what is known as a normal heart.

He had reached the place where he knew that God is life and that God-life has nothing to do with what is called physical form. When Brown Landone left this experience, it was neither through disease nor accident, but only because he felt the time had come and that he was called to do some other work. He turned to his secretary and said, "I am leaving you"; and without ever having had even a sick moment, sat down and left. He was then ninety-seven years of age, plus.

These things are possible if, in your consciousness, life has been lifted above the physical plane, but do not think for a minute that a practitioner can give a treatment and have a person hear without ears or live without a heart. No practitioner can do that any more than can a doctor. But if the practitioner catches this glimpse of life as God, then there is no longer any living in a body or through a body. The body then is merely the vehicle. Life is within, or as, consciousness, and that is completely independent of physicality.

If you have no inclination to accept the two above mentioned experiences as possible, or if you are the kind of person who believes only what you can become aware of with your physical senses, that is, if you deny the validity of spiritual experiences, then you must accept the theory that life and consciousness end with the grave, because if consciousness and life cannot go on separate and apart from what is known as physical form, then of course there is extinction at the grave. What you wish to believe is up to you. You can take your choice, but unless you can accept what I am telling you, your belief in immortality is going to be badly shaken.

The Christ

To the average metaphysician, the Christ still is an unknown factor. Most people think of the Christ more as a person than as what It really is. The Christ really and truly is one's individual identity, one's real being. The Christ is individual consciousness when it has been purged of all love, fear, or hate of error of any nature. When you no longer love, fear, or hate error in any form, you are Christ-consciousness. Too many believe that Christ, or Christ-consciousness, is something separate and apart from their own being—something that is not an integral part of their being, but which may perhaps be attained.

As a matter of fact, Christ-consciousness can be attained, but it can be attained only in one way, that is, through our recognition of the nature of error which causes us to lose our love, our hate, or our fear of it. Just as we have to arrive at an understanding of God appearing as man, so we also have to realize Christ as immanent, as the Christ of our own being, the Christ of our own consciousness. Otherwise, there will be a patient or student *and* a God separate and apart, or a patient or student separate and apart from the Christ.

The Difference Between Prayer and Treatment

Another important aspect of The Infinite Way which students should be led to understand is the difference between prayer and treatment. In *Spiritual Interpretation of Scripture*, it has been made clear that these are not synonymous: Treatment consists of statements of truth which we may make for the purpose of reminding ourselves of the truth of being and for the purpose of gaining a conscious realization of the truth of being, either through the spoken word or through meditation or cogitation. Prayer, on the other hand, only begins when we have finished with thinking, with making statements or reviewing thoughts or ideas.

Prayer is that which takes place when we have come to the end of the treatment and sit with that listening ear and receive impartations, receive a message or a feeling, an awareness from within. Prayer is the word of God, but He speaks it to our individual consciousness, or within our individual consciousness. Therefore, those who have developed the listening ear, the attitude of receptivity, are those who receive the word of God, called prayer, and that results in healing and regeneration—in any change necessary in the outer picture.

Improvement Comes Through the Introduction of the Christ into Consciousness

Remember that there is no change in the outer scene until there is a change in our state of consciousness, and what change can there be unless something higher enters to change us? And where does that come from? Our thinking mind? No, we have to resort to something higher than the thinking mind.

Humanhood will not improve humanhood. Something higher is necessary, because it is only through spiritual sense, or the Christ, that a person can be improved. Even if you could make a person a better human being, you would have done nothing toward spiritualizing him. Never forget this. A better human being is a better human being, no more, no less: He is not spiritual consciousness.

Therefore, if you tell a person, "Oh, if you only had a better disposition! If you could just overcome impatience, then you would get a healing! If you would just get rid of jealousy, if you would only get rid of hate!" he might well reply, "Yes, I'd just love to get rid of all those things, but how can I?" Tell me, how does a person overcome jealousy, hatred, and impatience, or get rid of intolerance or injustice? How does he become more grateful? He doesn't, if he is looking to his humanhood to do it for him because if that were possible, he would have done it long ago.

There is no way humanly to overcome undesirable personal characteristics, except by will power; and when you do that you risk damming them up in one place only to have them break out again in a worse form at another time, in another place. Only the introduction of the Christ into individual consciousness will destroy jealousy, hate, enmity, injustice, dishonesty, immorality, and sensuality. Sometimes this is accomplished through the reading of metaphysical literature or scriptural writings. Sometimes just one statement registers in a person's consciousness, and it makes him a new man. Sometimes, as was my experience in 1928, it may be brought about through meeting an individual of such high consciousness that when his consciousness touches yours your whole human past is wiped out—that part of it that you wanted wiped out or which needed to be wiped out.

Over and over it happens that when people come to a practitioner who is in a high spiritual state or is normally of high spiritual consciousness, automatically they feel their fears drop away, or they feel their antagonism, or their hate, enmity, dishonesty, or sensuality just fade away. That is because they have been touched by the Christ of the person known as a practitioner, teacher, or lecturer.

An individual can do this for himself sometimes merely through the reading of spiritual literature which either suddenly or gradually brings about a change in his entire nature because it is introducing the Christ into human consciousness. Any way in which an individual is brought into the conscious presence of the Christ serves as an avenue through which that human improvement takes place.

Our first work with the young student is bringing to light the truth that God is the mind of the individual; God is the life, the Soul, and the Spirit, even the substance of the body of the person appearing for the moment as patient or student. In other words, in

our work the main point is that there is no God *and* man. Probably this approach is unique in that. You cannot give a treatment to
man because in this approach man is not separate and apart from
God, but God appears as man.

So it would be an impossibility for a practitioner to give a treatment to a man, woman, or child if he understood clearly that all
that is appearing as man, woman, or child is God, the one Life, the
one Soul and Spirit, and that even the body of that individual is the
temple of the living God, and the mind Its instrument.

Spiritual Integrity Is Vital

The subject of error should be very lightly touched upon with the
young student and not dealt with in its deeper aspects until he is
well prepared for it. It is not an easy subject and certainly cannot
be taught to anyone until the practitioner or teacher himself has
really mastered it.

Spiritual teaching is not the transfer of thought from one individual to another. It is the impartation of consciousness from God,
and in that lifting up of consciousness, all necessary knowledge is
received.

The teacher must be careful never to pass on to a patient or a
student quotations or statements, which might be considered in the
nature of clichés, until he has at least demonstrated the truth of
them in some degree. There is nothing worse in this work than
hollow phrases and statements. In their enthusiasm, many practitioners are likely to retort glibly to any call made upon them, "Oh,
you know it isn't real!" Of course a person asking for help doesn't
know it isn't real, and, moreover, had the practitioner known that
whatever he was talking about was not real, the patient would have
been healed in that moment, and he would never have had to voice
it.

Most of us make too many biblical or metaphysical statements to
our patients and students, many of which we ourselves have not

mastered. True, the authority of our statements may be Jesus or some metaphysical teacher or writer, but even so, before we quote them, we ourselves should have some understanding of them. Then these statements come forth from our own consciousness, and our patient or student understands and accepts them readily. Otherwise, they are very likely to reject any statement we make which we have not in a measure demonstrated.

It was Emerson who said, "What you are ... thunders so that I cannot hear what you say." And that is the truth about us. What we are within our own being is so much a part of our consciousness that if we attempt to voice anything not fully a part of us, nobody will believe us.

Suppose I declare as a spiritual truth, "There is only one Self; there is only one life," and yet, when some occasion arises, I lie or cheat a little. To whom am I lying and whom am I cheating, since there is only one Self? Whom am I deceiving, since there is only one mind and one life?

A good human being might go through life without ever cheating anyone of a single nickel, but that would not be spiritual integrity. That would be just human goodness. Spiritual integrity is living up to one's understanding of spiritual truth and living the Christ-ideal. That does not mean merely living a good human life or being a good moral person. Human good is not what I mean by spiritual integrity, because one could be humanly perfect and not measure up to the standard of spiritual integrity.

Spiritual integrity is the realization of the one Self as the Self of me and the Self of all men, of the one mind and the one life as the mind and life of me and of all men; and therefore, the interests of one are the interests of all. That is living up to spiritual integrity because that is making thought and action conform to our understanding of oneness.

Suppose I accept spiritually the teaching that all that the Father has is mine, and then I envy somebody his possessions. I am then violating my own spiritual integrity. I am not injuring the person I envy; he is not affected by it at all; but I am violating my own conviction that all that the Father has is mine because I am not acting on my own conviction. I am double-minded. I am saying in one breath, "Life is one," but at the same time I am setting up two—myself and the person I am envying, cheating, or defrauding.

In other words, spiritual integrity means living according to the Sermon on the Mount, "Whatsoever ye would that men should do to you, do ye even so to them."[1] But the reason for living the Sermon on the Mount is not for the sake of being a good human being, but because you realize that the other Self is you, and you are the other Self.

If you maintain this oneness in your consciousness continuously, living out from it, you are maintaining your spiritual integrity. If you never said a word to anyone, if you never preached a sermon on honesty, integrity, or loyalty, all those touching your consciousness would sense those qualities emanating from you because that is your state of consciousness, that is what you are.

Never indulge thoughts or acts that violate the teaching of the one Self. What about criticizing, judging, and condemning another person? When you do that, you are only doing it to yourself, and it is bound to come back to you. Do not ever believe that your own errors will not come back to you. They will. In judging or condemning anyone or anything, you are violating your own understanding that there is only One and are in reality judging and condemning your own being.

When you accept the spiritual teaching of oneness—of the one Self, of the one mind, as the mind of every individual, of one Life, one Soul, one Spirit—and live it, you can see that you will be helping to usher in the millennium, bringing about the time when no one could possibly act or think or do to another that which he would not do to his own being, because he would know that the Self of the other person is the Self of his own being.

[1]Matthew 7:12.

Ordination

Two statements from the Master I give you: "My kingdom is not of this world . . ."[2] and "I have overcome the world."[3]

Three men who are known to have had their own revelation of the complete secret of life are Lao-tze of China, about 600 B.C.; Buddha of India, about 550 B.C.; and Jesus of Nazareth. Through Jesus, the full revelation came to the beloved disciple, John, on the Isle of Patmos.

It was through Jesus that I, too, received this same unfoldment through his statement in the Bible, "My kingdom is not of this world," and this statement together with, "I have overcome the world," became the subject of my meditation for many months. I did not choose them; they clung to me, and finally came the realization of their meaning. I have never known this to be taught since it was received by John, except in his own veiled writings, and so if you can receive and accept this teaching, God has indeed blessed you beyond all men and women.

To overcome the world means to overcome, or rise above, all sense desire, to be free of world attraction, to live in the world but be not of it, to attain freedom from bondage to personal ego, and to understand the spiritual world and thus gain freedom from the false sense of God's universe. As we humanly see this world, we are seeing God's heaven, but seeing it "through a glass, darkly."[4] To overcome this world means to rise above the human, finite, erroneous sense of the world, and see it as it is.

It was John who told us, "When he shall appear, we shall be like him; for we shall see him as he is."[5] In this enlightened consciousness, we shall see God face to face, even though it is God appearing as you or as me, God appearing as individual man or woman.

These words clearly show forth the higher consciousness of life,

[2]John 18:36.
[3]John 16:33.
[4]Corinthians 13:12.
[5]I John 3:2.

but only as you can be reached within and open your consciousness spiritually can you come into the actual awareness of them. This is spiritual baptism, the Pentacostal experience of receiving the Holy Ghost. From it you will emerge as men and women who have seen through the mirage of sense testimony to the underlying reality in which you actually live and move and have your being.

This life you live is God seen "through a glass, darkly," but now, in this instant, face to face. You can now enjoy friendships, companionships, marriage, business associations, but all without intense attachment. The great successes of your friends or families will not unduly elate you, and their failures will not too greatly disturb you.

You will use dollars as a medium of exchange, but never again will you, who overcome this world, hate or fear or love them. You will handle dollars as you handle streetcar transfers—necessary and desirable paraphernalia of daily experience. You will always possess more than you need, without taking any anxious thought. Even the temporary absence of dollars will not embarrass or trouble you because nothing in your world is dependent upon them. All that you require comes to you through grace and as the gift of God.

In overcoming this world, you overcome the beliefs which constitute this world, including the belief that man must earn his living by the sweat of his brow. You are joint-heir with Christ in God to all the heavenly riches, to every idea of infinite Wisdom.

In overcoming this world, you lose your fear of the body, thereby freeing it to live under God's law. You overcome the world's beliefs about the body—that it is finite or material, that it lives by bread alone or by so-called material foods, or that it must be catered to in any way. Bathe it, keep it clean, inside and out, but drop all concern for it. It is in God's eternal keeping. It is living and moving and having its being in God-consciousness. Take no thought for your body, for it is God's concern to preserve and maintain the immortality of His own universe, including His body, which is the only body.

What you physically see as your body represents your concept of body, but there is only one body, the body of God, and this is the secret of secrets.

God's health is your health. God's wealth is your wealth.

Your family is the household of God, your consciousness of God's infinite, individual being. There is only one Being, and that One is God, and every person you meet represents your concept of that One, individually expressed.

Your spiritual freedom means your freedom from the false and universal beliefs about your body, your affairs, and your relationships. You are then no longer under the law of universal belief: You are set free in Christ, that is, you have overcome or risen above the erroneous beliefs about God's world, and therefore, you have overcome this world, the false sense of the world. You now see the world as it really is and not as "this world."

"My peace I give unto you: not as the world giveth."[6] *Spiritual peace I give you, the peace that passeth understanding, the peace that is not dependent upon person or outer condition. Now, nothing in this world can affect you who are free in Christ, in spiritual consciousness. You will walk up and down the world, come and go freely, and none of the world beliefs will kindle upon you. The flames will not harm you; the waters will not drown. I have put My seal upon you, and you are free. Walk up and down, in and out. Spiritual law upholds your being, your body, your business.*

Tell no man what things you have seen and heard. Do not explain or tell people of your freedom from "this world." Move in and out among men, as a blessing, as a benediction, as the light of the world. Let this life and mind be in you which was in Christ Jesus. Be receptive. Be expectant. Be always alert to receive inner guidance and direction and support. Keep attuned to your world within, yet fulfill all your duties without. Fulfill all your obligations without, but keep alert within.

There are those of you who have been called to God's work. It will be given you what to do and when. I have put My Spirit upon you. This Spirit will be seen and felt by men. It will not be you, but the spirit they will discern, although they will think of It as you.

My Spirit will work for you and with you and through you and as you. It will work to accomplish My purpose. You will be My presence on earth.

[6]John 14:27.

I will not leave you, nor forsake you. In any appearance I will still be with you. Fear nothing of this world. My guiding Spirit is ever with you.

Of Lao-tze it is said that when he was 1200 years old he grew weary because the world could not accept freedom from the grind of mortal living. He decided to leave the city, but before going through the gate, the gatekeeper, suspecting that he would never return, asked him to write down his teaching, which he did in a short message. Then he went out into the wilds of China and was never again seen.

Of Buddha, it is said that he taught his disciples, but found they could not fully realize the import of the message, so one day he sent for them, bade them farewell, and left this human plane.

Jesus asked, "Could ye not watch with me one hour?"[7] He also said, "If I go not away, the Comforter [the spirit of Truth] will not come unto you."[8]—meaning that even the disciples had not grasped the significance of his message.

Again, now, the Message is repeated on earth to you. Will you also sleep?

[7]Matthew 26:40.
[8]John 16:7.

Questions and Answers

Question: Is there any way of judging as to when a practitioner should take a case or have the person go to someone else?

Answer: From the very moment that a practitioner takes hold of a case, something begins to happen. Within twenty-four hours he knows, and the patient knows, whether there is a feeling of something at work. If there is not and the patient has any urge at all to change practitioners, let him go; or if the practitioner himself can see that within a day or two or three there is any sign that the patient would like to make a change, he should encourage it. The wisest thing in the world is for a practitioner never to believe that a patient belongs to him, or, in other words, that he has "a patient."

No patient is mine beyond the call that he has just this minute made. Five minutes later he is free to go to anybody else with no feeling on my part. I do not believe that there should be such a thing as personal feelings in the relationship between practitioner and patient. A person, who may be a patient this minute and asks for help, is under no compulsion to come back and explain tomorrow that he wants another practitioner. He is not obligated to me one moment beyond the minute he has asked for a treatment. If he comes back the next day, he comes of his own accord; but I have absolutely no hold on him and want none.

Sometimes I have had cases that do not seem to respond immediately, but the patient says, "I want you to go on with the work." In a case like that, you can be sure he is feeling something or he would not want the work to be continued. The healing may not have come through, but nevertheless there is something which causes the patient to say, "No, I want you." There is some bond. As long as he wants your help, continue the work; but at the first indication that you are not making any progress, and he realizes it, let him know that he is released and free and that he is not to feel any attachment or obligation to go on with you. In this work, it is all according to the inner response you feel.

Question: How far do you go with patients if they want *materia medica* help or want to resort to medicine?

Answer: That is a question that has to be answered by the individual case at the time. For example, my background being what it is, I naturally do not believe that we should mix medicine and metaphysics. On the other hand, it is apparent that many cases and situations are not being met through spiritual help. Many metaphysicians wear glasses, which certainly is a reliance on *materia medica*. This is a "suffer it to be so now" with them because it is undoubtedly better to wear glasses than it is to go around half blind waiting until the demonstration is made. However, even though glasses continue to be used, no one should be satisfied to accept this condition permanently; he should always continue his efforts to free himself.

Similarly, there are people who, in their early stages of coming into metaphysics from *materia medica*, may be taking sleeping powders or depending on digitalis or insulin, which according to *materia medica* "is keeping them alive." If they are young in the work, my procedure is not to upset them about that, but to do my work and free them from these material dependencies. But if I do not free them very quickly and I see that they are going to keep clinging and clinging to these dependencies, then I let them go.

If someone comes who has a cancer or a condition which, unless surgery is performed, would result in death, according to medical belief, or when there may be a broken bone and the patient wants to have it set, in my opinion it is far better for the patient to resort to surgery, get it over with, and get back on the path than to die because of a superstitious belief that it is better to die than to undergo surgery.

Every time, however, that you go back to *materia medica* you are failing in your demonstration. As I have said before, when I do not meet a case, I am honest enough to acknowledge that in that particular case I did not rise high enough. I offer no alibis. Whatever the case, I am sure that Jesus would have met it, and that indicates that anyone with the fullness of the Christ-mind could have met it. There is no use dodging the issue. So I freely admit, "Well, I didn't rise high enough, but I'm going to keep on in this work and try to do better next time."

So, if someone comes along with a fear so great that he feels he must undergo surgery, or as often happens, he or she may not particularly want it but may have a wife, husband, mother, son, or daughter who insists on medical attention and who may feel honestly: "No, we're not going to let you take this risk; you have to have medicine"; then stand by with those people—they need your help more than ever.

If someone that you know in this work has failed to make his demonstration and has had to go to a hospital, stand by with him. Your spiritual help may pull him through where the hospital or the surgery would not. Never cast off any person. Always remember this, and again Jesus is my authority, "Therefore all things whatso-

ever ye would that men should do to you, do ye even so to them."[1]
If you yourself should reach the point where you could not make
the grade and felt you needed some medial aid and found it necessary to go to a hospital, would you want your practitioner to refuse
to help you? Would you want him to say, "You are in a hospital,
so I wash my hands of you?"

Furthermore, suppose someone you know falls from grace, com-
mits some crime, and is arrested. What are you going to do? Are
you going to say, "Ho, ho! I'll have nothing to do with you!" No!
That's the time he needs you more than ever—when he is in the
deepest trouble. Jesus said, "I was sick, and ye visited me: I was in
prison, and ye came unto me."[2]

My attitude is entirely different when people become chronical-
ly dependent on *materia medica*. If they are habitually taking sleeping powders, cathartics, and all the other remedies prescribed for
an ailing body, they are not on this path, because obviously they
are seeking only the "loaves and fishes." Remember how the people came to Jesus the next day after he had just fed them with the
bread and the fishes, seeking to be fed again. It was then that he
said in substance, "What are you looking for? Not the truth. You
saw the miracle of the loaves and the fishes and you want some
more of that."

No Infinite Way worker should cater to people who want to try
a little of both *materia medica* and spiritual help. How can such
people be helped? But with those who are beginners, stand by and
have patience with them until they demonstrate their freedom.
Remember, it is not a crime or an irredeemable failure to be unable
to make a demonstration. What we have to do is to begin again.
Many of us are required to repeat a grade in school, and that is
what sometimes happens in this work. We go along and think we
are making remarkable progress, and than all of a sudden something comes along and there are our feet of clay. But that is when
we need our friends on the spiritual path the most.

[1]Matthew 7:12.
[2]Matthew 25:36.

So that is my attitude. Do not cater to the medical thought and do not go along indefinitely with people who are trying to benefit continuously by both *materia medica* and spiritual help. But on the other hand, do not reject anyone because he is failing in a demonstration. Rather stand by and help him get back on this path, because love is the principle of this work.

Question: If God is mind, or even if He is consciousness, is His activity not mental?

Answer: No, mental activity is a reasoning and a thinking activity. Consciousness is not a mental activity; consciousness does not reason or think: It is just aware.

Two times two is four. God, infinite Consciousness, does not use a mental process in arriving at that answer. It is just a state of is. There has never been a time when it was other than that, nor was there ever a time in creation when two times two *became* four. There is no process of making two times two, four, and, therefore, no mental activity is necessary to establish that fact. Two times two has always existed as four, and the only mental activity involved in that concept is the activity of awareness.

When I stated that we do not work on the mental plane, what I meant was that the only activity of the mind is one of awareness. We become aware that we are spiritual, that we are divine beings, that sin, disease, and death are illusions—just nothingness, or mesmeric suggestion—but we do not go through any mental process to make this so.

We do not indulge in any kind of a mental process with the idea of making a sick man well or a poor man rich or an unemployed man employed. If there is any process at all, it is the process of awareness, the process of becoming aware of that which already divinely is, and that is not a mental process.

From the human standpoint, we cannot look at a sick person and mentally assert, "You are well." That is hypocrisy and ignorance and is obviously untrue. It is only with inner spiritual discernment that we can look through the human appearance and see the divine reality which underlies that appearance. So it is not through a mental process that we become aware of perfection, and our work is to become aware of perfection. It cannot be done humanly with the human mind because nothing that the human mind will ever know will be perfect. It is only when the human mind is not at work, when in the very stillness of our innermost being, our Soul-senses and spiritual awareness are aroused, that we behold the perfect man.

That is why spiritual healing is not a mental process. None of your or my thinking will add health to you or to me. Again we go back to Jesus: "Which of you by taking thought can go back to Jesus: "Which of you by taking thought can add one cubit unto his stature?"[3] Who by taking thought can make "one hair white or black?"[4] Take no thought for your life ... "[5] In other words, a mental process has nothing to do with spiritual truth, and that is really the crux of this whole presentation of truth. Human mental activity has nothing whatsoever to do with this particular approach. No amount of knowing the truth will help you—no amount of declaring the truth. No human mental process enters into this presentation.

The Infinite Way is concerned first and foremost with the development of the Soul-sense. When we are still, sitting back with that "listening ear," when we are in meditation, giving what we call a treatment, the inner Thing comes to life and shows us the inward spiritual perfection, and that outwardly becomes interpreted as a healthy, sane, or wealthy human being.

Right there is the meat and the substance of the whole Infinite Way. We do not indulge in any mental processes for self-improvement, and that is where we depart from the entire metaphysical field. It is a question of developing our spiritual sense so that ultimately we arrive at the consciousness of a Jesus Christ who could look at the cripple and say, "Rise up and walk!"[6]

[3]Matthew 6:27.
[4]Matthew 5:36.
[5]Luke 12:22.
[6]Luke 5:23.

What do you think would enable a man to say that? Do you think any mental process anyone could use would instantaneously raise up a crippled man so he could walk? No, only the divine Fire within, only the very Spirit of God could do that.

It might be possible to give a person a year's treatment and gradually turn him from a cripple into a healthy man by mental manipulation—by a pounding and pounding and pounding away at him mentally. But no human being could instantaneously do that—only the fire of God in him.

That is why we must make love the dominating influence in our experience. All the divine qualities of the Christ must become active in us; all personal desires—all hate, envy, criticism, and condemnation—must be relinquished. There can be no indulgence in those human qualities. We must not fear them, for we are then missing the opportunity to bring forth the divine qualities of the Christ. Why should we go around indulging in these human things at the expense of cheating ourselves of having that mind that was in Christ Jesus?

The mind that was in Christ Jesus does not engage in any reasoning or thinking process. To the palsied man it says, "Arise, and take up thy bed, and walk,"[7] and might have added, "What is to hinder you? Is there any power apart from God?" This mind of Christ Jesus is awareness without a process.

The truth is that there is no power apart from God, but we could say it and say it and say it, and nothing would happen. In fact, a metaphysical teacher may sit and talk these truths from now until doomsday and not bring out any measure of spirituality in his class; or a clergyman may preach spellbinding sermons and yet the members of his congregation go on being the same kind of human beings year in and year out, with just as many ills, just as many crimes, just as much cheating in business, just as much corruption in politics. Why are not the congregations in these churches and centers improved spiritually? For the simple reason that they are sometimes hearing only an intellectual presentation of truth, and

[7]Mark 2:9.

even though many times this comes from a very good human being, if that person has not a developed Christ-consciousness, or spiritual sense, he cannot quicken the minds and hearts of his followers.

What is most important is not to criticize the human faults, but rather to lift people up to the place where they are not human any more. You cannot do that by means of human reason. You can tell a person not to steal; you can tell a person not to lie or cheat; you can tell him anything you want to tell him, and many of you probably have, but usually it has not and does not have any effect upon his conduct.

Improved conduct is only brought about by reaching the individual through the Spirit. You must attain such a degree of spirituality that when a sinner is touched by your consciousness, he loses all desire to sin. When that happens, you are functioning as a spiritual teacher. You are then not teaching new truths and new mental processes: You are giving forth the age-old truth that has been tried and found effective—effective by Elisha, Elijah, and Isaiah, by Jesus and John.

Truth is so simple that it can all be summed up in less than one thousand words, but it is only through developing our own spiritual qualities that spirituality can be brought out in those we meet.

Question: Why does God take us down into "Egypt"?
Answer: God is not a person sitting around manipulating the world: God is our very own consciousness. God is forever imparting Its truth and Its guidance to us, but because we are not always listening, sometimes we are compelled to take a roundabout way to reach our goal. It is not God who is responsible for this: It is our own obtuseness. God is always right where we are, imparting His impulses until ultimately we reach the goal.

It is not that there was a God who made his brothers sell Joseph into slavery, but undoubtedly there was such a state of consciousness in Joseph that ultimately he was destined to be the king's right-hand man, and in some way, he had to be brought to the proper place in order to function in that capacity. Similarly, the circumstances which we define as our "Egypt" may later be responsible for our becoming a "prince." In other words, had we not had some particularly trying experience, we would not have learned the necessary lesson, heard the Voice, and set our feet again upon the path.

You can take all you have read so far in this book and immediately begin to put it into practice and gradually, through that understanding, come into perfect harmony; or, on the other hand, you can say, "Yes, I'll practice as much of it as I can, but I must indulge in this bit of humanhood today, or I must indulge in that." True, you arrive at your proper place ultimately, but often only through much suffering.

For example, you could at this moment stand on this truth: "All that the Father has is mine, and never again do I have to take thought for supply." You could take that stand right now and demonstrate it, but most of you will not do this. Most of you will be a little bit worried about next month's bills and continue to take thought for this, that, or the other thing; and to the degree that you take thought, you are violating your understanding. To that degree, then, there will be a period of suffering, though ultimately you will arrive at your goal.

That is what happened to Joseph. Had he been sufficiently attuned, he might have said: "I think I'll move to Egypt." But he didn't. Instead, he perhaps thought that he was always going to remain with his father and his brethren, so he had to be picked up and forced into his rightful place—Egypt.

Then when he was in the household of the Pharoah, he could just as well have said to himself, "I am going to live as pure spiritual being and never let mortality enter my thought." But he didn't. He had to go down into prison and there learn that the indulgence of any form of mortality has no place in the experience of a spiritual being. When he was in prison, he had time to think, and that is when he finally came to the realization, "Well, if I'm spiritual, I guess I'd better act like it." Sometimes it takes the very depths of human experience to bring us to an awareness where we are willing to let the spiritual light gleam.

Question: I was called to the bedside of a very sick man, and I began with the first chapter of Genesis, explaining to him the perfection of God's creation. I then asked him if he could accept what I had told him, and he replied in the affirmative. The man who had taken me there asked me to work for him for a couple of days, which I did. How do you account for the healing in such a situation?

Answer: I would say that it had to do with your receptivity to truth, which is the highest form of treatment there is, but when we begin to work mentally and then call it God-healing, it is ludicrous. When we reach a state of receptivity, however, so that when any case comes, the ear is open, and the impartation comes like a flash, telling us how to work or what truth to reveal, then that is God-healing.

Question: Then you think that was God healing?

Answer: There is no question about it, because it came to you without any thought process; it was not conscious thinking. It was a state of receptivity which revealed that truth to you. This, I call being divinely led, because it did not consist of sitting down and giving a treatment to a disease or a condition. I do not believe in that kind of treatment. Turn to God and let God show you the need of the moment.

Can you imagine what a man wrongly imprisoned would feel if I told him that there is no injustice, that man is perfect? He would want to throw such words right back at me. But when one is led to tell him the story of Joseph and his brethren, then he might begin to understand the spiritual sense of forgiveness. The higher sense of forgiveness is looking through the human being and his activity and seeing that there at the center of his being sits God, which at the moment is being misinterpreted.

In all treatment, never do I permit myself to think a thought, to make a denial, or to affirm a truth. I take the attitude: "Speak,

Lord; for thy servant heareth. ... [8] Be still, and know that I am God."[9]

Take the attitude that this is God's universe; let God do something about it; be a witness to God in action. Then you are led to say the right thing, think the right thing, or do the right thing.

That is how the book, *The Letters*, came into existence. Whenever letters came from patients out of town asking for help, no matter what the problem was, I would sit down and turn within and let the Father speak. Then I would write a letter to the patient about the problem, but I always exemplified a particular point of what we call truth. The more you live in this state of receptivity, the more you live and develop this receptive ear, the more the divine Voice will speak to you at every point and at every call, although not always in words.

Jesus' words are literally true: "I can of mine own self do nothing ... If I bear witness of myself, my witness is not true.[10] ... My doctrine is not mine, but his that sent me."[11] That is our attitude. As human beings, we do not have enough power even to heal a simple cold. The power is that divine Impulse, that Thing we call God, or the Christ.

The only way we can bring the Christ to bear on a case is to set aside our human thinking and permit ourselves to become the vehicle for the activity of the Christ. Then the right words come, the right thoughts, or the right feeling.

Throughout these many years, I have observed with so many different kinds of cases that if I could just be receptive enough, the answer would come with the first call for help, and the results would be instantaneous. But in other cases it might require a second or a third call. Sometimes, it may even take two or three years. It all depends on the situation. I have had cases that have been long-drawn out and which took a great deal of patience and long

[8]I Samuel 3:9.
[9]Psalm 46:10.
[10]John 5:30, 31.
[11]John 7:16.

hours of work. There have been cases where, in the beginning, I have had as many as ten, fifteen, or twenty telephone calls in a twenty-four-hour period—incessant calls. Then I would watch as these calls gradually decreased from ten to five to two and then one every other day, and so on.

The process was always the same, always letting the Christ do the work, letting this inner infinite Thing we call the Christ—the Comforter, the Holy Ghost, the Spirit of truth—do the work and not trying to make of myself a metal worker using mental processes or treatments. While the mental approach may probably work for some people on certain levels of consciousness, it is not the approach of The Infinite Way.

None of this is said in any spirit of criticism, condemnation, or judgment, but only from the viewpoint that mental activity has nothing to do with the particular approach to truth as taught in The Infinite Way. And naturally, I do believe that this approach will bring the greatest reward. The reason this work has grown and spread so rapidly is because the results do come, and they come because of this infinite Thing which dispels the illusion.

From

The Master Speaks

God

When we say, "*I* am God," or "*I* am a law unto my universe," we are not saying that a human being is God, or that a mortal is spiritual. Never forget that it would be nonsense to try to spiritualize mortal man, or to make God out of a human being. That has been one of the mistakes of religion throughout the ages—setting apart some individual and making him God, taking some person, some human being, and making of him a God. The truth is that only God is God; but God is the individuality and the identity, and the reality of each one of us when we have overcome our sense of humanhood. Often when you see people who work from the standpoint of "I am," you will find them confused, walking around saying, "I am God." They are the very people who are apt to be walking around with an empty purse, a diseased body, or a pair of eyeglasses, and yet they continue to say, "I am God." You can see how ridiculous that is, because that is not God at all. *I am God.*

That *I* is a universal, infinite, omnipresent Being, and It is the reality of your being and of mine when the human sense of self has been overcome. You do not lift the human sense up and make it immortal or spiritual. That is the reason treatments that say, "You are spiritual," or "You are perfect," or "You are rich," are of so little value. Such statements are not true at all. If they were true, you would not find it necessary to repeat them. Can you imagine Rockefeller or a Carnegie or any man of recognized wealth, walking around saying, "I am rich?" And you almost never hear a healthy person say, "I am healthy." When you make these affirmations, it is because you believe you are the opposite; you are trying to fool yourself into believing that you are something that you really are not. When you simply repeat the words, "I am God," that is not true; but when you *hear* those words *within* you, that is Truth. That is God announcing Itself as the reality of your being. When you hear a voice saying, "Know ye not that I am God?" you have heard Truth; and in hearing that Truth, all that is human, all that is mortal, disappears. At least it disappears in a measure; and as, more and more, you hear the still small voice there will be less and less of the human or humanhood to be dispelled.

This is confirmed in the statement of the Master, "I have overcome the world."[1] He did not say, "I have improved myself in this world's goods," or "I have improved the health of this world or the wealth of this world." He said, "I have overcome the world." And again you will find that same idea in his statement, "My kingdom is not of this world."[2] "My kingdom"—the Christ kingdom, the spiritual kingdom—is not of the human world. You cannot bring the Christ into the human world, but you can overcome the human world, and find that kingdom within where the Christ is king.

In our favorite passage in Luke, you will find: "For all these things do the nations of the world seek after"[3]—things to eat,

[1] John 16:33.
[2] John 18:36.
[3] Luke 12:30.

things to wear, and things to possess. What are the nations of the world? Who are the people of the world? Are they not those whose consciousness is centered in things, the people who dwell in an atmosphere of things, acquiring things or needing things—*things, things*, always *things*. The nations of the world are seeking things; but not you—not "ye, my disciples," ye of spiritual consciousness. You are not seeking things; you are seeking the conscious awareness of God as the reality of your being. That is all you can ever seek in this work, and that attitude reaches its ultimate in Paul's declaration: "I live; yet not I, but Christ liveth in me." When you say, "Christ liveth in me," that is not a mortal speaking. The mortal, the human being, the planner, has faded out of existence, and you have become the witness to the activity of the Christ—to the life of the Christ. You are now watching the Christ work *in* you and *through* you and *as* you.

You are setting aside humanhood and living in your Christhood, when you are not thinking, planning, worrying, fearing, doubting—in other words, when the human mind is less active as a thinking apparatus and more active as a state of awareness. When your thinking is the witnessing of God in action, watching God unfold, then you are living more of the Christ life and less of the human life. The more you find it necessary to plan your days, weeks, months, and years—the more you have to take thought for your life—the more of humanhood is in evidence and the less of spirituality. On the other hand, you are living your Christhood in the degree in which you find your work given to you to do each day, your supply provided, and all your activity unfolding in a normal, natural way; and when this happens you can then say, "I, God, is the reality of my being." You have reached a place in consciousness where you understand the meaning of "*I am God*." This *I*, which becomes the law unto your being, is not the conscious thinking you or I. It is the divine Consciousness of our being, revealed in the degree in which conscious thinking, in the sense of planning and struggling, fades out of existence.

God is Infinite Individuality

We do not annihilate ourselves or destroy our individuality in this way; we increase it. But at this point, we must understand that God is infinite in Its individuality, and that, therefore, God is expressing that individuality as individual you or me. It is still God, but it is God appearing as you or as me. Because that is true, you can say, "I have overcome the world," or "I and my Father are one," or "I live; yet not I, but Christ liveth in me," or "I am the way"—anything that will give you this sense of *I*, and that will, at the same time, subordinate human selfhood, not glorify it:

> "Glorify thou me ... with the glory which I had with thee."[1] Glorify thou me with all *Thy* glory. Let everything I am, or do, be God in manifestation—not the glorification of my personal knowledge, or awareness, or achievement.

To be glorified with God's glory leaves no room for us to glorify humanhood and to call that humanhood God, or even to call it spiritual. Humanhood is not to be spiritualized; humanhood is to be overcome. It will never be necessary to overcome anything of a spiritual nature. But you must overcome this world; you must overcome personal selfhood. You must understand the Master when he says, "I can of mine own self do nothing."[2] He was turning away from his own personal powers, or conscious thinking, and recognizing, "The Father that dwelleth in me, he doeth the works."[3] That Father within is the *I* or *I am* or *reality* of being.

Only *God* is *God*. This is the teaching of The Infinite Way: Only God is God; man is not God. The Infinite Way never teaches that man is God. But God being infinite, God appears as infinite individuality—God appears as the allness of you and of me *when we*

[1] John 17:5.
[2] John 5:30.
[3] John 14:10.

have overcome the world. When we have overcome the temptation to be concerned about that little "I", when we are not longer taking thought for that little self, then we can say, "*I* am God," because then it is actually true.

Heretofore, our attention in the world has been centered on persons and things. It did not make any difference in what form the things appeared. The emphasis has always been on health, wealth, harmony, home, or companionship. The transformation that is necessary now is a complete about-face to where thought is focussed on our *consciousness*, and the ability to let that consciousness flow forth in whatever form is necessary to our unfoldment.

We do not take thought for any thing, for any person, or any demonstration. Nothing that appears in the world of form is our concern. That does not mean that we are eliminating persons or things from our experience. On the contrary, as concern for the people and things of this world lessens, we usually find ourselves with more of them; only now we utilize them in their right sense. For example, if a ring comes to me, I wear it and enjoy it, but there is no sense of possession, no sense of its being mine or no sense of desiring it. It just comes; I put it on, and I enjoy it. Now, the same thing can be true of clothing or of friends or relatives. It can be true of marriage. Whatever consciousness brings to me, I use and enjoy. But there is no sense of possession, no sense of needing anything, requiring anything, or desiring anything. There is only the realization that God, as my consciousness, is appearing to me at all times in every form necessary to my experience, watching as it unfolds from day to day. In this way, all power is placed in consciousness rather than in things.

We take the first commandment and realize that all power is in God—the Consciousness of my being—and because the nature of God or Consciousness is infinite intelligence and divine love, It not only knows our need before we do, but It has the love necessary to provide whatever is needed for our unfoldment. Therefore, when we are centered in the truth that "I and my Father are one,"[1] the

[1] John 10:30.

Father is revealed as the infinite, divine, spiritual consciousness of individual being. Its nature is infinite wisdom, divine love; and It is, therefore, forever pouring Itself forth as my harmonious daily experience. God, my consciousness, is appearing to me each day in the form necessary for the fulfillment of that day.

God is Fulfillment

The word "fulfillment"—filled full—is an important one for us. We are always filled full; we are always a state of fulfillment, since it is God fulfilling Itself as our individual being. It is God fulfilling Its glory, Its grace, Its power and dominion as our individual experience. We must come to that place where God pours Itself forth as us, through us, in us, and for us; and God must become a living reality.

There is a teaching which states that God is divine mind, a formless substance, and that we impress our desires upon this mind, and then our desires come forth into form. This teaching makes of God a vehicle through which we can get what we want. The Infinite Way approach is a reversal of that. In our work, we have no desires, no wants, no wishes; we have nothing to impress upon the divine Mind. We are not taking thought for what we need, because we do not know what we need. We do not know where we should be tomorrow. We have no idea, furthermore, of what place we are destined to fill in the spiritual scheme of existence. Therefore, our attitude is the reverse of any such teaching which would *use* God. The divine Intelligence or Consciousness, being infinite wisdom and divine love, knows our need, and because the nature of God is to fulfill Itself as our individual unfoldment, It does all things needful without our even being aware of what we need, want, or desire, or where we should be.

This is not an attitude of "let God do it," since that would involve a sense of separation from God. It is rather the understanding that since God is my very intelligence, I am always intelligently governed. Since God is the divine law of my being, then my experience is always expressing divine love, perfection, harmony, or good. Since God is infinite good, and all that the Father hath is mine, this infinitude of good is pouring itself through into expression as my experience.

This teaching is not fatalism; it is not a resigned acceptance that "Whatever happens God did it"; or "I will take whatever God sends me." Such an attitude is duality or two-ness. *This* way is the affirmation and reaffirmation of the great truths:

> I and my Father are one.[1]
> All that I have is thine.[2]
> The placed where thou standest is holy ground.[3]

God is forever fulfilling Itself as our individual experience. Then, in that consciousness, we can say: "Let Truth manifest Itself as It will, since Its will is only in the nature of infinite wisdom and divine love." Do you see the difference? There *is* a God. God *is*. Harmony *is*. We cannot create that harmony with our thinking, but through thought we can become aware of the fact that God is infinite law, that God is infinite, divine principle, forever expressing Itself as the harmony, wisdom, intelligence, and love of our experience.

That is knowing the truth, and the truth, then, makes us free. *Know the truth*. Do not be concerned with the things of the world—whether they be a home, money, a job, or opportunity. Be concerned only with the realization that God is fulfilling Itself as your individual experience; that God, the consciousness of your being, is always appearing as the form necessary to your unfoldment. Keep thought steadfastly on God; keep thought continuously on the Source and Substance, and not on the *effect in* which or *as* which God is to appear.

[1] John 10:30.
[2] Luke 15:31.
[3] Exodus 3:5.

Omnipresence,
Omnipotence, and Ever-Availability of God

The secret of this principle with which we are working—called the Christ Principle—is the omnipresence, omnipotence, and ever-availability of God. The entire message of The Infinite Way can be summed up in the words: *The omnipotence, omnipresence, and ever-availability of God.* That is the whole of it. Once you have attained the consciousness of the presence of God, you can take all The Infinite Way writings and throw them away, or give them away. You will no longer need them, because you will have the essence of their teaching: the understanding of the infinite nature of God, Its omnipotence and ever-availability.

This sense of God's presence and power is the principle that you will want to give your children, or that your patient or student will want to give his children. It must be built into the fiber of the child's consciousness from morning to night, and from night to morning. A child should never be permitted to go to sleep without a conscious remembrance of God as omnipresent in one form or another. Those who want their children to grow into a better sense of manhood and womanhood than these last few generations have experienced will have to do this by some means other than by human teaching, or through a purely human code of conduct. I do not believe children can be taught morals or ethics merely through human codes. But the person who once catches the consciousness of the presence of God never again has any excuse to violate any moral or ethical principle of life.

The real principle of life is this: your own will come to you. Your own state of consciousness will always be made manifest as your experience, and no man can take that away from you. No man can take your consciousness from you any more than he can take your knowledge of mathematics or music from you.

The greater the awareness of God which you attain, the greater degree of desirable things and persons will appear in your outer world. These things and persons will be your own consciousness appearing to you. Looking at your present state of affairs, you might say, "Then I have a very poor state of consciousness." That may be so. In that event, it is up to you to acknowledge that, and change it. It is up to *you* to change it. "Seek ye first the kingdom of God."[1]—the conscious awareness of God. Seek this consciousness of God and make it an ever-increasing awareness. God is here in Its infinite, but we attain that consciousness only in a measure. What the measure is, is up to us.

Everyone on earth has, potentially, the same consciousness as Jesus Christ. It is infinite; it is here; and it is awaiting us. The question is: are we willing to put in the hours of devotion; are we willing to put in the hours of devotion; are we willing to make the effort required to train ourselves to be conscious of the presence of God, instead of seeking some *form* in which God is to appear. There is the whole secret. *It is up to us!* If we can rely wholly on the Principle, on Consciousness, we can attain the consciousness of the Christ.

No man could ever steal after he has caught the consciousness of God as his supply. No man would ever murder, if once he caught the consciousness of God as eternal life, as the life of individual being. It is only the belief that someone has a life of his own that causes a person to kill, even in self-defense. Even to kill in self-defense is an acknowledgment that we have a life of our own which is in danger. Such a thing would not be possible if the truth that God is life eternal were realized. You cannot destroy life eternal; no bullet or bomb can destroy that. The consciousness that God is the reality of our being dispels every condition leading to sin, disease, and death. The cause of the world's troubles is the sense of separation from God. The antidote for the world's troubles is the conscious awareness of God as omnipresent, omnipotent, omniscient—the reality of being.

When we worship persons and personalities—whether we do so

[1] Matthew 6:33.

in the form of a religious character, national or international characters—we are laying the foundation for our own destruction. Only in the degree that we can realize God as a universal presence, as an impersonal and impartial presence, as the life of *all*, as the mind and Soul of *all*, as the consciousness of *all being*, can we overcome the conditions of this world.

Is not the teaching of one God, and that God omnipotent and omnipresent, the only religious teaching that can end the quarrels among churches, end not only religious warfare, but all other warfare? The antidote for war is the realization of God as individual presence and power, God as our individual experience. This realization brings an awareness of spiritual power. Once we, as individuals, have proved that there is a spiritual power which heals our personal ills, lacks, and limitations, we shall begin to see that there is a spiritual power which can overcome any evil in human society.

God Appears as Teacher, Healer, and Saviour

Consciousness is infinite. Consciousness manifests itself as individual being—your being and my being. If I tell you that consciousness has manifested itself as my particular being, and as my particular state of consciousness, and that that consciousness through me or as me is imparting to you this truth, you will probably agree. If you can sit in your office or home and help someone else, you will agree that the consciousness imparting itself to you as truth, as spiritual power, was that which enabled you to help your patient, neighbor, friend, or relative.

Now, let me carry this one step further, and show you that Consciousness is manifesting Itself as individual being within my consciousness and yours. Therefore, every moment of the day and every moment of the night, God is imparting Itself to you, within you, in an individual way, in some individual sense of person or power, as guidance and direction, and as a healing agency, as well as a supporting and supplying agency. At no time are you without your teacher and healer. God is manifesting Itself in your consciousness as teacher and as healer. Wherever you go, with or without a human being, with or without a book, you are carrying in your consciousness God's manifestation of Its own being as teacher, healer, supplier, protector, saviour.

Whether It appears within you as the idea of some personality in the past, present, or future; whether It appears to you as an externalized teacher or teaching; whether It appears to you as a position or as an investment, please remember this: God is omnipresent in your consciousness *as individual form*, as individual individuality. At all times and in all places, God is present within you as your teacher, as your teaching, as your companion, as your *everything of this existence*.

At this moment, I am thinking more particularly in terms of teacher and healer, since what appears outwardly to you as teacher or teaching is not that at all. Teacher and teaching are *God manifesting in your own consciousness as divine idea*. It has always been present in your consciousness awaiting your recognition, and It will always be there *manifesting in whatever form is necessary*, to the extent in which you are willing to recognize God manifest as divine idea within you, and are not afraid if that divine Idea appears to you in some form which you have not heretofore experienced.

Consciousness never dies. The consciousness of any and every individual never dies. Individual consciousness never disappears from the face of the globe. Therefore, that consciousness which is known as Jesus Christ or Krishna or Buddha—that consciousness which is known as any great religious spiritual light or character—is omnipresent within *you*, and may appear to you at any moment that you open your consciousness. It may take the form of words or thoughts. But do not be surprised if it appears to you as a person, as the very image and likeness of some spiritual being.

Consciousness may appear to you as the form of what you conceive to be Jesus Christ or any other great spiritual leader, but it will not be the form of any of them, as their forms were known on earth. It will be their form as God made their form, and it will be visible to you in proportion to your interpretation of it. If you have been a Christian from birth, it may well appear to you as the form you have seen in pictures or paintings of the Master, Christ Jesus. On the other hand, if you have been reared in the Hindu teaching, it may become visible to you as Krishna or Buddha. If you have come by way of Judaism, it may appear as what the world called Moses.

Whatever the form, it would merely to be your *interpretation* of the Christ—of Christ consciousness. It may come to you as someone you have never known or never heard of—some ancient or modern teacher. And on the other hand, it may not come in the form of a person: it may come as ideas, words, or statements. But in your own thought do not limit the forms of expression; and do not rule out anything as impossible, because God is infinite, and God has a way of appearing infinitely. The Bible is full of references to God as *light*, but it also emphasizes the fact that God is *truth*. Therefore, God can just as well appear as a sense or statement of truth as a sense of light. But do not forget that God, or Truth, has always appeared on earth as an individual. God can appear to us in *any* form.

God is infinite individual being: God is omnipresent as your individual consciousness. This omnipresence may appear to you in any form which your consciousness can accept. Do not limit the form in which truth, guidance, health, healing, can come to you, because God is *infinite* in Its activity; God is infinite in form and appearance.

Accept the truth that God can appear to you individually: God can appear to you within your consciousness; God can appear as teacher, healer, saviour; God can appear as direction, wisdom, guidance. Accept God in any form in which He may appear to you in your consciousness when you are in the silence. Do not be afraid of any inner visitation. The greater degree of unfoldment that you receive in this work, the greater will be the *inner* revelation of an individual nature coming to you. You will receive your individual unfoldment from God, and God will appear to you in an individual way.

So far as I am concerned, the healing of disease, the healing of sin, and the healing of poverty, are only the proof that the message of Omnipresence is true. The healing of the body is not the main function of this teaching; the purpose of this teaching is to make God evident and real to you individually as a living experience. God *is* a living experience. God is a living person and power—not "person" in our sense of person—but God is an infinite individuality to be realized by each one of us.

We can live and move and have our being twenty-four hours a day in God consciousness. That is the purpose of this work. The health, the wealth, the harmony, the peace, and the joy always accompany the consciousness of the presence of God.

Abraham called God "Friend." And Jesus called God "Father." Ramakrishna called God "Mother Kali"; the Quakers called God "Father-Mother." In whatever form these people have realized God, they realized It not as a name, but as an *actual experience* to which they gave the name "Father," "Friend," "Father-Mother," or "Mother." It was an actual experience which took place in their consciousness, like the descent of the Holy Ghost at Pentecost, an experience to which they then gave the name "God," or "Father-Mother."

What we have been doing in our religious life has been merely to *say* the names "Father," "Mother," "God," and "Christ"—without actually having had the experience of God in our inner being—all of which is but a hollow shell. The purpose and message of The Infinite Way is to make God a living reality, so that whether you close your eyes or open your eyes, you will always have the sense and feeling of this divine Presence, guiding, leading, directing, and instructing you.

Spiritual Existence

Meditation is valuable, even if the meditation lasts for only one or two minutes—even if it is only a few minutes snatched for this purpose during the noon hour. It is important, furthermore, never to retire, never to go to bed, just as a human being; because then you would have nothing more nor less than a night of human sleep, which might or might not be restful. Acquire the habit of never doing anything without first opening consciousness to the inflow of Spirit, of never engaging in any human activity without first opening consciousness to the inflow. Never begin any human activity—whether at the beginning of the day on awakening, whether it is preparing a meal, whether it is going out into the business world, whether it is undertaking household duties, or whether it is retiring for a nap or for a night's sleep—without specifically opening consciousness to the inflow of the Spirit.

For a while you may not get any results; that is, you may not be consciously aware of any results. But you will never open your consciousness to God without getting a result, even though at the time you may not be aware of the result. In other words, you may meditate, you may open your consciousness, and you may feel no response. Do not let that disturb you. That has nothing to do with it. I went on in that same way for eight months, meditating five and six times a day, and never in all that time, having any answering response. Of course, I did it alone. I did not receive my inner teaching until after the meditation had been successfully accomplished. I only found my inner Teacher when I found the ability to "be still, and know that I am God."[1] For you it will be much more simple.

As you continue meditating—especially as you have the opportunity to do it with others who have achieved the ability to meditate—it will become more and more simple, and you will feel the response much more quickly. But do not be discouraged if there seems to be no answer, if you seem to be no more spiritual after the meditation than before, or if you do not get any response. Remember that behind you there are hundreds of generations of people who have lived in the outer world, living completely in the realm of effect. That is the heritage of a human being, and that is the thing that you must break through. In time, if you persevere, you will find yourself automatically settling down into the center of your own being; and from that point on, you will feel yourself to be an avenue through which all of the Spirit continuously pours Itself. You can almost feel how it flows out from the center of your being.

Remember not to be too concerned about human beings. You are not on the human plane of existence. That does not mean that you should become cold and heartless. It does not mean that if somebody needs food, you are to give him a treatment and withhold the food. If somebody needs clothing, do not withhold it because you are so metaphysical. I do not mean that. I mean that even while suffering it to be so now, do not accept the appearance

[1]Psalms 46:10.

as the reality, but always stand fast on the inner plane, realizing the presence of God.

Continuity of Individual Identity

Now we come to another question: "Do you believe that you would be living as an individual, if you had never experienced human birth?" Regardless of what you may now think, ponder that idea in the weeks to come. What would have happened to you had you had not been born humanly? Where would you be? What would you be doing? It may give you an insight into what you may experience after the world says that you are dead. In reality, you will never be dead, but there may come a time when the world will believe that you are dead; and it would be wise for you to have some idea of what you will be doing, and where, and when and how.

"Before Abraham was, I am."[1] That means that Jesus existed as an actual, individual entity and identity before Abraham's human existence. It means that, before Abraham, you existed as an individual, as a spiritual entity, as a spiritual identity. God, in manifesting Itself individually, could not begin to express Itself at a certain time in a certain place. God's manifestation of Its own being has always existed. God's manifestation of Its own being has existed since time began, since God, Itself, began—not that God ever did begin, because God is timeless and spaceless, God is infinite; God is eternal. But God is eternally expressed; God is eternally manifested, and has been, ever since God has been God. That manifestation, that expression, is you, and it is I. Nothing can be added to God and nothing can be taken from God. God has been and is fully manifested from the beginning. Therefore, if you are the God-entity, in any form, the God-identity, or the God-individual, before Abraham was, you have had conscious identity. I have had conscious individual identity ever since God has. And that

[1]John 8:58.

is forever. By that same token, "I am with you alway, even unto the end of the world."[1] In other words, as long as God is God, God will individualize Itself, or individually express Itself, as individual being—spiritual being. Do you see how pointless it is to look at a human being and begin thinking about his age or his condition? That picture before the eyes is the illusion of human sense.

The fact that we have been drawn together from every part of the world, representing almost every religion, with varying degrees of education and from diverse backgrounds, is sufficient indication that somewhere on the path we have touched each other in consciousness. We have existed before this experience. How could we be of one mind, of one Spirit and consciousness, if somewhere, somehow, we had not touched each other in consciousness? Once you catch the realization of this truth of your immortal individuality, of the fact that you have existed, pre-existed, co-existed, since God began, and that you will individualize the life that God is unto eternity, you will begin to understand the spiritual universe and spiritual existence.

Then will come the realization of why we are on this spiritual path, why we have been drawn together. It cannot be for the purpose of developing a heart that beats a little more normally according to the world's standards, or that ten or a hundred dollars a week should be added to our income, or that we should find a more comfortable house in which to live. It surely was not to that end that we have come to this study, although the effect of this study will be better health, more happiness, a greater sense of peace within, probably a better home in which to live, and perhaps a greater sense of supply. These will be some of the effects of our study. But the real purpose is to awaken us to our true identity; to awaken us, so that when we are awakened, we shall see Him as He is, and be satisfied with His likeness. The "He" to whom we are to be awakened and which we are to recognize is our own spiritual identity as Christ—our identity as the Son of God, as the spiritual image and likeness of God.

[1]Matthew 28:19.

It is our individual being—our spiritual identity—to which we are to be awakened. That identity has existed and co-existed with God from the beginning. That individual identity will continue to be individual you and me until the end of the world, that is, until all mortal concepts disappear, and we realize the spiritual universe. That was the vision of John. That was the vision of Paul who wrote about the "house not made with hands, eternal in the heavens."[1] That spiritual identity is the *I* which has existed throughout all time and which will continue to exist for all time to come.

According to human values, we all appreciate motherhood, fatherhood, and parental and filial relationships, but we know from experience that they are not always as beautiful as they are sometimes pictured. For many years I, myself, was unable to discover any reason for my having been born. Others may not have had this experience, but at one period of my existence, I had to find some reason for living. Furthermore, as I looked about, I wondered why other men and women were living—working eight hours a day, nine, ten hours a day, with their only recompense a place to sleep, and ultimately, a hole to crawl into. It did not seem very purposeful or meaningful. Now I see what life can be when it is lifted above that mortal, human, finite, physical sense—when consciousness expands, and we catch the vision of each other as spiritual beings. We find a joy in human companionship hitherto unknown. That comes when we are seeing through spiritual light, not through the dark glass of humanhood. Because of this vision, I am more than ever convinced that spiritual friendship, spiritual companionship, would be a part of our existence even without the process of human birth. In fact, I know from the inner companionship I have experienced, that all who have existed as individuals—as God manifesting Itself as individual being—all of those still exist. They not only exist, but they commune with us; they tabernacle with us. We are not aware of this until we open the spiritual center of our being, and find them there; we are unaware of their existence, because they do not exist as mortals; they do not exist as

[1] II Corinthians 5:1.

human beings; they do not even exist as dead spirits, or the spirits of the dead. They exist, as I exist, as individual being, but as individual beings who have always been alive and have never died. On that higher plane of consciousness, you will never meet those who have lived and died; they have always been immortal. You find them in their immortality and not in the human sense of manhood or womanhood.

Healing work, which is the proof of our work and of the rightness of the message, becomes easier, less labored, and much more fruitful, as we perceive the spiritual nature of the *You* that you are and the *I* that I am, as we learn to drop this physical sense of existence. Now all this may sound abstract, or absolute, but please believe me, it is not. It is possible right here on the level where you are now, and where I am now; and it is brought into manifestation and expression in the degree that you and I realize that our function in this work is not merely to make a physical body more comfortable physically, or to make a material purse richer. As you rise above that stage of the work, you will no longer center your thought on the material plane of satisfaction—on the physical, mental, or even on the financial plane. Then you will begin to think of the spiritual significance of individual being and spiritual supply, and you will find an entirely new world. That new world will appear here as improved humanhood. It will appear as an improved body, or as an improved pocketbook; but it will not be an improved anything and you will know it. You will consider these outward effects of no importance, because you will know that they are just the translation of the divine law into human terms.

As you open your consciousness for the inflow, you will find that the Spirit will really go before you and do that for you which you had expected to do humanly. Ultimately, you will find that you rarely have much to do humanly—that always the Spirit goes before you to make the crooked places straight, to open and do those things that, heretofore, you have thought you had to do. Spirit is a reality. Spirit is a power. Heretofore, we have merely said so; but now we really have to draw It forth and watch It at work.

Spirit is God; Spirit is truth; Spirit is omnipresent, omniscient, omnipotent. Once we have the conscious feeling of the Presence, It lives our lives for us. But there must be the conscious communion. There must be the conscious oneness or conscious at-one-ment. There must be a conscious awareness of the Presence, and that all takes place through the opening of consciousness to Truth through meditation in one form or another.

No Predestination in God

Sometimes the question is asked: "Do you believe that each one of us must go through certain experiences during our lives, that certain pictures present themselves to us, or are destined for us, according to a foreordained pattern, even to the experience of our coming into some form of truth work at a particular time?"

No, I do not believe that there are any such patterns or pictures. God is Spirit, and God has no awareness of human pictures. It is an impossibility that God could believe that we have to be run over by an automobile, or that we must become ill with a certain disease. It is impossible to believe that God ordains that we should marry, be unhappy; or that we should work hard, faithfully, honestly, sincerely, accumulate some degree of financial competence, and then have a panic or a depression or something beyond our own control wipe it out for us. No, these things I do not believe, nor do I believe that God ordains that some children should come into the world healthy and wealthy, and that others should come into the world poverty stricken or deformed.

God is individual, spiritual consciousness. If we were consciously aware of that, then our experience would be God experiencing Itself as us, and our life would contain nothing but the harmony of God. The experience of the prodigal son is one to which I often refer. The son probably became tired of receiving all his good from the father, and wanted to go out and make a name for himself. That state of consciousness is our humanhood. Humanhood is the "prodigal son," wandering around in life, claiming to be Mary, Joe, or Joel. It sets up a separate entity and it creates for itself all of the experiences through which it goes. Yet, all the time it is really God made manifest. The proof of this is that everyone in the history of the world who has touched God consciousness has been freed of these mortal patterns—has been freed of sin, disease, lack, limitation. Life to such a person takes on an entirely different pattern— a pattern of freedom, wholeness, abundance, and happiness.

Some people, however, who have already touched God consciousness, have had other forms of suffering come upon them, perhaps because they later accepted a limited concept of life, and set out to reform the world. In so doing, they brought upon themselves persecution and crucifixion. If each one of us were to realize this God consciousness and, at the same time, set the other person free to realize this for himself as well, then the religious leaders of our world would not have had to go through such struggles. If I were to attempt to attract crowds to this message by preaching on the street corners, I might receive a very unpleasant reception, because I would be trying to bring Spirit to the human mind which is antagonistic to It.

On the other hand, if I abide in the center of my being, if I sit in my office or home and rest content in my conscious oneness with God; one here, another there, and two or three in another place are attracted to me; and just as a remnant of those who had not bowed their knees to Baal was saved out for Elijah, so do I find the remnant that my state of consciousness has drawn to me. Then there are no antagonisms and no arguments—only a state of receptivity.

I do not believe that human problems have anything to do with God, and for that reason they are not foreordained. They are only foreordained from the standpoint of humanhood. If we adopt stealing as our means of a livelihood, it is foreordained that we will end up in jail, if we live long enough. But that is a pattern that we have drawn, not one that God has drawn. There is a striking example of that in the man, Starr Daily. The foreordained climax to the pattern he had established was a twenty-year prison sentence; yet one touch of the Christ nullified the whole human pattern. Three years after the moment of his Christ realization, he was released on parole, even though a parole board stated that he could never be paroled. A human pattern is never spiritually ordained, nor is it ordained to be permanent, even humanly; it is merely a question of when and how soon the Christ comes.

The theme of this message is: *spiritual identity, spiritual activity, spiritual power*; their development within our own being; and the need for touching within ourselves that spiritual Center from which flow spiritual activity and spiritual power. Once that spiritual Center has been touched, and the power of Spirit has been released, It really lives Itself as our experience. What Paul says becomes literally true: "I live; yet not I, but Christ liveth in me";[1] or the Master, "I can of mine own self do nothing.[2] . . . My doctrine is not mine but his that sent me."[3] The essence of this message is that the Father is really living our life, doing all things, and being all.

Sincerity and Integrity Prerequisites for the Search for God

Spirituality, however, does not come forth in a day, in a week, or in a month. Yes, it is true that Saul of Tarsus became Paul in a blinding flash. But remember the number of years that Saul of Tarsus had been studying truth under the guidance of a spiritual teacher. That his spiritual guidance may or may not have been correct is not the significant factor. What is significant is that Saul was God-hungry, that Saul was so intent on God that he was willing to be a party to the persecution and murder of others for what he considered to be Truth. There was an inner devotion to Truth or God. So with us: what is important is the motive and the intent. If we persist in following a religious or metaphysical study for some material good that we are seeking, we shall never be a Paul; we

[1]Galatians 2:20.
[2]John 5:30.
[3]John 7:16.

shall never have the experience of the illumination. If, however, we are God-hungry, if we are intent on learning the true nature of Cause, rather than demonstrating effect, then it really makes no difference whether we pursue that path as a Roman Catholic, as a Hebrew, as a Protestant, or as a follower of some one of the numerous metaphysical movements: we will reach the goal—realization. Our search will carry us from one stage of consciousness to another; it may even take us from one church to another, or one teaching to another, but in the end it will carry us out of the human sense of church. Just think how wonderful it is that a man who was so intent on Judaism as Saul should have been the very one to destroy the belief that it was necessary to be a Jew before one could become a Christian. The light in his consciousness was so complete that Judaism faded out in his vision of Christianity.

If we could learn all the truth that is contained in all the scriptures of the world, it still might not lead us to the spiritual experience. But as long as we are on the path of seeking the Spirit, and the spiritual way of life, then the more we associate with those on the path, the better it will be. The more we can be together in the fellowship of the Spirit—whether it is in the form of attending lectures, classes, or group meetings—the more helpful it will be. Such fellowship leads to the unfolding of consciousness, unless somebody should attempt to crystallize these associations into an organization, so that the Spirit is lost in the outer form. It is unfortunate that it is necessary to have even as little organization as there is in The Infinite Way to keep the message printed, published, and recorded. That does require some organization, but I am sure it will never become a church organization with church memberships, and for this reason: I long with all the intensity of my being to see every individual free in Christ; I long to see every individual so at-one with God that we are only companions to each other on the way—helpers when one of us slips a little or needs encouragement.

Therefore, let us never indulge such human pastimes as judgment, criticism, or condemnation of each other, because each one of us is going to have to work out his own spiritual unfoldment in an individual way. The way that I work mine out may not appeal to all of you, but that is my individual demonstration, so let me have the freedom to see and do things in my own way. Each one of you in turn will do things with which some of the other students may not agree. Let each one have the privilege of working it out and even failing, if that is necessary. Failure may serve a very good purpose in revealing the incorrect things we may be doing. Instead of criticizing or judging or condemning, let us support each other in this activity. No one could be in this work with any motive but that of spiritual development. To do otherwise would be a violation of spiritual integrity. We cannot put on the Robe, and then violate its ethics or teachings or morality. Any such violation will prove to be a boomerang. Out in the world men can lie, cheat, steal, or defraud, and their evil deeds may not return to them for a long period of time; but it is not so with one who is on the spiritual path.

A person who has opened his consciousness to spiritual truth, pays a heavy penalty for any conscious error in which he indulges— even for the mistakes he makes. An honest mistake will bring a degree of suffering to him, since that mistake must be pointed out to him in order for him to change. But conscious error—ambition for place or position, greed for money, lusting after the flesh— indulged in while wearing this Robe carries with it a heavy price. Let us as individuals live up to our highest developed sense of spiritual right. Do not think for a minute that I claim that I am or that anybody I have ever known is fulfilling the fullness of the Christ. Our responsibility is to make the effort to live up to our highest developed sense of spiritual good. As long as we are doing that, we are on the right path. It is only when we come down from that level, and through some human means or some human desire, find our selves in conflict with the action of the Spirit that trouble descends upon us.

The Spirit is a freeing action, and It frees us from material concepts and material forms of existence; but this activity can be a terrifying thing when it strikes up against the opposite quality of spiritual dishonesty. I think that is why I use the term *spiritual integrity* so much. We can do many things humanly that may not seem right to the world; but when we are on the spiritual path, it is then necessary to live up to our highest unfoldment, our highest developed sense of spiritual good. Then we do not have to fear what mortal man can do to us; we do not have to fear the past, the present, or the future. Here, too, our history as human beings may not always conform to our spiritual heritage. Therefore, let us learn not to judge according to appearances. Let us not be too concerned about each other's human history. We come out of varying backgrounds of sin or purity, disease or health, and ignorance or wisdom. But though the sin be as scarlet, it will be white as snow once we touch the spiritual level of consciousness.

One of the great sins of organization is that often after it accepts an individual in Christ, it then proceeds to ferret out his past and sit in judgment upon him. Instead of working through a sense of forgiveness and understanding, it still applies the same code of human conduct or human punishment or human action as before. Even on this spiritual path, we make human mistakes. It has been done over and over again in the Protestant ministry, in the Catholic ministry, in the Hebrew ministry. And we all know that in the metaphysical ministry people well along the path have been subject to temptation and have fallen.

So let us not adopt the attitude of the world—criticism, judgment, or condemnation. Rather let us see if we cannot work together, and with our enlightenment lift each other up so as to make it impossible for any one to fall by the wayside again. In other words, even though there is a sense of humanness among us, let us not judge humanly. Let us not act as the human world acts. Let us not work from the standpoint of expulsion or ostracism. Let us rather take the attitude that we are all one; and, therefore, our purpose is upliftment, not punishment, or excommunication. This is a very important point. Remember this, because it is only that state of consciousness which will know how to forgive an enemy, how to forgive those who despitefully use us, how, in other words, to fulfill the Christian doctrine of "love one another."[1] Love not only your friends and your neighbors, but love those who persecute you and hate you. Love! Love! Love! Forgive! Forgive! Forgive! And then, finally, reach that state of consciousness in which you no longer take the mental sword of criticism, judgment, or condemnation. When that time comes, your consciousness will have become the light of the world, because in it there is neither love, hate, nor fear of error.

The Allness of God

The primary purpose of our work is to bring forth our true identity as Spirit, as God made manifest, as life, individually expressed in all of life's harmony and perfection. We, in our work, do not attempt just to turn sick people into well people, or poor people into rich people. Improving humanhood is not our main object. The fruitage of our work is improved health and supply, but the improvement of material conditions is not its prime object. These are only the "signs following." The primary object is to reveal God as individual being, to reveal that there are not God *and* man, but that there is only God, God appearing as individual you and individual me to reveal that "I and my Father are one."[1] There are not both a God *and* you, but since God is infinite, and God is all, then God must express Itself, manifest Itself, *as* you and *as* me.

In this oneness, there is no room for sin, disease, lack, or limita-

[1]John 10:30.

214

tion. There is no room for war or for unfair competition. There is no room for the evils of capitalism or the evils of communism. There is only room for the understanding of true being—the understanding of what it means to be God manifested individually, in all of God's glory. You will remember the prayer of the Master: "Father, glorify me with thine own self, with the glory which I had with thee."[1] Think what it would mean if we could stand forth here and now in all of God's glory. Think how impossible it would be to lack anything if we were showing forth the allness of God, if we were showing forth the truth of that statement, "Son ... all that I have is thine."[2] According to Scripture, it is true that all that the Father hath is thine and mine. Once you and I begin to show forth that allness of God, how impossible it would be for any form of envy, jealousy, malice, or strife to enter into our daily experience. And that is the object of this work. The Infinite Way is not merely for the purpose of setting up better human beings, but to reveal the allness of God as individual you and me.

In all religions there are promises of Imnipresence. We have to go one step further; we have to *demonstrate* Omnipresence. To us the presence of God must become a living reality; God must become as real to you and to me as we are real to each other. It must ultimately be as possible for you to tune in to God as for you to tune in to your practitioner on the telephone. God, through this study, through meditation, and through inspiration, must become, not a word that we talk about, not a being to whom we pray, but an actual companion on our pathway, through life.

The object of this work is to make God real—to make God as real to you and to me as he was to Abraham, Jacob, Moses, Elisha, Elijah, Jesus, John, Paul, or Peter. God becomes an absolute living reality—a presence, a power, a companion, a healer, a supplier. We shall not find God in books and we shall not find God in churches. Books and churches are merely the avenues which enable us to open our consciousness to the inflow. God ultimately will be

[1]John 17:5.
[2]Luke 15:31.

revealed where Jesus said It would be revealed—within: "The kingdom of God is within you[1] ... I can of mine own self do nothing[2] ... the Father that dwelleth in me, he doeth the works."[3] Where is the Father? Within me. Of course, that does not mean inside this body. God is not in our physical body, but God is within us in the sense that God is our very own being. God is not separate or apart from you or me. In this case, the word "within" does not actually mean within some part of the body such as the brain or heart: it means that God is not something outside or separate or apart from our own being. God is not separate or apart from our consciousness. And before long we shall see very clearly God *is* our consciousness.

Man is Not a Reflection

Most metaphysical teachings would call us "man." Their synonyms for the word "man" include idea, image, likeness, reflection, expression. Nearly all of them teach that you are an idea of God, but The Infinite Way teaching does not agree with that concept. This teaching stands on the fullness of the Master's unfoldment, on the fullness of his realization that in his humanhood, he, of himself, could do nothing:

> I am the way, the truth, and the life.[4]
> I can of mine own self do nothing.[5]
> The Father that dwelleth in me, he doeth the works.[6]
> Have I been so long time with you, and yet hast thou not known me, Philip?[7]
> I and my Father are one.[8]

[1]Luke 17:21.
[2]John 5:30.
[3]John 14:10.
[4]John 14:6.
[5]John 5:30.
[6]John 14:10.
[7]John 14:9.
[8]John 10:30.

Did you ever see one? Hold up one of your fingers—just one finger and not two. Think of that one finger as the symbol of the oneness expressed by the "I and my Father."

Always remember: I and the Father are one. Unless you can agree with that teaching of oneness, understand it, and feel the rightness of it, you will never be able to take the next step and realize: All that God is, I am; all that the Father hath is mine. Now hold up two of your fingers and notice that no matter how close together you can bring them, you do not have one, or oneness. You still have two-ness. As long as you have two, you will be striving to bring them together, or expecting one of them to pray to the other, or to have one of them worthy of the other. But if you can agree that I and the Father are one, as much as one finger is one, then you will find that all that the Father is, I am, and all that the Father hath is mine; you will understand that when you pray, believing that you already have, you do already have. Two fingers represent God *and* you. One finger is our symbol—God manifest *as you*. It is the Word made flesh—not the Word *and* flesh, but the Word *made* flesh.

The basis of our work is oneness—omnipresence. It is not one thing present together with another thing. It is omnipresence—"I and my Father are one." In this oneness is your completeness. In this oneness, God is made manifest as individual you and me in all of Its glory. "Glorify thou me with thy glory." The first important concept that must be changed in coming from any metaphysical teaching to The Infinite Way is that you are *not* an idea; you are *not* a reflection. Look at a reflection of yourself on the wall and ask yourself how you would like to be that reflection.

We are not reflections; we are not ideas; you and I are life eternal. If we were other than life eternal, there would be a law, a God, a something, acting upon us, whereas: I am the way, I am the law. I was given dominion over the things of the sea, over the things of the earth, over the things of the air, and over the things of the sky. In that oneness is dominion—the dominion of God made manifest as individual you and me. You should study this very carefully, turning to the Father within, and praying for light and guidance on this point, because on this revelation rests the entire demonstration of harmony.

The moment you believe that there is some other power—some power outside of yourself, separate from yourself—that can act upon you, even if you believe it is a good power, you are exposing yourself to the possibility of its opposite, an evil power. There is no power acting upon you. Life, God, or Soul is the *only power;* God, Soul, Spirit, and Truth are the reality of your being. If there is only one Life, and that Life is your life, then God is your life. If there is only one Mind, then God is your mind. God is your Soul. God is your Spirit. We are told that even "your body is the temple of the Holy Ghost."[1] What else is there to you but life, mind, Soul, Spirit, and body? And all this is God—God infinitely manifested in all Its glory as you and as me.

The history of the world, and surely the history of the religious world, contradicts any such teaching. But history has very little proof of harmony to offer us. We have only to look at the history of the world to find a continuous record of the belief that we are something separate and apart from God. On every side there are wars and other chaotic conditions. if there is to be any hope for us as individuals, it will have to be found in the message and the mission of the Master; and that message and that mission without misinterpretation. The Word itself must suffice. We must accept as our principle the words of the Master, not as a teaching applying to an individual of two thousand years ago, but as a principle of life which we can follow. On that point of oneness, of conscious oneness with God, rests the foundation of all else that is to come.

The Human Mind Is an Avenue of Awareness

A second important point in the message of The Infinite Way is also in disagreement with most of the teaching of the metaphysical

[1] Corinthians 6:19.

world: The human mind is not a power; human thought is not a power; even good human thought is not a power. Those who have attempted to heal with good human thought will testify to the fact that it is not a very great healing agency. If we are dependent on the human thought of a practitioner, we are in a very precarious situation. You know that many practitioners, at some time or other, prove to be very human. If that should happen to be the case when you need help, how would you get your help? If the practitioner happened to be asleep when the call came, what hope would there be for the patient? No, human thought is not a power. Human thought cannot make two times two become four. The principle of mathematics establishes that fact. Human thought cannot violate the principle of mathematics by making two times two become five. God's thoughts are not your thoughts, and your thoughts are not God's thoughts. "Which of you by taking thought can add one cubit unto his stature?"[1]

If in treatment we use the human mind to bring about a healthy heart, liver, or lung, we may possibly achieve our objective. But tomorrow is another day, and why should not one or another of these organs become sick tomorrow, even though it has been restored to health today? Next month is another month, next year another year, and before we realize it, the years have added up to three score and ten. After that, of course, there is no use praying for a good heart or liver or lung; it is too late. Even scripture tells us that. It has been said that the study of metaphysics prevents untimely death, but what is a timely death? If you believe in the timeliness of death, can you pray for a good heart after seventy, eighty, or whatever your conception of a proper life span is? No, unless we actually take the Master at his word and understand that the life which is God is our individual life, then we shall be praying each month, or each year, for a renewed heart, lung, liver, blood vessel, or for a renewed something else.

There is only one way to avoid the necessity of repeating

[1]Matthew 6:27.

demonstrations year after year, and that is to come back, first, to the basis of this work: "I and my Father are one";[1] and, therefore, all that the Father is I am, and all that the Father hath is mine. We must really trust and rely on the truth, and gain such a conscious awareness of it, that it becomes so much a part of our being that it is second nature to us. Then we no longer have to make demonstrations week in and week out, month in and month out. Secondly, and a major point, we must catch the vision that the human mind is not a power—either for good or for evil. If we understand that it is not a power for evil, we shall never fear it; we shall never fear malpractice; we shall never fear the individual or collective thoughts or beliefs of the world.

There is only one reason why anyone of us has ever experienced sin, disease, death, lack, or limitation and that is universal mortal, or human belief. There is a universal belief, a human belief, that we can live only three score years and ten, and according to medical law and insurance statistics this is correct, because the average life span today is approximately only seventy or seventy-five years. There is a universal belief in catching cold from sitting in drafts. There is a universal belief in infection and contagion from certain germs. There is a universal belief in vitamins and calories. There is a universal belief in anything and everything under the sun, except the power and presence of God. That is not so universal. There are only a few of us trying to maintain our firm faith in and reliance upon that truth.

If we understand that the human mind is an avenue of awareness, we will not make the mistake of trying to do away with the human mind; but we shall be grateful that we have it to use as an avenue of awareness. Through this mind and its thoughts, we can become aware of the truth of being; we can become aware of the beauties and bounties of the world. It is through thought that we become aware of each other. Through thought, God, Truth, imparts Itself to me and to you. Through thought, we become receptive to the divine ideas, the spiritual ideas of life. Therefore, we are not trying to negate or eliminate either thought or the human mind, but rather are we going to utilize it as one of those avenues given to us for the harmonious expression of daily experience. However, we are not going to use that mind as a power; we are not going to use that mind to demonstrate health or wealth or opportunity: We are merely going to use that mind to become aware of the health and the wealth that already exist as the natural state of our being. This teaching cannot be built on the old metaphysics, because no amount of human thought-taking is going to bring about health or wealth. Only God can do that, and God *is* the very life of our being.

Difference Between Prayer and Treatment

We shall go on now to another point in which there is a lack of agreement—perhaps not disagreement, but in which there is a difference in language and a difference in application. In The Infinite Way, prayer and treatment are not the same thing. Treatment is not a synonym for prayer; prayer is not a synonym for treatment. In this teaching, treatment is the truth that you and I know, the truth that we think, declare, or affirm in contradistinction to the error that is appearing. In other words, when I say that God is the law and the reality of my being, that God is my life, my Soul; when I say that God, the life which is God, is the eternality and immortality of my being; when I say that Christ is the law unto my being, and there is not a material law to act upon me; when I declare or affirm my oneness with God; when I declare or affirm the nothingness, the nonreality, of any form of error, that is treatment. In some metaphysical teachings, this would be considered prayer, but not in our work.

In The Infinite Way, affirmations and denials have not been entirely eliminated. We do not do away completely with affirmations and denials, but we do not think of them as prayer; they are treatment, a statement or restatement of truth within our own thought. The purpose of the treatment is to remind ourselves of the truth of being, thereby lifting ourselves to that place where prayer is possible.

Prayer is the word of God which comes to us. Prayer is not something we do. Prayer is not a voicing of anything for God to hear. Prayer is not a petition nor is it an affirmation. Prayer is really the word of God coming to us. It is the "Peace, be still,"[1] that is voiced within our consciousness. It is an assurance that comes to us within, which says: "Be still, and know that I am God. I am on the field. Stand still and see the salvation of the Lord." When a practitioner or a teacher says to you, "Stand still and see the salvation of the Lord." When a practitioner or a teacher says to you, "Stand still, and see the salvation of the Lord," that is treatment, not prayer. You are being reminded of some truth, the purpose of which is to bring about a certain stillness in your thought, a certain quietness, and an ability to be receptive, so that you may hear within you a voice saying, "This is the way, walk ye in it."[2]

But when you hear this voice within your own being—and when I say hear I do not necessarily mean audibly hear; I mean hear in the sense of becoming aware of, sensing, feeling, or becoming conscious of—that is the Word. If you become aware of something stirring within you, if you become aware of a sense of peace descending upon you, that is prayer; that is the Word coming to your consciousness. That is communion. Prayer, or communion, is the relationship existing between God, the Father, and God, the Son. It is the relationship between the universal infinite Being and you. It is infinite, yet individualized in expression. This is the relationship which makes it possible for you to hear and receive divine guidance, divine healing, divine direction, divine protection, or whatever it is that is necessary in your experience.

I know from my own experience that healing takes place for my patient when something within me says, "All is well"; or "I am on the field"; or "Do not worry; I am there, too." To the Master it

[1]Mark 4:39.
[2]Isiah 30:21.

came as: "I can of mine own self do nothing."[1] In other words, even though the Father and I are one, this part of me that appears to the world as a human being is not really the presence or power of God. The presence and power of God is that which is invisible to your eyes, but is very, very visible and audible to your spiritual senses. When I am still, when I am quiet, when I am receptive, this assurance comes to me. Sometimes it comes in words, sometimes in quotations, sometimes in original thoughts, sometimes just in a feeling of well-being; and then I know that all is well with those who have called on me for help. Emerson called it the "Oversoul." It is really Omnipresence—the very infinite presence and power of God, consciously realized.

God is omnipresent; God is always present. But it is our conscious realization of this that does the work. It is not simply the fact that God is omnipresent. God is omnipresent on every battlefield in the world, right where men are being killed. That God is omnipresent, that God was in reality on the battlefield, did not help those needing help. No, it takes conscious realization of the presence of God in order to make God available in whatever need there may be. Never think for a minute that there is any place in the world that is not filled with the presence of God; but never think for a moment that that is going to be of much help to you, except in proportion to your conscious realization of that truth. It is conscious realization that is prayer. Praying and repeating the 23rd Psalm or the 91st Psalm, or voicing all the metaphysical truths you know, such as "I am rich, and I know it," or "I am well, and I know it," will not do the work. Some of you know what could be happening to you at the very moment you are making these statements. Repeating words does not do the work. It may lift your thought to that place where the work can be done—to that place where you have a conscious realization of the presence of God.

Right here is a point of demarcation between this and much of

[1] John 5:30.

the metaphysical work in the world. The Infinite Way is an unfoldment which says that you and I, as well as Jesus, Moses, and Elijah, must have a conscious realization of the presence of God. It is
not going to do us any good to walk around saying, "God is love,
and God is present; God is love, and God is present." Unless, and
until, we actually feel the presence of God, unless we can lift ourselves to a state of consciousness in which God becomes tangible
and visible and evident in our own experience, it is all in the realm
of treatment and not prayer.

Treatment is correct in its place, and all of you who are familiar
with my writings know that a considerable amount of space is given
to the subject of treatment. I am very thorough in the teaching of
treatment; because I believe that at certain stages of our experience,
it is not only necessary to treat, but that treatment forms the very
foundation of our understanding of truth. At least, it is the letter
of truth, upon which we may build the structure of spiritual understanding.

To know the correct letter of truth is a good foundation for the
revelation, unfoldment, and spiritual discernment of truth, the spiritual consciousness of truth. Naturally, after a while you will have
no more need for treatment than you have use for stating or
repeating the multiplication table. When you have occasion to
know the product of 12 times 12, 144 comes to thought immediately without conscious effort.

No matter how much you learn of treatment in any metaphysical work, no matter how perfect you become in stating the truth as
it is found in The Infinite Way writings, please do not have too
much faith in it, or you may stumble and fall. It is not the statement of truth that does the work; it is the inner realization of truth.
It is not how much you can declare God, affirm God, or petition
God. it is not how many statements of truth you know. On the
contrary, it is much better for a student to use two or three statements as reminders of truth; meditate upon them; ponder them;
and then rest, and let God do the work. Let spiritual consciousness
unfold.

All this repeating of statements of truth is self-hypnosis—auto-suggestion. No one ever has to use force or power in this work. Nothing is more true than that it is "not by might, nor by power, but by my spirit, saith the Lord of hosts"[1]—not by physical might, and not by mental power, but by *My* Spirit.

Regardless of how much you may declare that I and the Father are one, it does not have any real power unless you know what the Father is, and unless you know who *I am.* Two things must be known: Who am I? and, What is God? Ultimately, in the end, we will know that they are one. But until we have reached that point, let us not accept blindly some statement about God or about ourselves.

That word *I* contains the entire secret of Hebrew Scripture. That word *I* contains the entire secret of the ancient Hindu Scripture. That word *I* contains the secret of the Master's revelation. Only through this understanding of the word *I*, can you understand that "I and my Father are one," or "I am the the way, the truth, and the life." And without that understanding, what good would any treatment be? What good would any treatment be that did not embrace within itself the wisdom of truth! It is assumed that a treatment is the embodiment of truth, or expression of truth. Unless we know the truth about the *I*, unless we know the truth about the Father, unless we know the truth about body, a treatment is not really worth the time it takes to give it. Even a mental treatment, even a statement of truth, must be literally true to be even a little bit effective; and, in order to lead to the consciousness of truth, a treatment must be a declaration of truth.

The Deep Things of God Revealed Through Meditation

We now come to the subject of meditation. If you follow along the path of The Infinite Way, you will learn a great deal about meditation and its practice. Without it you are merely living as a

[1]Zechariah 4:6.

human being, and as such you are subject to all of the conditions of humanhood, just as is every other human being in the world. When, however, you develop the ability to meditate, to open your consciousness to the inflow of the Spirit, then you have the conscious awareness of the presence of Spirit, of God, of Life, Truth, and Love, with you from morning until night, and from night until morning. it is this *conscious awareness* that is your safety and your security.

God is infinite good. But this good is experienced only through the conscious recognition, or conscious awareness, or the presence and power of God. Therefore, as we follow the instruction in the chapter on "Meditation" in *The Infinite Way*, we shall find that from waking in the morning until retiring at night, never for a moment do we leave God out of our consciousness. We make God the very center of our consciousness, the very activity of our consciousness. When we do that, something happens to most of us. Very few of us who have been in this work any length of time are permitted to sleep a whole night through. Somehow we are awakened with another reminder of God's presence and power; and it is that reminder in the middle of the night that often proves a benediction to our friends and family and patients, since in that stillness and quietness of the night it is easier to receive this conscious awareness of divine Presence and divine Power. Naturally, that blesses all those who are a part of our consciousness.

As we fill our thought, our consciousness, with this realization of God, an extraordinary thing happens to us. A greater sense of quietness descends upon us, a greater sense of peace. With the realization of God's presence we have a confidence that all is well, and we know why. We cannot escape from God once we have made God the reality of our being. That makes it possible for the deeper meditation. It is in this deeper meditation that we really learn the deep things of God. There are deep things of God to be known, and these deep things of God are shown forth in our experience. For example, we were not born to be only business men and housewives. We were all born for a spiritual purpose—to perform a spiritual function, to be some part of God's plan. In the degree, however, that we are attached to the human world, we are not about our Father's business. And that is one of the reasons we are in this work—to get back to the Father's house. Instead of living this prodigal experience, instead of earning our living by the sweat of our brow, one of these days we shall return to the Father's house and the Father consciousness, and there find a jeweled ring and a purple robe—find that we have nothing to do but bask in the Father's love.

From

MAN WAS NOT BORN TO CRY

Spiritual Dominion

Truth is within ourselves.
There is an inmost center in us all,
Where the Truth abides in fulness; and to know
Rather consists in opening out a way
Whence the imprisoned splendour may escape
Than in effecting entry for a light supposed to be without.
                                        —Robert Browning

Practically all human experience testifies to the very opposite of
Robert Browning's words. In a human sense, forces outside our
own being are continually acting upon us. We are affected by
weather, climate, and food; by racial, religious, and nationalistic
beliefs; and by national and international economic conditions. We
are acted upon by germs; we are acted upon by the belief of age,
heredity, environment, and by education or the lack of it.

Because all these things are conditions or circumstances over which we apparently have no control, it is easy to blame all our ills and troubles on someone or something else. And oftentimes, if there is no person or thing on which to blame the calamities befalling us, the superstitious may resort to astrology, to looking up to the stars in an attempt to determine in what position they were on the date on which they were born, and then reach the conclusion that their problems can be laid at the door of the stars; or if they are wont to delve into the occult, they may believe that someone who has passed on has put a curse upon them.

To what ridiculous ends we go in an effort to find an alibi for our personal failures, and what weak excuses we make to ourselves and to others in order to avoid personal responsibility! As a matter of fact, in the human picture, there is only one reason for our ills, misfortunes, and discords, and that is ignorance—*spiritual ignorance*. We have never been taught the truth and, being in ignorance of the truth, we have had nothing with which to meet the vicissitudes of life; therefore we have become victims of persons and circumstances.

The entire human race is in the same situation. People throughout the world may really believe that they are being truthful when they claim that they are not responsible for their troubles, but that is because they have never been taught that they do not have to be victims of forces external to themselves. That is a truth which has never been taught to mankind. It is only those who have been fortunate enough to come in contact with a mystic or with mystical teaching, and who have been taught the truth of being, who know that the power to control their destiny lies within themselves, and that no person, no group of persons, no nation, conditions, or circumstances can operate to harm, destroy, or to prevent the truth from being manifested.

Taking the Journey Back to the Father's House

The question naturally arises: Where is that truth to be found on earth? And it must be admitted that it can be found in very, very few places. If this truth be so hard to find, we must conclude that it is only those who through some inner Grace are led to spiritual teaching who become immune to the things of this world. Actually, then, no one in the human picture is to blame for his troubles so long as he is ignorant of the truth of Being. After he learns the truth of Being, however, he can no longer put the blame for his problems on someone else in the past, the present, or at any time.

The truth of Being is that God created all that was made and all that God made is good. He made man in His own image and likeness and gave him dominion over everything on the earth, in the sky above, and the sea below. Empowered with this spiritual dominion, man, the image and likeness of God, can never claim that his troubles come from anyone or any condition because he himself has been given dominion.

But the human race lost that dominion and sank to the state of the Prodigal Son who wasted his God-given heritage and ended up with the swine. The human race became enslaved, engulfed by war, depression, poverty, disease, and sin, all because of surrendering its dominion through ignorance of its true identity.

All this is the prodigal state which continues to be a part of the human experience until the individual, like the Prodigal Son in Scripture, begins to wonder, "Is this the way life is meant to be? Why, even the servants in my Father's house are better off than I am." Then he begins to work his way back to the Father's house and, as he approaches, he is robed with the cloak of divine Grace and given the ring of divine authority. Once again he finds himself in possession of the dominion bestowed on him at birth.

So when a person discovers a spiritual teaching that puts him on the spiritual path, it will ultimately bring him back to the truth that dominion is within himself. Immediately, then, he loses the fear of "man, whose breath is in his nostrils."[1] He begins to realize:

> *I shall not fear any conditions existing in the world, for I and the Father are one, and that Father is greater than he that is in the world. The Father within me doeth the works.*

[1] Isaiah 2:22.

When a person perceives this truth, he has already begun the long journey back to the Father's house where he will once again become conscious of his God-given dominion. Then he will not fear people—individually or collectively—or conditions or circumstances, for he knows that he is master of these by right of his God-given dominion.

The Power Within

The basis of all mystical teaching is: "I and my Father are one.[2] ... Son, thou art ever with me, and all that I have is thine."[3] To take these passages into consciousness and abide with them, living with them day after day, restores to an individual the awareness that the grace of God has been bestowed upon him and that, because of that Grace, he has dominion. The moment the student ponders the idea, "*I* have dominion," the word *I* begins to work in his consciousness, and then he remembers: "I will never leave thee nor forsake thee.[4] ... Lo, I am with you always, even unto the end of the world.[5] ... If I make my bed in hell, behold, thou art there.[6] ... Though I walk through the valley of the shadow of death, I will fear no evil: for thou art with me."[7]

So the student begins to realize the nature of that word *I*:

I *in the midst of me is mighty.* "I am the way, the truth, and the life.[8] ... I am the bread of life.[9] ... I am the resurrection and the life."[10] *This* I *within me, this* I, *this Truth, this grace of God, this son of God, this oneness with God—this is my bread and my wine and my water, and therefore I understand what the Master meant when he*

[2]John 10:30.
[3]Luke 15:31.
[4]Hebrews 13:5.
[5]Matthew 28:20.
[6]Psalm 139:8.
[7]Psalm 23:4.
[8]John 14:6.
[9]John 6:35.
[10]John 11:25.

said: "*Take no thought for your life, what ye shall eat, or what ye shall drink; nor yet for your body, what ye shall put on.*"[11]

What the Master really was saying is: "do not pray for supply: I am the bread; I am the wine; I am the water. Do not take thought for anything concerning your human life, for I am the substance of it and the activity of it. Dwell only in Me, in the realization that I abide in you, that I really am you. I constitute your being—I. I in the midst of you is your Grace, the grace of God unto you."

I need not look to "man, whose breath is in his nostrils"[12] for anything; I need not fear what mortal man can do to me. I need not plot and plan and plunder, for this I that I am, this divine Presence, this He that is within me, this It goes before me to make the crooked places straight. It prepares a place for me; It walks beside me; It walks behind me as a rear guard; It goes with me whithersoever I go.

"He that abideth in me, and I in him, the same bringeth forth much fruit."[13] Does the Master say that this has to be only in time of prosperity or in peacetime, or does he say plainly and unequivocally: "He that abideth in me, and I in him, the same bringeth forth much fruit"? Wherever we are, whether it is in heaven or hell or in the valley of the shadow of death, wherever it is and whenever it is: "*I* will never leave you, nor forsake you. When you go through the waters or through the flames, you will not drown, nor will the flames kindle upon you, for *I* am with you." This divine Power which is God in action—the son of God in us, the God-Being, the divine Presence within all of us, the *He* within us—is greater than any circumstance or condition of the outer world.

So when a Pilate of any name or nature says to us, "I can crucify you," quick as a flash our replay should be, "'Thou couldest have no power at all against me, except it were given thee from above.'[14] There is no power outside of me that can act upon me.

[11]Matthew 6:25.
[12]Isaiah 2:22.
[13]John 15:5.
[14]John 19:11.

All power is within me acting upon this world. This power within me can still the storm, and can prevent any enemy from touching me because it reveals that there is no power and no enemy without. *All* power is given unto me from on High."

Deny Thyself

The spiritually awakened person realizes that God's grace is his sufficiency in all things and for all things: food, clothing, health, harmony, protection, safety, security, peace, companionship, and home. Such an enlightened person no longer looks to man for supply, for companionship, or for home, but is willing to share the supply, companionship, and home he has. He does not look to anyone or believe that it is his right to receive these from anyone, but having returned now to the Father-consciousness and become "dead" to himself, "dead" to personal self, personality, and personal possessions, he comes to the realization that "the earth is the Lord's, and the fulness thereof,"[15] and that all that the Father has is his. Therefore, instead of seeking things or persons, he now seeks to share and to give. It is an *outflow* rather than a seeking for an *inflow*. He is now living in this truth:

> *Truth does not come to me: it is within me. Supply, infinite supply, God-supply, is within me. It does not come to me: it flows out from me. The companionship of God is within me—it does not come to me—and all I seek is to share that companionship which God has given me.*

A dry seed of itself is nothing and never can be anything in its seed state. Only when it gives itself up, surrenders itself, and permits itself to be broken open by the natural elements, does the seed change its form and eventually become a whole tree full of fruit. So it is that we—insignificant you and I, who of ourselves are really nothing—suddenly become the source through which flows infi-

[15]Psalm 24:1.

nite wisdom, love, companionship, supply, forgiveness, and infinite good in every form.

Jesus was quick to admit that of his own self he was nothing, but we all know what has gone out through him to this world because of that very denial of self and the acknowledgment that it was the Spirit of the Father that did the work. It is much the same with us because as long as we insist on living to ourselves, trying to be something and claiming something, we will be just a seed. How different life becomes for us when we are willing to deny ourselves and admit that of ourselves we are nothing and can do nothing, but that through the Christ we can do all things!

Think what Saul of Tarsus was—less than nothing. Then think what St. Paul was, and you will see how a little nothing of a Saul became the great light Paul. Think how unimportant Jesus must have been as a Hebrew rabbi; then recall how great he became as the founder of Christianity. As a rabbi with an established position in the world, he might have been tempted to look upon himself as something. It was only when he perceived that he was nothing that he became all.

One of the first realizations that comes to every person who has a spiritual experience is his unimportance as a person. How small a part an individual can play in the world's history by means of his own human capacity! But suddenly in that nothingness and seemingly from nowhere, the light dawns, and something begins to flow out from within him to the whole world! When that happens, a Gautama becomes the Buddha, a Jesus becomes the Christ, a Saul becomes Paul, a John becomes the Revelator. A shoemaker, Jacob Boehme, uneducated, a nobody, becomes the father of a long line of mystics. From a shoemaker to a mystic! Brother Lawrence who wrote that masterpiece *Practicing the Presence of God*—Brother Lawrence, a nothing, a nobody, a monk in a monastery, cooking for other monks—has lived in history for hundreds of years. Walt Whitman, a little insignificant printer in a print shop, is one of the half dozen people of his generation who has survived in the minds of men and been accepted throughout the world as a great mystic.

The very moment that the Spirit of the Lord God touches an individual, he becomes the son of God. Paul says: "They that are in the flesh cannot please God. . . . but as many as are led by the Spirit of God, they are the sons of God.[16] . . . Therefore, if any man be in Christ, he is a new creature: old things are passed away; beyond, all things are become new."[17] Then he becomes the son of God; he becomes less than he was of himself; and then this Light goes before him and It either gives to the world some new religious teaching or some new way of practicing an old religious teaching, or It produces something new or greater in music, art, or literature. But in one way or another, it is always the power of the Presence that does it.

Practice and Not Conversation

To help us learn how to become the sons of God and to experience the flow of this Power, we should begin to live and apply the promises of Scripture until they become flesh of our flesh, blood of our blood, bone of our bone, until they become so much a part of us that we become the Truth. Truth Itself dwells in us, feeding us and all those who come to us. Then we no longer blame anyone or anything; we no longer criticize, judge, or condemn anyone, any group, any nationality, or any race or religion, but we accept the responsibility which comes through knowing that "I and my Father are one."[18] That all that the Father has is ours, and that He that is within us is greater than he that is in the world. Once that is acknowledged within us, we then have to begin to *live* and to *practice* it.

The kingdom of God is within me. Through the grace of God, I can feed multitudes, I can share supply, companionship, friendship, service—all good. From the Infinity which is my being, I can begin to

[16]Romans 8:8, 14.
[17]II Corinthians 5:17.
[18]John 10:30.

pour out, rather than to expect someone or something in the external to provide for my needs.

Every day we must practice letting Infinity flow out from us, even though it be giving only a penny or a bit of service here or there, or sharing a few moments of companionship. If, for any reason, there are those who are unable to do that, they can begin to share forgiveness. They can look out at the ever present world of enemies—personal, national, racial—and begin to forgive them, praying that God's mercy open their consciousness. They can begin to pray, not so much for their friends and relatives, but for the sick and the sinning of the world, for those who are downtrodden, dejected, and rejected.

One reaction to such a program may be, "Oh, but I'm further down in the scale than are these people for whom I am supposed to pray." In this realization, we forget that: we give what we have to give, and if we have nothing to give but prayer, then we pray. If we have nothing to give but forgiveness, we give forgiveness. If we have nothing to give but service or dedication, we give it—but we *give!*

This is a practice. This is not conversation; this is not reading a book and exclaiming, "How lovely!" This is taking it out of the book and putting it into practice. In other words, it is acknowledging that Infinity dwells within, and if we have only one dollar's worth of Infinity at this minute, let us give ten cent's worth of it away. It makes no difference how little we may have at the moment. What counts is that we make the acknowledgement that Infinity is the measure of our being and act as though that were true, even though we act only with pennies, or if we act only with forgiveness or prayers or service.

The way of the spiritual life was presented to the world by the Master, and that is why he is called the Way-shower: "I came down from heaven, not to do mine own will, but the will of him that sent me."[19] He practiced doing the will of the Father by healing and

[19]John 6:38.

feeding the multitudes, forgiving sin, praying for the enemy, and by teaching the lessons which he had learned of God. If he is the Way-shower, then we have to follow the way he showed us, and that way is the way of acknowledging that while we of our own selves are nothing, all that the Father has is ours, and we can begin to share that Allness.

The World Loses its Hold on Us

It will not take too long a period of this kind of practice before things begin to come into our experience which prove to us that we have regained some measure of dominion, that now the world is not doing to us quite the same things it formerly did, and certainly not doing them to us in quite so hard a way. Eventually, we realize, "The world is 'dead' to me; it can do nothing to me or for me. 'My kingdom is not of this world.'[20] Therefore, it has nothing good to give me, and there is nothing evil that it can do to me. This world has nothing for me, for my kingdom is a spiritual kingdom, and I receive my good from the spiritual Source."

Too many truth-students believe that their study should bring them more material good, so they continue to dwell in "this world," only now they are dwelling in the good aspects of it instead of the bad. But they have not yet reached the Kingdom, and they never will reach the Kingdom until they are "dead" and this world, or as the Master phrased it, until they have "overcome this world."

There may be some truth-students who are not ready to go so far on the spiritual path as to be willing to give up the good things of this world, or even to acknowledge that they should not be seeking health, happiness, and abundance through the Spirit. Interestingly enough, however, being in the world but not of it does not mean asceticism: it does not involve sackcloth and ashes; it does not involve living in poverty or in hovels—not at all.

We can be in this world and use all of its good, and yet not be dependent on it, or even desire it, but as it takes place in our expe-

[20]John 18:36.

rience stand by watching and let it be of use and help to us. In other words, there is nothing of good that this world can do for us, and there is nothing of evil that it can do because although we are in this world, we are not of it.

As we come to that place in consciousness where we are not trying to use God to attain some form of human good, but where we accept the Master's revelation that we are to seek only the kingdom of God, we shall then find that the good things of the earth are added to us, and they do play a part in our experience.

Dwelling in the Kingdom

The real beginning is made when we can accept the revelation that the kingdom of God is within us, when we begin to realize that his divine Grace which is the presence and power of God in us can, does, and will supply us with everything necessary to our unfoldment, and when we come to that place where we no longer not only do not blame anyone for our troubles, but no longer dwell on them.

When this truth has been realized in some measure, we take the second step which is one of sharing. We no longer look for companionship, but rather give companionship; we no longer seek supply, but share supply; we no longer seek to gain, but see, only to be that instrument through which God's grace flows in the world.

Ultimately, we come to the experience described by Paul: "I live; yet not I, but Christ liveth in me."[21] It is then that the student touches one of the very high rungs of the ladder of the spiritual life. Without effort, without labor, and without toil and sweat, divine inspiration is always at work within, performing that which is given him to do, and he can, therefore, do it without strife, without struggle, and without even a fear of failure because even though he may seem to be doing it, it is not really he that is performing it but the *He* that is within him, and he himself is but the instrument through which it is being performed.

[21]Galatians 2:20.

It makes no difference whether his work is giving forth a truth-message or being the instrument for healing, or whether it is in music, art, literature, bridge building, or newspaper publishing. It makes no difference what the work is: there is this spiritual intuition at work within one to perform it, to provide the inspiration, the wisdom, the knowledge, and the power, even to draw unto one the very capital that may be needed for the particular enterprise. After realizing that the Presence within is the power unto all things, one finds that everything comes by the grace of God.

Actually, the teaching of Jesus is a teaching of individual responsibility. In other words, our daily outer experience—success or failure—is the effect or result of the activity of our own consciousness. Therefore, the degree in which we are willing to abide in the Word and let the Word abide in us is the degree of harmony on the outer plane, and so if we decide to set aside a half-hour a day for truth, we can count upon one forty-eighth of a day of perfect harmony. And if we decide that one hour is the measure of truth we will take in, we can expect one twenty-fourth of a day of peace, joy, and love.

When we come to the place of praying without ceasing, living in the World, letting the Word abide in us, dwelling in the secret place of the most High, living and moving and having our being in the consciousness of truth, we can look forward, then, to about twenty-three twenty-fourths of a day of harmony. There is always a little bit left for the future—we do not ever quite attain complete fulfillment. Jesus attained his fulfillment only after the Resurrection, and we, too, may first have to be entombed in our troubles and resurrected out of them before we attain the fullness of the God-head bodily.

Across the Desk

The Infinite Way is dedicated to revealing innate, individual, spiritual freedom which appears as freedom from bondage to the senses: to the body, to the purse, and to circumstances.

Acquiring some knowledge of truth is the raft on which we travel to "*My* kingdom" where all receive freedom, peace, and immortality. There is a story from the Chinese to the effect that when a person travels and comes to a deep stream, he builds a raft and crosses the stream on it, but once he is on land again he drops the raft and leaves it behind lest it become a burden to him. So do we use the letter of truth as a raft to carry us across the river of our ignorance. Then, upon reaching, "*My* kingdom," we drop the letter of truth and clothe ourselves with the Spirit, thus attaining freedom. Our real freedom is not freedom *from* anything, but a freedom in Christ which *appears* as freedom from fear, from the body, from the purse, and from limitation of every nature:

Every human being will demonstrate the continuity of life after death, but only the spiritually free attain immortality.

Every human being may achieve health, abundance, and a measure of happiness, but only the spiritually free attain life by Grace—"not by might nor by power," but by the realization of Omnipresence.

Almost every human being believes in God, but only those enlightened through the continuous realization of Omnipresence attain the grace of God in daily life and experience.

Few ideas contain the inherent power of spiritual freedom that is found in the constant remembrance of the words, "Emmanuel, or God with us." To *live* in the continuous awareness of Emmanuel is to float on a safe raft into "*My* kingdom," the realm of eternal freedom and peace.

Sing the song, "Emmanuel, God with us," morning, noon, and night, and cross the river of ignorance to "*My* kingdom," and know forever "*My* peace."

The Meaning of Prayer

For many years after the Crucifixion, the majority of Jesus' follow-ers resisted all efforts that were made to bring them into confor-mity with the teachings of the Master. They continued to live by the Hebraic laws, many of them insisting that no Gentiles be admitted to their brotherhood, that all men must be circumcised, and that all members observe their dietary rules. It was only years later, with the advent of Paul and his teaching of "neither circum-cision availeth anything, nor uncircumcision,"[1] that the Judaic laws were dropped and the Christian teaching accepted.

Today, too, we find that it is not easy to give up teachings and traditions of our childhood, regardless of how erroneous they may have been, and we therefore often continue to cling to them throughout our lives. I will remember the day when my mother told me that there was no Santa Claus and that there was no use

[1]Galatians 5:6.

244

hanging up my stocking on Christmas Eve. No Santa Claus! I knew better than my mother. I was not going to believe it for a minute; therefore, I proceeded to hang up my stocking. Even my mother could not break a belief that had been implanted in me from the time I came on earth. I was looking forward to Santa Claus coming on Christmas and bringing me a whole tree full of gifts, and no one was going to take that away from me.

So, also, do we cling to our early religious teachings relative to the nature of God. God has been set up as a kind of superhuman parent to whom we can go and cry, asking for what we want, and if we just cry hard enough, sacrifice, tithe, light a candle, take off our shoes, put our hats on, or perform some other ritual, we may get what we ask for. Each group or denomination has its own way of persuading God to do its will; each one has some way in which it tries to appease God and thereby hopes that God will open up His bag of gifts and hand out health to one, supply to another, a husband to one, a divorce to another, or a child to one, and so on and on and on.

This is based on the belief that God has something that He is withholding and that He is not going to give it up until we manage to wheedle Him into the right frame of mind, or until we succeed in pleasing Him in some way or other. Surely, in our spiritual adulthood, we must know that there can be no such God, because to entertain such a concept of God is to humanize Deity.

It is not easy to take a Santa-Claus-God away from people who still expect that God is going to do something for them if they tithe, if they are sanctimonious or look holy. That is a difficult habit of thought to break; nevertheless it has to be broken. God is omnipresent wherever we are, and we do not have to roll our eyes up to Him or make a pretense of being good to receive his blessings.

Our State of Consciousness Returns to Us

Let us get over the idea that there is a rewarding or a punishing God. There is no God to reward or to punish anybody for anything. God is not a man or a woman; God has no human instincts. God is Spirit and God is love, and when we remember how parents love their bad children as well as their good ones, how much less cognizance must God take of goodness or of badness!

It is true that we do receive punishment for our wrongdoing, but from what source does that punishment come? The punishment is never from God: it is from the state of consciousness that brought about the sin. In other words, if we believe that we lack to such an extent that we are willing to steal to satisfy our needs, it is our belief in lack that is punishing us; or if we think that taking somebody else's property can enrich us, we are going to suffer from that belief because we cannot avoid suffering from what we accept in our consciousness.

Whatsoever we mete out, that is the way it is going to be measured back to us—not by God, but by our own sins, by our own state of consciousness. It is the state of consciousness that we express that returns to us. The bread that we can cast upon the water is the bread that returns to us. So it is important that we cast fresh bread with good fresh butter on it, for it is going to come right back to us, and if we have not put good out, there is no good to come back to us.

Praying for Spiritual Bread

The Master made it clear that God has no pleasure in our sacrifices. He also made it clear that man was not made for the Sabbath, but that the Sabbath was made for man, that worshiping in holy mountains, or even in holy temples, has no value, and above all things he made it clear that we should take no thought for our life, what we should eat, or what we should drink, or wherewithal we should be clothed, and he may even have gone on and added, "housed," too.

It is true that over and over again he said, "Ask, and it shall be given you; seek, and ye shall find; knock, and it shall be opened unto you,"[2] but he also explained what we were to ask for: bread, and he told us what "bread" is. The bread that he was talking about had no relationship to baker's bread or to the kind a cook or housewife can turn out; the bread to which he referred was the bread of life; and he said, "*I* am the bread of life."[3]

Not long ago after a lecture, someone totally unfamiliar with The Infinite Way came up to me and said, "I can go along with you in most things, but not with what you say about prayer. You say that we must not pray to God for anything, but Jesus prayed, 'Give us this day our daily bread.'[4]"

And I replied, "Yes, I can understand your feeling that way, but probably no one has ever explained to you what bread is. Just what is bread? Jesus said, and nearly every Christian church repeats this in its communion service, 'I am the bread.'[5]"

He wondered why he had never seen this before, but it was because he had read the Bible with the conditioning he had received in his childhood and from his early religious teaching, and not with an unconditioned mind. Somebody had perhaps pointed out this passage and told this man what he understood it to mean, and that is as far as he had ever gone. That is the way with many of us: we have accepted our childhood teachings, never questioning them and never realizing that we ought to think for ourselves.

Thus it is that when we pray for daily bread, we are to remember what bread is and that we are praying for Christly substance which is understanding, praying for the Spirit of God to be in us, praying that light be given to us, that God's grace be made evident to us, praying as though we really understood the Master's teaching of two thousand years ago that the kingdom of God is within us:

Father, even though I know that the kingdom of God is within me, reveal it to me now. If I have forgotten this great truth, if the mes-

[2]Luke 11:9.
[3]John 6:35.
[4]Matthew 6:11.
[5]John 6:35.

merism of human living has separated me from it, open my eyes that I may see, open my ears that I may hear.

All we have to do is to turn within and pray, but not as though we were praying to a human being, to a human mother or father who has a piece of candy to give us, a toy, or a new dress. To pray in that way is to humanize God. It is trying to make God over into the image and likeness of a Santa Claus, but we may as well know, once and for all time, that our God is not in the business of putting presents under Christmas trees—not even for good children.

God *is*—this we must know. God is good—this, too, we must know. And God is closer to us than breathing and nearer than hands and feet—this we also must know. The Master further stated that God knows our needs and that it is His good pleasure to give us the Kingdom. Let us, therefore, stop begging, asking, and seeking for things, and seek "first the kingdom of God, and his righteousness."[6] The only legitimate asking, seeking, and knocking is that which we direct within ourselves.

Laying Up Spiritual Treasures

The whole basis of prayer in The Infinite Way is that we cannot pray for anything to come to us because in the beginning, "before Abraham was," God established the whole Kingdom within us. Nothing can be added to us, but we can pray that the kingdom of God, which is within us, find expression and outlet through us. It is much like turning to our memory in order to bring to mind some fact which has escaped us, and we bring it forth from within ourselves even though temporarily we had lost sight of that fact that we knew it.

So it is with any form of good. It cannot come to us: it must flow out from us. Many of us have experienced temporary forms of good that have come to us apparently for no reason at all. Sometimes

[6]Matthew 6:33.

money, position, and fame have been almost thrust upon us, but because we have not brought them forth from within ourselves, they do not really belong to us, and very often we have the sad and unpleasant experience of finding out that they really were not ours because they were not the fruitage of our consciousness and, therefore, they were not permanent.

That which we bring forth from within our own consciousness, we will never lose. As a matter of fact, we will take it with us when we leave this scene. Jesus was not indulging in fanciful poetic language when he said, "Lay not up for yourselves treasures upon earth, where moth and rust doth corrupt, and where thieves break through and steal: But lay up for yourselves treasures in heaven, where neither moth nor rust doth corrupt, and where thieves do not break through nor steal."[7] This is great wisdom; this is a divine principle of life, which should be heeded. It does not mean that we should not have money, and have it by the billions, if it flows to us. What it means is that we should not store it up in the sense that it is our supply or that we are dependent upon it, because after all the barns and storehouses have been filled and then we build more and fill those, what are we going to do with them? Eventually, they must all be left at the door of the Probate Court.

We cannot take our wardrobes or our jewels with us, our storehouses or barns; we cannot take our money or any worldly possessions with us. What then have we to take with us? How do we go forth, and with what? The answer is that if we have not stored up spiritual treasures, we go out of this world a blank, and when we enter the next life, we may have to start off on a lower level than when we came into this world. It is the spiritual treasures that we have laid up in our consciousness through prayer that we carry with us wherever we go, and those treasures will ensure that our entry into the next life-experience will be on a higher plane than the level on which we came into this one.

[7]Matthew 6:19, 20.

God Is Not Responsible for Evil

God is not to be prayed to in the sense of praying to Him to do, give, or bestow something or someone at some time. There is no such God. In the last war, hundreds of thousands of families prayed for the safety and the security of their sons at war, but their prayers were primarily personal and selfish, concerned only with the safety of their own, and many of those fathers and mothers lost their sons in one way or another.

Does this not show how useless it is to go to God for anything of a personal and selfish nature and to believe that there is a God who cares whether we are of one country or another, whether we are Jew or Gentile, Protestant or Catholic, Buddhist or Moslem? What kind of God would make a distinction between one racial, national, or religious group and another?

As a matter of fact, in order to overcome the religious superstitions people have accepted, we must eventually overcome the belief that God cares more for good people than for bad people. All we have to do is to travel this world for a while to find out that the good people are suffering just as much as the bad people: they have just as many colds and just as much cancer, tuberculosis, and polio. Even innocent little children suffer before they know enough to be either good or bad. God is not holding innocent children in condemnation, or innocent men and women, and letting the rascals go free. God has no part in any of that. God is not responsible for evil.

God does not enter the human scene until an individual returns to Him. In the fifteenth chapter of John, the Master taught: "If ye abide in me, and my words abide in you, ye shall ask what ye will, and it shall be done unto you."[8] But if you do not abide in this Word, if you do not let this Word abide in you, you will be "cast forth as a branch and [be] withered."[9] There we have it! It does not say on which side of the boundary line we are; it does not say which uniform we are wearing, which church we are entering, or

[8]John 15:7.
[9]John 15:6.

what the color of our skin is: it says that we either abide in the word of God and let the word of God abide in us, or we are cut off, and it makes no difference whether we are humanly good or humanly bad, humanly white or humanly black.

Isaiah says, "Thou wilt keep him in perfect peace, whose mind is stayed on thee."[10] No distinction is made. The only requisite is to keep our mind stayed on God and thereby bring God into our experience. God fills all space, but God is available only where the mind is stayed on God, where the presence of God is maintained in consciousness, and where contact is made with Him.

The Prayer of Acknowledgment

When we begin to perceive the nature of God, we will know how to pray. When we know how to pray, all of God's grace will manifest Itself in our life because prayer is the connecting link between man and God. It is through prayer that we bring God's grace into our individual experience and are enabled to share it with others so that they, too, benefit in some degree by the Grace that we have received.

The Master said, "The Spirit of the Lord God is upon me, because he hath anointed me to preach the gospel to the poor; he hath sent me to heal the brokenhearted, to preach deliverance to the captives, and recovering of sight to the blind, to set at liberty them that are bruised."[11] Wherever a person makes contact with the Spirit of God, in some degree he, too, is anointed, not necessarily to do healing work—some will comfort, some will support and supply, and some will bless in other ways—but in one way or another, everyone who has been ordained of God and who has received the Spirit of God in him is at the same time ordained to bless and bring blessings to others.

As human beings, we are imbued neither with the life nor the wisdom of God: we do not receive the blessings of God, nor do we

[10]Isiah 26:3.
[11]Luke 4:18.

come under the law of God, until, at some moment of our experience, the Spirit of God dwells in us, and then do we become the children of God, and a children, heirs, and as heirs, joint-heirs of Christ—"if so that the Spirit of God dwell in [us]."[12] Then, prayer becomes an acknowledgement:

> *The very place whereon I stand is holy ground. Here where I am, God is. If I mount up to heaven, God is there; if I make my bed in hell, God is there; if "I walk through the valley of the shadow of death, I will fear no evil,"[13] for God is there. Wherever I am, God is—up in the heavens, down in the hells, walking the earth, even in "the valley of the shadow of death."*
>
> *Where God is, I am; and all that the Father has is mine. God can set a table for me in the wilderness.*
>
> *"The heavens declare the glory of God, and the firmament sheweth his handywork"[14]—and man is his greatest creation. That very place where God stands, stands I, for I and the Father are one: God, the Father; God, the Son—here, where I am. Underneath me are the everlasting Arms.*
>
> *"I will never leave thee, nor forsake thee.[15] . . . Before Abraham was, I am,"[16] and that I Am is with me, and that I will be with me to the end of the world; It will never leave me, nor forsake me. I can never die because that I is my life eternal. "Whither thou goest, I will go"[17]—whithersoever I go, God goes with me, inseparable, indivisible—one.*

When we have prayed that kind of prayer, we can rest in quietness and in confidence. Then we can listen for a moment or two as the answer comes from within. Always something wells up from

[12]Romans 8:9.
[13]Psalm 23:4.
[14]Psalm 19:1.
[15]Hebrews 13:5.
[16]John 8:58.
[17]Ruth 1:16.

within to bring assurance that this word of God is true, and that there is a Presence that is ever within us, and yet that goes before us to make the crooked places straight and to prepare mansions for us.

This kind of prayer never comes down to the level of dishonoring God by implying that God is withholding something from us and that we must use some coercive method to persuade Him to let loose of it.

Prayer Reveals the Eternal Relationship of Oneness

God is the same yesterday, today, and forever. What God does is from everlasting to everlasting: there is no beginning to God, and there is no ending to God. Therefore, it is useless to expect God to do something for us today that He did not do yesterday.

God's work is done. When there seems to be an absence of health, harmony, wholeness, completeness, or perfection, our attitude should be not that God is withholding any of these things and that he must do something that He is not already doing to bring them to us, but rather should we accept the fact that a *sense* of separation has sprung up between God and us, and we are therefore going back to the kingdom of God within us to re-establish our sense of oneness—not to re-establish oneness because that is, always has been, and always will be intact. The human mesmerism that was brought about by accepting the belief in two powers has created a sense of separation from God which, at times, is so great that it makes us feel that God is a billion miles away upward, and we are a billion miles away downward, and that there is no possibility of spanning the gap.

Actually, this is not true. "I and my Father are one" is an eternal relationship, but if we have forgotten it, if the mesmerism of world beliefs has taken it away from us, then we have to go back within ourselves, where eventually we shall find the kingdom of God, and there, pray, ask, and knock:

Father, reveal Thyself. Break this mesmeric sense that I may pierce the veil of separation. Open my eyes that I may see; open my ears that I may hear. Glorify Thou me with the glory that I had with Thee in the beginning.

Then we are not asking God for anything. What we are trying to do through this prayer is to break that mesmeric sense within ourselves until the glory of God, which is already established within us, can once more be evident in manifestation. Truth, light, love, happiness, joy, peace, dominion, companionship, home—all these are established within us. Our only task is to let them flow out from us.

The way of doing this differs with each individual. There are some who have developed such love of money and such great fear of the lack of it that it is only with reluctance that they can part with it. They may have to open a way for the infinity of God to flow forth into expression by being willing to take a few dollars and begin to give them out without fear, with a sense that these dollars belong to God, and they are going to share them.

With some persons, the thing that they are not letting flow out from them is less tangible. They may have to learn to pray for their enemies or for those who persecute them or despitefully use them, and above all to forgive even until seventy times seven in order that they may be the children of their Father which is in heaven. There are others who have developed a pseudo-loyalty to their nation or church, and they will have to learn the meaning of the true brotherhood Jesus taught when he said, "Call no man your father upon the earth: for one is your Father, which is in heaven,"[18] God is not a sectarian God, a nationalistic or a racial God.

We must make sure that we are fulfilling the demands of the Master, and even if we have to wear out our kneecaps on the ground in order to do it, we must bring ourselves to the place where we understand that God knows no such thing as boundaries,

[18]Matthew 23:9.

nationalities, races, or creeds, that none of those things has a place in the kingdom of God.

In that Kingdom, there is no race or creed of any nature: there is only the relationship of God and His son, universal and intact. If we have any other idea of God, we shall have to work to eliminate it from our consciousness, and this we will be able to do when we learn the true nature of God and realize that God cares just as much for the daisies in the field as for the orchids, for the blades of grass as for the most luscious of fruits. God is the same to all those who bring themselves under the reign of God.

The Humility of True Prayer

There is no way to pray other than to make of oneself a stillness, a quietness, a peacefulness, and a listening ear. Prayer that contains words and thoughts meant to reach God is not really prayer at all. True prayer has neither words nor thoughts because it has no desires except one: to know God's will, to know Him aright, to be a fitting instrument for His grace. With that one exception, prayer is desireless. It is a desireless state of being which opens the way for God's will to be known and made evident.

Prayer is an inner stillness that waits for God's thoughts—"for my thoughts are not your thoughts, neither are your ways my ways."[19] Therefore, let us be still with our thoughts and our ways, and let us hear God's thoughts and, by listening, let us come to know God's ways:

> *"Thou wilt keep him in perfect peace, whose mind is stayed on thee."[20] Thou wilt keep me in perfect peace in proportion as my mind is stayed on Thee. Thou leadest me beside the still waters. Thou makest me to lie down in green pastures.*
>
> *What must I do? Only acknowledge that because the Lord is my shepherd I need not fear. He feedeth me in the wilderness and setteth*

[19]Isaiah 55:8.
[20]Isaiah 26:3.

a table before me. My function is not to tell that all-knowing Intelligence, but rather to listen and be still.

Prayer is acknowledging God as Omnipotence, Omniscience, and Omnipresence—All-power, All-knowledge, and All-presence. Prayer is being still so that Omnipotence may establish Itself in our consciousness, Omniscience impart Itself to us, and Omnipresence reveal Its presence to us. Prayer does not bring God to us. Prayer does not bring God's grace to us: prayer reveals God and God's grace to be active where we are.

The most important part of prayer is that listening or receptive attitude which is a state of pure humility:

Speak, Lord; Your servant is listening. I am not turning to You to have You do my will, as though You were my servant and I could direct You to provide me with supply, health, home, or companionship. I am not coming to You as though I had greater wisdom than You and, therefore, knew what to pray for. I come to You in true humility, for I realize that I can of my own self do nothing. I do not even know how to pray, or what to pray for.

Therefore, Father, let Your Spirit make intercession with my spirit. Speak, Lord, that Your will may be made manifest in my experience. You are my Shepherd; I shall never want. Your grace is my sufficiency in all things.

And so in this state of receptivity, in this state of opening ourselves in humility to the will and the grace of God—whether it happens the first day or the hundred and first day is not important—eventually it happens, and we are filled with the Spirit of God. There is an inner warmth, an inner stillness, an inner peace. Sometimes there is even the still small voice assuring us, "*I* have never left you. *I* will never leave you," or sometimes, "*I* am your bread and your wine and your water." It does not make any difference whether it comes in words, whether it comes in thoughts, or whether it comes just as a feeling, a sensing, or a release. But it is an assurance:

God is closer to me than breathing and nearer than hands and feet. He knows my need before I do, and it is His good pleasure to give me the Kingdom.

Prayer is attunement, at-one-ment, with God. Through prayer, our eternal relationship with the Father is revealed. But for that oneness to become realized consciousness, we must go to the throne of God pure of heart, free of desires, with every barrier removed, seeking only communion, and praying the prayer of acknowledgment. In that purity, selflessness, and desirelessness, we enter the inner sanctuary, and from that high point of vision behold His kingdom on earth as it is in heaven.

ACROSS THE DESK

Life really begins for a person when he faces fairly and squarely these questions: Why am I on earth? What came I here to do? Is there a goal to be attained? Have I begun to fulfill God's plan for me on earth? Until the beginning of such self-questioning, one's life is like that of a vegetable.

Each person has a unique destiny in life, but only a few have concerned themselves with their destiny, and fewer still have attained any awareness of their real Self. Because of this, men are sheep and follow leaders, occasionally to a better way of life, but more often to their own destruction.

It is true that labor unions have given workmen better wages and greater security, and that civil service employment has provided economic security of a sort, but this has at times stultified ambition and initiative and has been coupled with such a sacrifice of individuality that it has imprisoned the spirit of adventure, pioneering, and of achievement. To have become a power in the religious, political, or economic world tends, too, to limit one's freedom of choice, decision, movement, and growth.

In countries throughout the world, millions have died that others might survive in order to pass on to coming generations political and economic freedom, but often, after this sacrifice, the survivors have immediately imprisoned themselves in new forms. Men have fought for what they believe would result in religious freedom only to find themselves bound more securely in mental slavery. The unthinking masses fight because they follow leaders who promise liberty, justice, and equality, not knowing that even victory may mean greater serfdom and domination under still more autocratic leaders.

At some time or other, if we are not already conditioned to serving out the balance of or time on earth as vegetables, we begin to question the meaning of life, and soon receive answers which set in motion the process of freeing us. Those of us who reach the stage of self-questioning soon learn that they only wars that can be fought and won are those that take place within ourselves. Our first awakening reveals that our mind, conditioned as it is to superstition and tradition, is the prison-house in which we dwell. Then begins the warefare within ourselves between truth and error, the warfare that can result, if we are faithful, in the attainment of our complete freedom and the ability to help others.

Of all the blessings in heaven or on earth, the greatest of these is freedom. Those who would be free—physically, mentally, morally, financially, politically, and religiously—must be willing to face the truth that only the attainment of spiritual illumination will bring that freedom, and this enlightenment must take place within the consciousness of the individual.

In proportion as we attain some measure of transcendental consciousness, and only as we seek and find an inner Grace, do we discover our freedom, peace, and joy, and experience outer harmony. By human means, we cannot bring peace and abundance to our world, or intelligence and integrity to those who govern.

"My kingdom is not of this world." "My peace" is not the peace that worldly conditions can give, and yet when we discover "My kingdom" and attain "My peace," we do bring some measure of its reign to earth.

The great attainment is the awareness of the nature of life and our reason for being, the awareness of the nature of the Self and of the purpose of the individual.

If there are earthly fetters still binding us, we must cease fighting them, put up our sword, and begin here and now to undertake the transformation of consciousness that brings freedom and peace to Soul, mind, and body, begin to seek the awareness of the Presence within us, that Presence that has been with us since "before Abraham was" and whose function It is to reveal to us "My kingdom," "My peace," and "My grace."

The natural man, or human self, does not evolve into Christhood. The spiritual man is a separate being, newborn as the "old man" is put off through the renewal of consciousness.

From

Consciousness Unfolding

Meditation

Meditation forms a most important part of our work. Although there are many ways of achieving silence and meditation, I have found only one way that meets my own need. I sit quietly, with my attention centered somewhere between the eyes and a little above, and take some word such as "life," or "God," or "Spirit," and ponder it. As my thought tries to wander, I come back gently to the same idea. I feel no sense of impatience with myself, no sense of frustration. No matter how many times the thought wanders, I bring it right back to that one word.

If you try this method, eventually, you will find that outside, intruding thoughts do not come, and you are able to sit quietly in a peaceful state of meditation. It may take days or it may take months to acquire this steadiness of mind, but it will come if you have patience and perseverance. Do not try to remain quiet for more than from three to five minutes unless you feel like it. We are doing this only for a conscious realization of our oneness, or to make our contact with God. When we have achieved that, we have achieved our purpose. We are not trying to see "light," or to have "experiences." If they come, there is nothing wrong about them. The only thing wrong would be in becoming so fascinated with these experiences that we lose our way by making too much of them.

After we have had our few minutes of meditation and have achieved the "click" or feeling of the presence of God, we get up and go about our business. If at noon, we find that we have a few minutes to use for this purpose, we repeat it; we do the same thing again at night, and in the middle of the night. Why? Because, ultimately, through providing these opportunities three or four times a day, meditation is going to become so much a part of our being that we shall be in meditation twenty-four hours a day whether awake or asleep. Then we do not have to go through a process of "healing" when someone calls upon us. We shall have been through all the preliminaries, and we shall be able to say, "Thank you, Father." Then we understand the reason for all the preliminary practice.

Ultimately, treatment becomes a very simple thing. We learn to dismiss instantly every negative suggestion that comes to us. Let us suppose that I am walking through a store and am tempted to snatch some jewelry. The thought immediately comes, "What kind of nonsense is that! Where did it come from? That temptation is no part of my nature." I walk home and that ends it. I would not treat it. I would merely keep on walking and drop the whole thing after the flash of recognition that a temptation such as this is no part of my consciousness.

Inasmuch as sin, disease, lack, and limitation are really only universal beliefs that present themselves to us for our acceptance or rejection, we must treat these by rejecting them at once. If we attach the word "I" to these and say, "I do not feel well. I am getting a cold," we have accepted the temptation or the suggestion, and an hour later or a day later we find ourselves showing forth the results of this acceptance. Suppose we had said, "Wait a minute!

Where does a thing like this come from? A temptation out of universal nothingness! I will accept no thinking like that. It is no part of the law of God and it is no part of me." We, then, would walk on, our treatment of the belief having consisted of quickly turning away from it.

I wish that all of us had the courage to adopt that form of treatment. When any temptation comes regarding ourselves or another, we should say, "Oh, no! Good-by to you! You are temptation, suggestion, appearance; there is nothing real about you, and I am not accepting you." Then we would find quicker healing many times.

Whenever the Call to Meditate Is Felt, Meditate

It may be that sometimes while you are speaking to a person or lecturing to a group, you will find yourself impelled to stop in order to go into meditation for no human reason of which you are aware. it is not necessary that you know the reason for it. It is mind unfolding, and when your meditation is completed you can then go on with your talk or conversation. Do not be surprised to learn. later than some need was met, some call was made at the instant you felt impelled to meditate. It may have been from someone you know, or it may not.

Doctors in hospitals frequently tell us that their patients "miraculously recovered" for no reason known to materia medica. Sometimes they add that "somebody must have been praying." A patient who so recovers may know the reason, because possibly he had asked for spiritual help or had some friend or relative who was working in this way. Another patient is healed just be reaching out to his concept of God. In so doing he touched the level of consciousness of someone living the spiritual life. So, even though we may not know why, we should always respond to these inner promptings for meditation and silence.

How was it possible for a man like Starr Daily, engrossed in a life of crime, suddenly to find himself so illuminated as to be freed of the whole sense of sin and disease? My own thought after hearing his story was that this man, consciously or unconsciously, must have said to himself, "Oh, God! Isn't there an answer to all this? Can't I get out of this misery in some way?" Perhaps he was thinking seriously of God as God, or as some kind of Presence that could do something.

Of this we can be sure, that in his being, there was a crying out to something that appeared to him as a protective influence, a presence of Love. In doing this, he perhaps touched the consciousness of someone praying on the level of impersonal relationship and he received an answer. I am convinced there are many people who have wonderful experiences of a spiritual nature, who do not know where they have come from; they have made a contact on this plane with someone who is praying. One does not have to be praying "for" anyone; as a matter of fact, I do not think one *can* pray *for* any person. Prayer is conscious at-one-ment with God. Prayer is being in tune with the Infinite. Prayer is the realization of God disclosing and revealing Itself as an actual presence and power. While we are living in that state of consciousness, does not the infinity of God include anyone lifting himself into that consciousness which is so real in our thought? Why not?

When a person is trying to find some kind of God of Christ—some kind of help—with his whole being, why should he not touch your level or my level of consciousness when we are in the process of realizing and touching God, here and now? This is what happens to you when a practitioner is working for you. You do not know the minute or the hour when the practitioner is at work. You are not tuned in to any personal consciousness, nor to his "thinking." You ask for help and drop the whole matter. Sometimes you put a letter to a practitioner into the mailbox, knowing that he will not receive it for a day or for several days. But you have your healing that minute, or that hour, or six hours later. Anyway, you get it long before the practitioner receives your letter. How can this happen?

What you did was to tune yourself in to your highest sense of God consciousness, which at the moment you thought of and personalized as your practitioner. Your practitioner was living in the realization that *I* is God, and that *I* is omnipresent. Wherever and whenever someone reaches out for the unfoldment and revelation of God, he touches that Christ consciousness. A practitioner does not humanly have to know you are reaching out in order for you to receive help. You may have thought you were reaching out to Mr. Jones or Mrs. Smith, but you were not! You were reaching out to the Christ. The Christ is the practitioner's developed state of consciousness.

Is it not possible that someone else down the street, in the same moment that you reached out to God or to the Christ also reached out, touched the same Christ consciousness that you did, and had his healing? Neither of you made a human contact, for he may not have known of the practitioner, and your message may not yet have reached the practitioner. When you reach out to a practitioner for help, you must touch something higher than the thought or personality of the practitioner. You must touch that mind which was in Christ Jesus. That is where and when healing takes place.

Attain the Consciousness of God

The whole secret lies in attaining the actual consciousness, the actual feeling of God's presence. Without that feeling, we still do not have the assurance that the declarations, the affirmations, and the denials that we make are true.

You cannot fight error after you know God to be the only reality of being. You then realize that error exists as an appearance. You recognize that it exists to the ignorant sense of those not yet aware of their true identity, but that does not mean that you have to fight it. It means that you must sit at peace and realize the nothingness of it. None of this is of any importance at all—none of this truth about God and man, or about error, is of any importance—

unless you get the feeling of it, unless you have the actual feeling of this Presence.

It is so easy to repeat: "My life is God. God is my life," and five minutes later begin to fear that you are going to die. It is an easy thing to make the affirmation: I don't have to be afraid of germs, infection, or contagion. They are not power," and a few minutes later, it is just as easy to become afraid of those very things. The affirmations and the denials will not do the work. It is the feeling, the absolute conviction, the inner realization, and when it comes, it fills the whole body with a sense of reality, power, and dominion.

It is one thing to say to a little child, "Go on! Cross the street; Mother is right behind you and there is no danger." It is another thing for a mother to take the child's hand and walk across the street with him. In the first case, the child may or may not believe that there is no danger, or he may believe and still be afraid. But once he feels his mother's hand in his, all fear is gone. That is what I am trying to bring out. It is easy to say, "God is with you though you make your bed in hell." But there is no power in the words until you actually have felt God's presence when you are walking down the street, or going into a hospital to help someone.

Your words have to be God realized, God felt. Certainly, there is no presence of power apart from God, and our assurance comes when we have felt it. Over and over people ask, "Do you believe in God?" Certainly, we believe in God. But *what* do we believe? To feel God, to touch God, to have the actuality of God, is no longer to "believe" in God, *This is the experience of God.* The more you feel this, the less you can talk *about* God. We talk about It, when we ought to be able to look right up and see It. If we could, no one would have to talk about It. It should be like that with all of us. We should be able to see It and feel It, not with the eyes, at least with our inner sense—our intuition.

God is reality. In healing or in teaching, with a patient sitting before you, it is futile to make statements or recite quotations of truth for the purpose of filling or satisfying his thought. In teaching, it is futile to memorize a lot of things from books, and then go before an audience and recite things you known nothing of, things that are not a part of your consciousness.

These statements are not power; they are nothing more than the words that come forth out of the human throat. They carry no substance and no essence. Sometimes, you may come to a period where you have nothing to say, where the answer is not there. Then, go within to God. And if it is best to say nothing, then say nothing. Let God do it. Let the work be done in silence. There is more power in a second of silence than in an hour of conversation. "The letter killeth, but the spirit giveth life."[1] So, let it come through the silence, through the Spirit, rather than through words that can be made up.

[1]Corinthians 3:6.